ENSEMBLES
JSWD

Uta Winterhager
Nils Ballhausen

ENSEMBLES
JSWD

Uta Winterhager
Nils Ballhausen

jovis

Inhalt   Contents

Vorwort – Prof. Volkwin Marg — 6
Preface—Prof. Volkwin Marg — 8

Einleitung – Zusammenspiel — 11
Introduction—Interplay — 11

Neues Kesselhaus, Gelsenkirchen — 14
Vivawest Headquarter, Gelsenkirchen — 24
    Bekenntnis zu den Wurzeln — 28
    Commitment to the Roots — 28

Haus der Europäischen Geschichte, Brüssel — 32
House of European History, Brussels — 38
    Grenzgänger — 50
    Border Crossers — 50

Koelnmesse 3.0, Köln — 54
Koelnmesse 3.0, Cologne — 58
    Experiment Deutz — 62
    The Deutz Experiment — 62

The Icon Vienna, Wien — 68
The Icon Vienna, Vienna — 72
    Hochhäuser in der Stadt — 82
    High-rises in the City — 82

Neue Mitte Porz, Köln — 86
Porz' New Center, Cologne — 90
    Die große Sehnsucht nach Kleinteiligkeit — 94
    Longing for Small Scale — 94

Universitätsklinikum UKSH, Schleswig-Holstein — 98
University Medical Center UKSH, Schleswig-Holstein — 103
    Klinik der Zukunft — 114
    Clinic of the Future — 114

Haus und Platz — 118
Building and Square — 121
    Zehn Jahre Maternusplatz — 128
    Ten Years Maternusplatz — 128

Ecole Centrale Clausen, Luxemburg — 132
Ecole Centrale Clausen, Luxembourg — 137
    Gebaute Bilder — 146
    Built Images — 146

Neuer Kanzlerplatz, Bonn	150
New Chancellor Square, Bonn	155
Die geografische Mitte	162
The Geographic Middle	162
Konversionen	166
Conversions	170
Die Auseinandersetzung mit Veränderung	182
Dealing with Change	182
Thyssenkrupp Quartier, Essen	186
Thyssenkrupp Quarter, Essen	193
Fassade und Identität	202
Facade and Identity	202
Haus und Hof	206
House and Yard	208
Wohnen im Dorf	216
Living in the Village	216
Bundesumweltministerium BMU, Berlin	220
Bundesumweltministerium BMU, Berlin	224
Nachhaltige Quartiersentwicklung	228
Sustainable Urbanism	228

Anhang
Appendix

Ausgewählte Bauten und Projekte 2000–2020	234
Selected Buildings and Projects 2000–2020	234
Gründungspartner	240
Founding Partners	240
Associate Partner	241
Associate Partners	241
Mitarbeiter	242
Employees	242
Autoren	244
Authors	244
Dank	245
Acknowledgement	245
Bildnachweis	246
Picture Credits	246
Impressum	247
Imprint	247

Vorwort

Das Ganze ist mehr
als die Summe seiner Teile

Dieses Credo gilt seit jeher für alle komponierenden Künste: Poesie, Musik, bildende Kunst, Darstellung und allemal für die Baukunst. Vielfalt in der Einheit, Einheit in der Vielfalt – JSWD Architekten haben sich hierzu selbst verpflichtet und zeigen mit der Dokumentation ihrer Ensembles, wie weit sie es gebracht haben.
Kunstfertigkeit hieß im Altgriechischen noch *techne* und die Baumeister bezeichnet man seit damals als Architekten. Sie bauten nicht nur kleine Häuser, große Theater und bedeutsame Tempel, sondern auch ganze Quartiere und Städte. Deren Komposition hatte im Kleinen wie im Großen im richtigen Verhältnis zueinander zu stehen, das heißt in angemessenen räumlichen Proportionen zu individuellen und öffentlichen Belangen.
Diese dialektische Komposition der Synthese des Teils mit dem Ganzen haben JSWD zum Ziel. Sie verstehen sich als ganzheitliche Baumeister, die sich bei ihren Ensemblekompositionen nicht auf den architektonischen Solitär als bloßen Teil beschränken, sondern mit der Orchestrierung des Ganzen mehr anstreben. Sie ordnen und entwerfen sowieso im übergeordneten Kontext gesellschaftlicher, städtischer, landschaftlicher und ökologischer Zusammenhänge. Dazu befragt, haben sie im Interview für eines ihrer Bücher so geantwortet: „Wir bewegen uns an der Schnittstelle von Architektur und Städtebau." – „Wir suchen eine Ordnung, die sich aus einer gesellschaftlichen Struktur entwickelt. Architektur und Städtebau müssen deren Vielfalt widerspiegeln." – „Wo sich der Raum auflöst und indifferent wird, ist es weniger schön als an klaren Stadträumen und Orten, wo ich mich als Mensch in einer bestimmten Ordnung wiederfinde. Im Städtebau denken wir vom öffentlichen Raum aus, also von außen nach innen – und in der Architektur von innen nach außen." – „Es muss eine sinnvolle Abfolge, eine Hierarchie von Räumen und Größen geben, vom Platz zur Straße, zur Gasse, zum Haus." – „Wir folgen da dem klassischen Muster des europäischen Städtebaus. Wir haben auch keine Angst vor Größe: weder im Städtebau noch in der Architektur." Alle vier Partner äußern sich hier ebenso klar wie selbstbewusst.
Das spiegelt sich in den geplanten und gebauten architektonischen und städtebaulichen Inszenierungen, die in diesem Buch vorgestellt werden. Sie entwerfen unbeirrt von wechselnden Designmoden und unangefochten vom eitlen gleichförmigen Formalismus im Geiste einer von ihnen kontinuierlich fortgeschriebenen Moderne. Dabei entstehen sehr unterschiedliche und vielgestaltige städtebauliche und stadtlandschaftliche Ensembles, zum Beispiel das Thyssenkrupp Quartier in Essen. Es ist großzügig, großmaßstäblich, innen- und außenräumlich signifikant, hierarchisch axial eindeutig; und auf repräsentative Weise stiftet es Identität.

„Mit der Erweiterung der Hauptverwaltung von Vivawest in Gelsenkirchen ist ihnen ein stadträumlicher Dialog zwischen der denkmalwürdigen Industriearchitektur des 20. Jahrhunderts und deren Umwandlung zu einem Gesamtkunstwerk des 21. Jahrhunderts gelungen, und zwar durch raumbildende Neubauten, ausgreifende Gartenarchitektur – gekrönt durch skulpturale Kunst als signifikante Landmarke auf dem höchsten Förderturm.

Der Schwarz Projekt Campus in Bad Friedrichshall ist ein wahrhafter Campus – im ursprünglichen Sinne des Wortes: Inmitten einer üppig begrünten Topografie inszeniert er als stadtlandschaftliches Ensemble durch seine ringförmig gruppierten Gebäude für mehrere Tausend Arbeitsplätze einen äußeren Landschaftsring und im Inneren einen Park für die Belegschaft.

Ich kenne JSWD buchstäblich alle persönlich seit Studentenzeiten an der RWTH Aachen, durch die Arbeit am Lehrstuhl für Stadtbereichsplanung und in meinem Aachener Büro, nicht nur die vier Namensgeber, sondern auch die assoziierten Partner und leitenden Mitarbeiter. Mich beeindruckt der Teamgeist, der ihre partnerschaftliche Arbeit so fruchtbar und einfallsreich werden lässt. Das prägt nicht nur deren Arbeitsweise intern, sondern auch den Arbeitsstil mit ausländischen Kollegen aus Frankreich, Italien und der Schweiz bei Arbeitsgemeinschaften mit wunderbaren Ergebnissen. Befragt man sie dazu, sagen sie: „Man muss sich sympathisch sein. Die Chemie muss stimmen." – „Man sollte ergebnisoffen arbeiten können. Sonst funktioniert eine Arbeitsgemeinschaft nicht." – „Uns ist wichtig, dass wir eine gute Arbeitsatmosphäre in der rheinischen Tradition im Büro haben." – „Wir verlangen viel, geben aber auch etwas zurück. Leidenschaft gehört zum Kern unseres Berufsverständnisses." – „Unser Erfolg ist nicht nur aus uns geboren, sondern auch aus unseren Mitarbeitern." – „Ich wünsche mir Bauherren, die mich in der Verfolgung gemeinsamer Ziele unterstützen." – Das wünsche ich ihnen auch.

Neulich, beim Büroquartier am Neuen Kanzlerplatz in Bonn, waren wir Konkurrenten. Sie haben den Wettbewerb gewonnen. Das Team JSWD ist nicht nur sympathisch, sondern auch einfach gut. Das macht es leicht, ihnen jeden Erfolg zu gönnen.

Prof. Dr.-Ing. h.c. Volkwin Marg

Preface

The whole is more than the sum of its parts

This motto has always been true for the compositional arts: poetry, music, the visual arts, illustration, and certainly also for architecture. Variety in unity, unity in variety—JSWD Architects have committed themselves to this task. With this documentation of their work, they demonstrate how far they have come.
In ancient Greek, craftsmanship was called *techne*; the builders were described back then as architects. They did not just build small houses, large theaters, and important temples, but also entire districts and cities. Their compositions needed to have the right relationship on both the small and large scale, which means appropriate spatial proportions to meet individual as well as public demands.
JSWD have made this dialectical composition of the synthesis of the parts with the whole their goal. They see themselves as holistic builders, who do not restrict themselves to the architectural stand-alone intervention as a mere part of an ensemble composition, but strive rather to achieve greater things through orchestration of the entirety of the ensemble. In the overarching context, they naturally organize and design social, urban, landscape, and ecological relationships. When asked about this aspect in an interview for this book, they responded as follows: "We work at the intersection of architecture and urban design."—"We are searching for an order which has developed from social structures. Architecture and urban design must reflect these structures' diversity."—"Places where space breaks up and becomes indifferent are less attractive than clear urban places and spaces in which I as a human can recognize a certain order. In urban design, we always begin with public space, so from the outside in—and in architecture from the inside out."—"We need a sensible progression, a hierarchy of spaces and sizes, from the square to the street to the lane to the building."—"In this task, we follow the classical pattern of European urban design. We're also not afraid of going big: neither in urban design nor in architecture." All four partners expressed themselves with unequivocal clarity.
This is reflected in the planned and constructed architectural and urban design interventions which are presented in this book. They design in the spirit of a continually progressing modernism, unperturbed by changing design styles and impervious to idle repetitive formalism. The result is a large variety of very different and diverse urban designs and urban landscape ensembles, for example the Thyssenkrupp Quarter in Essen. It is generous, large-scale, significant on both the interior and exterior, clearly axially hierarchical; it creates a specific identity in a representative way.
With the expansion of Vivawest headquarters in Gelsenkirchen, JSWD were successful in creating an urban spatial dialogue between the historically

significant industrial architecture of the 20th century and their transformation into a 21st-century "Gesamtkunstwerk;" they achieved this through spatially incisive new construction and expansive garden design—crowned by a sculpture on the highest mine tower to create a significant landmark.

The Schwarz Project Campus in Bad Friedrichshall is a campus in the truest sense of the word: in the middle of a lush green topography, the urban landscape ensemble forms an outer landscape ring made up of the circularly organized buildings, which house several thousand workspaces, and provides a park for the employees in the interior.

I know all of the members of JSWD personally since they were students at the RWTH Aachen, both through my work at the chair for urban planning and my office in Aachen. I know not only the four founding partners, but also the associates and the managers. I am impressed by the team spirit which makes their collaboration work so fruitful and imaginative. This is not only a characteristic of their internal work culture, but also their working style in consortia with colleagues from France, Italy, or Switzerland—with wonderful results. If one asks them about it, they say: "You have to like each other. You need the right chemistry."—"You need to be able to work without prejudging the outcome. Otherwise a consortium will not work."—"It is important to us that we have a good work atmosphere in the office in the Rhenish tradition."—"We demand a lot, but we also give something back. Passion is a core aspect of our work."—"Our success doesn't just come from us, but also from our employees."—"I always wish for clients, who support me in the pursuit of common goals."—I also wish that for them.

Recently we were competitors in a tender for the office quarter at New Chancellor Square in Bonn. They won the competition. The JSWD Team is not only likeable, they are quite simply good. And that makes it easy to wish them every success.

Prof. Dr.-Ing. h.c. Volkwin Marg

Einleitung Introduction

Zusammenspiel

Ein kurzer Dialog zwischen Bonn und Berlin
über Architekten und das Büchermachen

Interplay

A short dialogue between Bonn and Berlin
about architects and making books

Uta Winterhager: Auf meinem Schreibtisch liegt eine Postkarte, auf der steht: „Wenn man einmal angefangen hat, geht's." Bevor wir beide anfingen, wir also noch überlegten, ob wir dieses Buch gemeinsam machen wollen, stand bereits der Titel fest: *Ensembles*. War darin etwa unsere Rolle als Autorenduo bereits angelegt? Wir kannten uns bis dahin schließlich nur dem Namen nach …

Nils Ballhausen: Aus meiner Zeit als *Bauwelt*-Redakteur kannte ich dich als Autorin, die sich mit Architektur und Architekten des Kölner Raums sehr gut auskennt. Von Berlin aus betrachtet, scheint mir Köln ein spezielles Feld zu sein, und so, wie man zum Mount Everest besser in Begleitung eines ortskundigen Sherpas aufsteigt, war es für mich naheliegend, dich zu fragen, ob wir uns für die Redaktion von *Ensembles* zusammentun wollen. Siehst du dich denn überhaupt als Teil der Kölner „Architektur-Community"?

UW: Jaja, wir tun hier in Köln wirklich alles, um dieses „Spezielle" zu kultivieren. Und da bin ich gerne mittendrin, obwohl ich zugeben muss, dass mein Schreibtisch eher am Rand, nämlich in Bonn, steht. Aber aus meiner Perspektive ist JSWD gar kein typisch kölsches Büro – wie sieht das der Berliner?

NB: Viele Berliner neigen dazu, Köln mit Attributen wie chaotisch, intransparent, verfilzt, leichtfertig oder feierwütig zu versehen. Nichts davon trifft meines Wissens auf JSWD zu. Ich hatte das Büro bis zu diesem Buchprojekt eher punktuell wahrgenommen. Sicher, die Veröffentlichungen über das Thyssenkrupp Quartier in Essen oder das Haus der Europäischen Geschichte in Brüssel konnte man in der Fachpresse kaum übersehen, aber als ich mich dann intensiver mit dem Portfolio beschäftigt hatte, war ich doch überrascht, dass ich nur so wenige Bauten und Projekte kannte. Woran das wohl lag?

Uta Winterhager: There's a postcard on my desk that says, "Once you've started, the rest is easy." Before we both started, while we were still wondering if we wanted to produce this book together, the title was already set: *Ensembles*. Was our role as authorial duo also predetermined? Until then we knew each other only by name…

Nils Ballhausen: I knew you as a writer who is familiar with architecture and architects in the Cologne area from my time as an editor for *Bauwelt*. Viewed from Berlin, Cologne seemed to me to be another country. And just as it is better to climb the Mount Everest accompanied by local Sherpas, so it was natural for me to ask you if we should team up to edit *Ensembles*. Do you even see yourself as part of the Cologne "architecture community?"

UW: Yeah, we really do everything here in Cologne to cultivate this "specialness." And I like to be in the middle of it, although I have to admit that my desk is more on the edge, namely in Bonn. But from my perspective, JSWD is not a typical Cologne office—what do you think about that as a Berliner?

NB: Many Berliners tend to describe Cologne as chaotic, intransparent, corrupt, reckless or party-obsessed. None of this applies to JSWD to my knowledge. I had only noticed the office here and there up until this book project. Sure, the publications on the ThyssenKrupp Quarter in Essen or the House of European History in Brussels could hardly be overlooked in the trade press, but as I worked more intensively with their portfolio, I was surprised that I knew so few of their buildings and projects. Why was that?

UW: I offer you two hypotheses: The fact that JSWD was not so familiar to you may be due to the fact that they do not focus on the optimal presentation of their work in architecture magazines, but rather on the particular needs and

UW: Ich biete dir zwei Thesen an: Dass JSWD dir nicht so vertraut waren, mag daran liegen, dass sie ihre Arbeit nicht auf die Darstellung in einer Architekturzeitschrift ausrichten, sondern auf die besonderen Bedürfnisse und Wünsche jedes einzelnen Bauherrn – Stichwort: Corporate Architecture. Das läuft vielleicht, auch wenn es sehr professionell betrieben wird, der eigenen Markenbildung in gewisser Weise zuwider. Zum anderen haben wir hier ein Büro mit vier Partnern, vier Charakteren, vier Handschriften. Dass sie nach 20 Jahren immer noch so erfolgreich zusammenarbeiten, mag auch an den Freiheiten liegen, die sie einander und auch der nächsten Generation, den vier assoziierten Partnern, zugestehen. Trotz vieler scharfer Einzelaufnahmen wird es dadurch aber schwieriger, das Portfolio als Ganzes zu betrachten. Wie ist dein Eindruck heute, nach sieben Monaten intensiver Beschäftigung mit JSWD?

NB: Die Aufgabe wurde mit der Zeit immer interessanter. Schon beim ersten Kontakt mit Kim [Steffens], die bei JSWD für die Öffentlichkeitsarbeit zuständig ist, hatte ich den Eindruck, dass es sich um ein anspruchsvolles und gut organisiertes Büro handelt, das zudem die eigene Arbeit professionell dokumentiert. Es gab reichlich gutes Bildmaterial zu sehen, das aber nicht prahlerisch oder *glossy* wirkte. Als wir uns zum ersten Mal im Kölner Büro trafen, wurde mir klar, dass es dort eine Begeisterung für Fotografie gibt. Die großformatigen Bilder von Christa Lachenmaier, die dort an den Wänden hängen, zeigen Baustellen und Zwischenstände und treffen eher eine künstlerische Aussage.

UW: Ja, gerade die Fotos des entkernten FLOW Towers in Köln sind sehr schön, deswegen waren wir uns auch schnell einig, dass sie in dieses Buch gehören.

NB: Sich selbst zurücknehmen und andere Sichtweisen zulassen – ist das typisch für JSWD?

UW: Bezogen auf die genannten Fotos, erkenne ich da eine große Wertschätzung für Ästhetik und einen wachen Blick, der das Schöne auch dort findet, wo man es normalerweise nicht sucht. Charakteristisch finde ich, dass sie auch in diesem Bereich mit Profis zusammenarbeiten und sich nicht selbst verkünsteln. Sie wissen genau, was sie gut können; sie sind aber zugleich offen für Leute, die etwas anderes gut können. Schon bei unserem ersten Treffen in Köln wurde deutlich, dass dieses Buch keine bloße Werkschau werden soll, sondern einen gewissen Mehrwert bieten muss. Das war doch genau das, was wir erhofft, aber nicht unbedingt erwartet hatten …

NB: Wir waren uns jedenfalls alle schnell einig. Viele Architektenmonografien kranken ja daran, wishes of each client—in particular corporate architecture. Even if it is very professionally driven, this is in a way contrary to their branding. On the other hand, JSWD is an office with four partners, four distinctive characters, and four different styles. The fact that they still work so successfully together after 20 years may also be due to the freedom they allow each other and the next generation, the four associated partners. Despite many clear individual portraits, this however makes it harder to look at the portfolio as a whole. What is your impression today, after seven months of intensive work with JSWD?

NB: The task became more interesting over time. From the very first contact with Kim [Steffens], who is responsible for public relations at JSWD, I had the impression that theirs is a sophisticated and well-organized office, which also documents its own work professionally. There were plenty of good images, but they did not look brash or glossy. When we met for the first time at the Cologne office, I realized that they have an enthusiasm for photography. The large-format pictures by Christa Lachenmaier which hang on the walls there show construction sites and intermediate stages and make more of an artistic statement.

UW: Yes, especially the photos of the gutted FLOW Tower in Cologne are very beautiful. We quickly agreed that they belong in this book.

NB: Holding back and allowing other perspectives—is that typical of JSWD?

UW: In terms of the aforementioned photos, I see a great esteem for aesthetics and a keen eye that finds beauty even where you do not normally look for it. I find it characteristic that they also work together with professionals instead of trying to do everything themselves. They know exactly what they are good at; but at the same time they are open to people who are good at other things. At our first meeting in Cologne it became clear that this book should not be a mere showcase, but must offer a certain added value. That was exactly what we hoped but did not necessarily expect…

NB: We all certainly agreed quickly. Many architectural monographs suffer from the fact that they remain locked in the specialist vocabulary of words and pictures, while simultaneously emphasizing how strongly the depicted architecture is geared to the context, the client, and the users. Readers only rarely have these connections demonstrated. The variety of topics that architects deal with in their work is unfortunately often omitted. And if then a creative claim to a formal and functional reduction to the essence exists, then the

dass sie in Wort und Bild im Fachvokabular verschlossen bleiben, obwohl zugleich betont wird, wie stark die Architektur doch auf den Kontext, den Bauherrn und die Nutzer ausgerichtet ist. Nur bekommen die Leser diese Zusammenhänge selten veranschaulicht. Die Vielfalt an Themen, mit denen sich Architekten bei ihrer Arbeit auseinandersetzen, wird leider zu oft ausgeblendet. Und wenn dann auch noch der gestalterische Anspruch in einer formalen und funktionalen Reduktion auf das Wesentliche besteht, dann droht die Komplexität der jeweiligen Aufgabe unsichtbar zu werden. Das wollten wir in diesem Buch vermeiden. Deswegen sollte es in jedem Kapitel einen eher beschreibenden Teil und einen eher freien Magazinteil geben. Bei dem Projekt Neuer Kanzlerplatz in Bonn, quasi vor deiner Haustür gelegen, hat es ja gleich gut funktioniert.

UW: Das war genau das richtige Projekt, um zu testen, ob unser Konzept aufgehen würde. Denn dort, wo gerade der Grundstein für den neuen Bürokomplex gelegt wurde, stand früher das Bonn-Center – in der Bundeshauptstadt eine Institution, nicht schick oder schön, aber ein Ort, der für viele die Hoffnung auf das Großsein oder Großwerden verkörperte. Und heute entsteht genau dort wieder ein Wahrzeichen und wieder sind die Erwartungen groß, die gewählten Mittel jedoch gar nicht so verschieden. Solchen Geschichten gehe ich gerne nach. Hatte ich eigentlich erzählt, dass sich dort im Keller das Pantheon befand, zu Schulzeiten unser bester Club?

Schön finde ich bei diesem zweiteiligen Format, dessen Grenzen wir zum Glück nie abgesteckt hatten, dass wir mit vielen Menschen ins Gespräch gekommen sind und dadurch mehr als nur unsere eigene Perspektive in das Buch eingeflossen ist. Sind wir damit etwa schon wieder beim Buchtitel *Ensembles* gelandet?

NB: Es ging uns jedenfalls darum, Zusammenhänge sichtbar zu machen. Ein Architekturbüro ist wie eine Blackbox: Es gibt einen Input, es gibt einen Output, aber was dazwischen geschieht, bleibt für Außenstehende meist im Dunkeln. Je mehr wir uns mit den Bauten und Projekten von JSWD beschäftigten, je mehr Gespräche wir führten, desto mehr Querverbindungen waren zu entdecken. Wie lässt sich eine bestimmte Denk- und Arbeitsweise auf unterschiedliche Bauaufgaben anwenden? Welche städtebaulichen Figuren, welche Materialien oder Grundrisskonzepte sind auf welche Weise adaptierbar, ohne dass es nach Wiederholung aussieht? Darüber ließ sich einiges in Erfahrung bringen, das wir nun gerne teilen.

complexity of each task threatens to become invisible. We wanted to avoid that in this book. That's why we wanted a more descriptive part and a more free magazine section in each chapter. On the first attempt with the project New Chancellor Square in Bonn, almost on your doorstep, it worked really well.

UW: That was precisely the right project to test if our concept would work. The location of the foundation stone for the new office complex was the former location of the Bonn-Center—a landmark in the German capital, neither ornate nor beautiful, but a place that for many embodied the hope of becoming whole or growing up. And today a new landmark is being built there and again the expectations are great, the selected means are however not so different. I like to work on these types of stories. Did I mention that the Pantheon, the best club in Bonn when I was in school, was there in the basement?

What I like about this two-part format, whose boundaries we fortunately never staked out, is that we spoke to so many people and thus were able to include more than just our own perspective in this book. Does that bring us back to the book title *Ensembles*?

NB: In any case, it was about making contexts visible. An architecture office is like a black box: there is an input, there is an output, but what happens in between is usually invisible to outsiders. The more we studied JSWD's buildings and projects, the more conversations we held, the more cross-links we discovered. How can a certain way of thinking and working be applied to different construction tasks? Which urban planning elements, which materials or floor plan concepts are adaptable in which way, without looking like repetition? We learned a lot about that, which we would now like to share.

Neues Kesselhaus
Gelsenkirchen

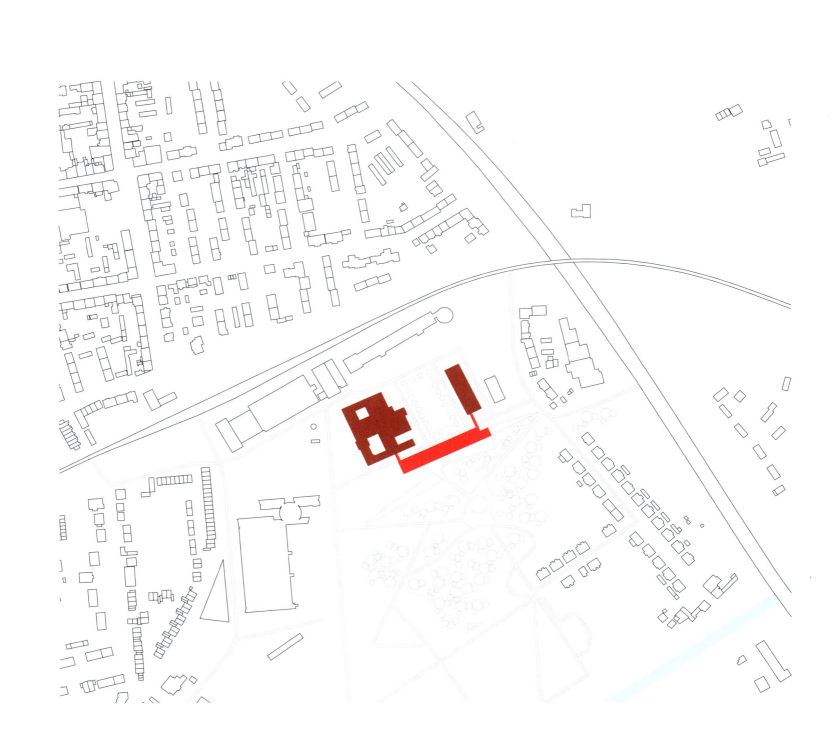

Der Transformationsprozess der Steinkohlereviere hat an vielen Orten markante Bauten freigelegt, die den Wandel von der Industrie- zur Dienstleistungsgesellschaft symbolisieren. Stehen gebliebene Zechengebäude verkörpern lokale Identität und gehören im Ruhrgebiet oft zum baukulturellen „Tafelsilber". Das international bekannteste Beispiel ist Schacht XII des heutigen UNESCO-Weltkulturerbes Zeche Zollverein in Essen-Katernberg. 1926, zwei Jahre bevor sie mit den Planungen für Zollverein begannen, entwarfen die Architekten Fritz Schupp und Martin Kremmer die Werkstatt und die Schreinerei für die Zeche Nordstern, wenige Kilometer nördlich im Gelsenkirchener Ortsteil Horst gelegen.

Nordstern, wo 1855 erstmals nach Steinkohle gebohrt wurde, war lange Zeit die nördlichste Schachtanlage des Reviers, daher ihr Name. 1993 verließ der letzte Förderwagen mit Nordsternkohle die Zeche, es folgten Abrisse, Umbauten und Zwischennutzungen. Im Rahmen der Bundesgartenschau 1997 wurden 100 Hektar des Areals in einen Landschaftspark umgewandelt. Die denkmalgeschützten Bauten von Schupp und Kremmer der Schachtanlage 1/2 wurden zum Kern eines neuen Gewerbeparks. Die Wohnungsgesellschaft THS, deren Wurzeln im Wohnstättenbau für Bergarbeiter liegen, ließ 2003 den Wagenumlauf und die Sieberei zur neuen Hauptverwaltung umbauen; 2006 wurde auch das Werkstattgebäude für Büroflächen hergerichtet. Weiterer Raumbedarf entstand, als 2012 nach der Zusammenlegung mit Evonik Immobilien die neue Dachmarke Vivawest gegründet wurde. Am Hauptverwaltungsstandort im Nordsternpark musste nun Platz für rund 600 Mitarbeiter geschaffen werden. Der erforderliche Erweiterungsbau resultiert aus einer Mehrfachbeauftragung, die JSWD Architekten mit ihrem Entwurf 2014 gewannen. Der 126 Meter lange Neubau, der wie eine Spange das Hauptgebäude mit der ehemaligen Werkstatt verbindet, steht an der Stelle des ehemaligen Kesselhauses, von dem nur noch das Stahlskelett vorhanden war. Das neue Gebäude, braunrot wie das Stahlziegelfachwerk der benachbarten Altbauten, ist von den Bestandsbauten abgerückt, um angemessene Lichtverhältnisse für die Büroflächen zu schaffen. Über zwei Brücken, die großflächig verglast sind und dementsprechend filigran wirken, wird die Berührung zwischen Alt- und Neubau dezent in Szene gesetzt. Über diese beiden „Gangways" gelangt man von den beiden Altbauten in das Flözgeschoss, einen sich über die gesamte Gebäudelänge erstreckenden Bereich mit Besprechungs- und Seminarräumen, einem teilbaren Konferenzsaal und einer kleinen Cafeteria. Der Begriff Flöz hält zum einen die Erinnerung an die einstigen Kohlenschätze unter Tage wach, lässt sich im übertragenen Sinn aber auch als Ort von Betriebsamkeit und Austausch begreifen. Die großflächige Verglasung erlaubt es, sowohl die Landschaft als auch das Baudenkmal zu erleben, und hebt dieses kommunikative Element vor allem bei Dämmerlicht hervor.

Im Kontrast dazu steht das mit Blechpaneelen blickdicht verkleidete Sockelgeschoss, das nur im Eingangsbereich gläsern und offen ist, und hier den Durchgang zum südlich anschließenden Landschaftspark ermöglicht. Das Eingangsfoyer sticht vertikal mit einem Luftraum nach oben und stellt die Verbindung zwischen Sockel- und Flözgeschoss her. Das ist überraschend repräsentativ für einen Nebeneingang, aber umso sinnvoller, wenn man an Veranstaltungen außerhalb der Bürozeiten denkt und das Hauptgebäude dann geschlossen bleiben kann.

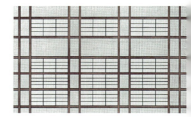

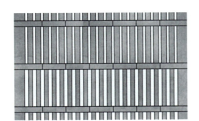

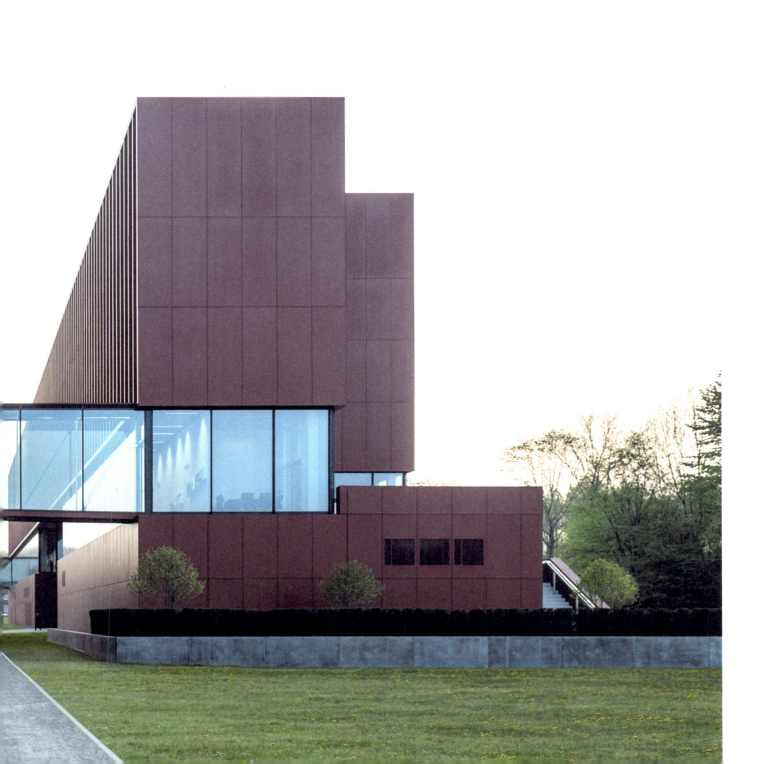

Oberhalb des Flözgeschosses sind vier Ebenen mit Zellenbüros aufgesattelt, wobei die beiden Bürostränge versetzt angeordnet wurden und eine tiefe Mittelzone mit Besprechungsräumen und Teeküchen umrahmen. Die rigide Rasterfassade wird durch das Achsmaß von 1,15 Metern strukturiert, das für heutige Büroetagen als effizient gilt. Die beeindruckende Repetition der Fenster veranschaulicht, vor allem in der Schrägansicht, die schiere Länge des Gebäudes, zitiert dabei aber auch die Architektursprache typischer Verwaltungsbauten der 1950er und 1960er Jahre. Jedoch handelt es sich hier nicht um eine formale Nachahmung, sondern um die geschickte Neuinterpretation einer bekannten Chiffre. Selbst wer nicht weiß, dass die Entwicklung der Neubaufassade auf den vorgefundenen Rastersystemen der Bestandsgebäude basiert, spürt intuitiv den Kontext, der sich in dem Neubau widerspiegelt – er ist die Synthese der verschiedenen Zeitschichten. Was den Industriebau der Zeche auszeichnet – seine sachliche Setzung, die funktionalen Anforderungen folgt, seine technisch bedingte Überdimensionierung, sein ehrlicher und effizienter Materialeinsatz –, all diese Eigenschaften machen den Neubau zu einer modernen und absolut ortsverbundenen Architektur.

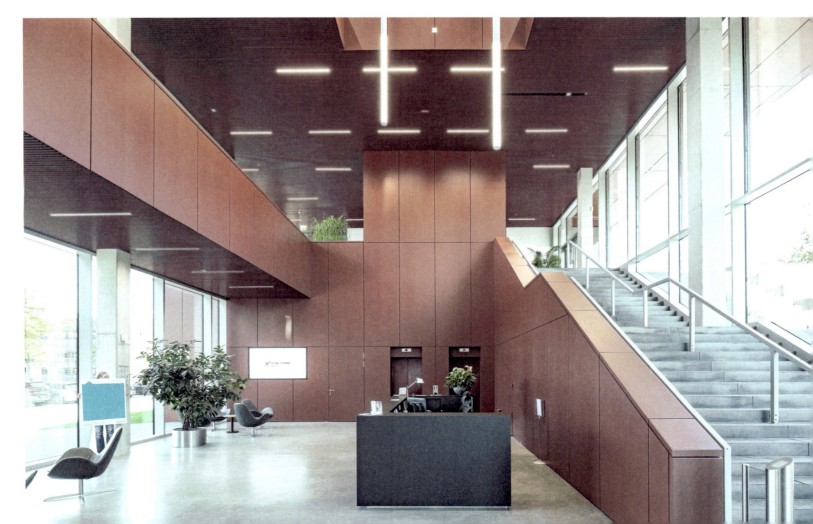

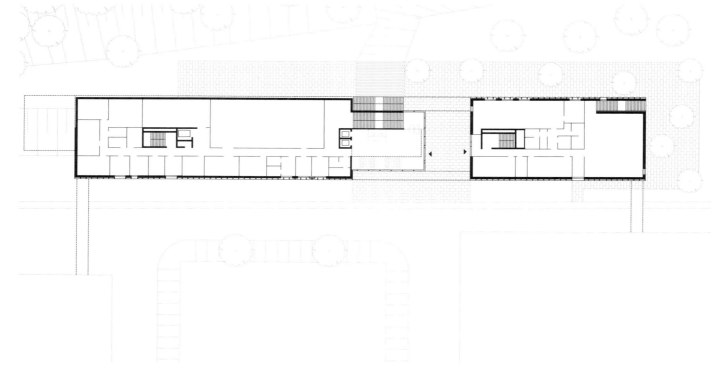

Ebene 0   Level 0

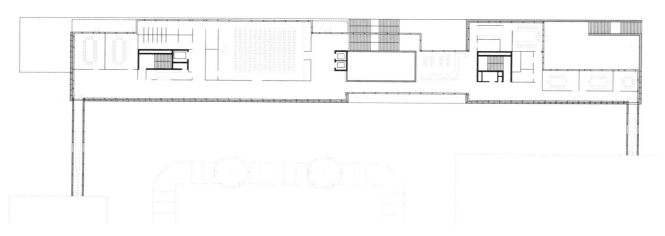

Ebene 1   Level 1

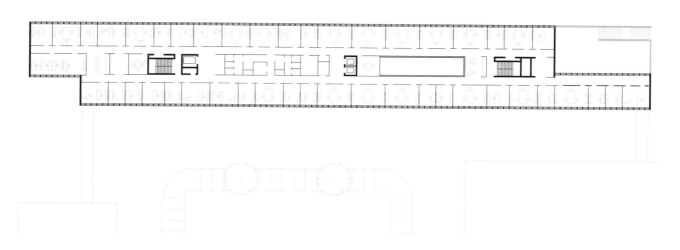

Ebene 2   Level 2

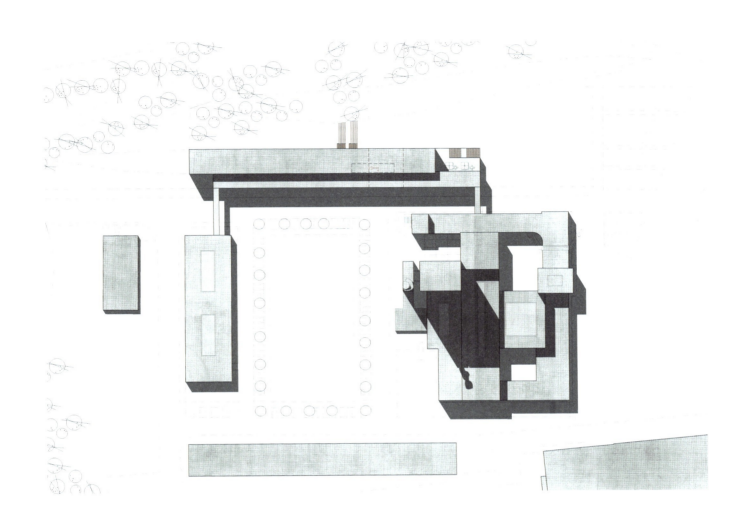

Vivawest Headquarter
Gelsenkirchen

In many places, the transformation processes in coal mining regions have uncovered striking buildings which symbolize the shift from an industrial to a service economy. Surviving mine buildings embody local identity and, in the Ruhr region, they are often part of the architectural-cultural legacy. The best known example internationally is Shaft XII of the Zollverein Coal Mine Industrial Complex (*Zeche Zollverein*) in Essen-Katernberg, which has been designated a UNESCO world heritage site. In 1926, two years before they began planning the Zollverein, architects Fritz Schupp and Martin Kremmer designed the workshop and carpenter's shop for the Nordstern Coal Mine, located only a few kilometers north of the Horst district of Gelsenkirchen.

Nordstern, where, in 1855, hard coal was mined for the first time, derives its name from the fact that for many years it was the most northerly mine. In 1993, the last cart filled with Nordstern coal left the mine; demolitions, modifications and intermediate uses followed. 100 hectares of the area were transformed into a landscape park for the 1997 Federal Garden Show (*Bundesgartenschau*). The listed buildings by Schupp and Kremmer from shafts 1/2 became the core of a new business park. In 2003, the housing association THS, which has its roots in housing construction for mine workers, had the tub circuit and the screening plant converted into a new administrative headquarters; in 2006, the workshop was also renovated and repurposed into office space. The 2012 merger between Evonik Real Estate and THS resulted in both a new umbrella brand, Vivawest, and a further increase in office space requirements. At Nordsternpark, where the headquarters is located, space for approximately 600 employees needed to be built.

The necessary extension building resulted from a multiple commission which was won by JSWD Architects in 2014. The 126-meter-long new construction, which connects the main building with the former workshop like a clasp, is located on the site of the former boiler house, of which only the steel skeleton had remained. The new building, which is red-brown like the steel-trussed brick of the neighboring historical buildings, is shifted back from the existing construction in order to afford the office space adequate light. The relationship between old and new is modestly framed by two delicate-feeling bridges with extensive glass surfaces. Over these two gangways, one can travel from the historical buildings to the "seam story" (*Flözgeschoss*), an area which stretches the length of the building and contains meeting and seminar rooms, a separable conference room, and a small cafeteria. On the one hand, the term "seam" serves as a reminder of the coal seams that once enriched the landscape here; on the other, it can be figuratively understood as a space for activity and exchange. The extensive glass surfaces allow observers to experience both the landscape and the listed buildings and highlight this communicative element, in particular at twilight.

This communicative transparency is contrasted by the ground floor, which is faced with opaque metal panels throughout with the single exception of a transparent glass section around the entrance; through this section, one can pass through to the landscape park, which connects to the space to the south.

The entrance foyer vertically connects the ground floor and the "seam story" through its double-floor ceiling height. It is surprisingly grand for a secondary entrance; this design choice, however, makes sense when one considers events outside of normal business hours, when the main building is closed.

Above the "seam story," there are four floors with small offices. The two rows of offices were arranged staggered around a deep middle zone with meeting rooms and tea kitchens. The rigid raster facade was structured using an axial dimension of 1.15 meters, which is considered efficient for today's office space. The impressive repetition of the windows illustrates the sheer length of the building, in particular when viewed on an angle, and makes reference to the architectural language of typical administrative buildings of the 1950s and '60s. However, this building is not merely a formal imitation, but rather a skillful new interpretation of a well-known code. Even those who are not aware of the fact that the development of the new building's facade is based on the raster systems of the buildings around it intuitively sense the context which is reflected in the new construction—it is the synthesis of various layers of time. All the qualities which distinguish the industrial construction associated with mining—its rational organization following functional considerations, its technically necessary large proportions, its honest and efficient use of materials—also make the new construction a modern and absolutely local architecture.

Bekenntnis zu den Wurzeln
Commitment to the Roots

Ein Gespräch mit Claudia Goldenbeld, Mitglied der Geschäftsführung des Wohnimmobilienkonzerns Vivawest, und Frederik Jaspert (Partner, JSWD) über das neue Verwaltungsgebäude auf dem Gelände der ehemaligen Zeche Nordstern in Gelsenkirchen.

A discussion with Claudia Goldenbeld, one of the managing directors of residential real estate company Vivawest, and Frederik Jaspert (Partner, JSWD) about the new administrative building at the former Nordstern mine in Gelsenkirchen.

Frau Goldenbeld, welche Absichten haben Sie mit dem Verwaltungsneubau verfolgt?
Claudia Goldenbeld: In erster Linie wollten wir mit dem Neubau attraktive Arbeitsplätze für die Mitarbeiter schaffen. Unsere Hauptverwaltung, die ehemalige Zeche Nordstern, sowie benachbarte, angemietete Räumlichkeiten boten für die Mitarbeiter am Standort keine ausreichenden Kapazitäten mehr. Wenn eine nicht unerhebliche Summe an Geld in die Hand genommen wird, um ein weiteres neues Verwaltungsgebäude zu errichten, ist das Unterfangen aber – nicht zuletzt für unsere Gesellschafter – ein Spagat zwischen ökonomischer Effizienz und ästhetischer, zu uns passender Architektur. Dieser ist uns gelungen. Wir kommen aus dem Bergarbeiterwohnungsbau, daher stehen wir zu unserem Standort Gelsenkirchen und dem Gebäudeensemble auf dem Gelände der ehemaligen Zeche Nordstern, das unsere Geschichte visualisiert. Der ergänzende Neubau ist kein Fremdkörper, sondern fügt sich harmonisch in das Ensemble des Vivawest-Campus ein. Darauf bin ich stolz.

Herr Jaspert, wenn Sie als Architekt mit Ihrem Büro vor der Aufgabe stehen, in einem solchen historischen Kontext zu entwerfen, welche gestalterischen Ausdrucksformen werden da herangezogen? Wie gehen Sie im Zuge einer derart spezifischen Aufgabe vor?

Ms. Goldenbeld, what were your goals with regard to the new administrative building?
Claudia Goldenbeld: First and foremost, we wanted to create attractive new workspaces for our employees. Our main headquarters building, the former Nordstern mine, and the neighboring rented spaces no longer offered sufficient capacity for employees working at this location. When you plan to spend a not insignificant amount of money in order to build an additional new administrative building, the challenge is—not least of all for our shareholders—to achieve a good balance between economic efficiency and aesthetic architecture which fits us. However, I would say that we have been successful. Our roots are in housing construction for mine workers; for this reason, we are committed to our location in Gelsenkirchen and the building ensemble at the site of the former Nordstern mine, which exemplifies our history. The supplemental new construction is not a foreign body, but rather blends harmoniously into the ensemble at the Vivawest Campus. I am very proud of that.

Mr. Jaspert, when you as an architect are faced with the challenge of designing a building in such a historical context, which creative forms of expression do you employ? What approach do you use in the course of a task which is a specific as this one?
Frederik Jaspert: Planning on a historical site or with historical

Frederik Jaspert: Das Planen auf historischem Grund oder mit historischer Substanz ist eine besondere Herausforderung. Anders als bei dem Bau eines freien Campus einer Konzernzentrale steht zunächst die intensive Auseinandersetzung mit der Bestandsarchitektur im Vordergrund. Hier sollte das existierende Quartier nicht nur weitergebaut werden, sondern der Neubau sich wie selbstverständlich in den bestehenden Kontext eingliedern. Aus unserer Sicht ist entscheidend, dass das Gesamtquartier mit Neu und Alt eine große Kraft entwickelt und nicht jeder Baustein nur für sich steht. Wir haben uns intensiv mit der Architektur, den vorhandenen Maßstäben, den orthogonal geformten Baukörpervolumen sowie mit Materialität und Farbigkeit beschäftigt, um den Charakter und die industrielle Rauheit in den Neubau zu transportieren.

Der Neubau auf Nordstern ist allerdings nicht nur eine einfache Adaption der bestehenden Gebäude, vielmehr haben Sie den Bestand hier in eine etwas andere Sprachlichkeit transformiert. Was war hierbei der Leitgedanke?

FJ: Eine wesentliche Idee war es, mit den vorhandenen Gestaltungstypologien zu arbeiten. Damit das Haus auch eine eigene Kraft entwickelt und weil es – unseres Erachtens – eines Kontrapunkts zum hohen Nordsternturm bedurfte, haben wir uns für einen äußerst klaren Baukörper und eine große Homogenität in Material und Farbigkeit entschieden.

Können Sie, Frau Goldenbeld, in Ihrer verantwortungsvollen Position über Aspekte wie Repräsentanz und Schönheit sprechen, ohne das Gefühl zu haben, sich im Zuge einer solchen Bauaufgabe entschuldigen zu müssen?

CG: Ja, das kann ich sehr wohl. Die Entwicklung des Standortes Nordstern stieß bei unseren Gesellschaftern auf große Zustimmung. Wir sind gemeinsam stolz auf diese einmaligen Gebäude. Jeder, den wir in das Hauptgebäude führen, ist begeistert, und diese Begeisterung habe ich mir auch für den Neubau gewünscht.

Der letzte aktive Tag der Zeche Nordstern, 1993
The last working day at the Nordstern mine, 1993

existing buildings is a particular challenge. First of all, as opposed to the construction of a freestanding campus or company headquarters, the intensive negotiation with the existing architecture is in the foreground. The existing quarter is not just supposed to be extended; the new construction should integrate itself into the existing context in a natural and self-evident way. From our perspective, it is decisive that the entire area with new and old develops a force as a whole, that the individual components are not just good on their own. We worked intensively with the architecture, the existing scale, the orthogonally shaped building volumes, the materiality and the colors in order to convey the character of industrial roughness through the new construction.

The new construction at Nordstern, however, is not just a simple adaptation of an existing building. On the contrary, you have transformed the existing buildings into a somewhat different vocabulary. What was your thinking behind this?

FJ: One essential idea was to work with the existing design typologies. So that the building could develop its own power and because, in our opinion, a counterpoint to the high Nordstern tower was needed, we decided to design an exceptionally clear structure and employ very homogeneous materials and colors.

Ms. Goldenbeld, considering your position of particular responsibility, can you tell us about aspects such as representativeness and beauty in

Zeche Nordstern in den 1960er Jahren   Nordstern mine in the 1960s

Anschluss eines Verbindungsstegs
Attachment of a connecting bridge

Herr Jaspert, wir sprachen eben über die alte, solitär stehende Fassade des ehemaligen Kesselhauses, die lange Zeit auch durch den Denkmalschutz gesichert werden musste, allerdings am Ende einvernehmlich abgetragen wurde. Wie gehen Sie als Architekt mit so einer Fragestellung um?
FJ: Diese Fragestellung hatte sich während der Mehrfachbeauftragung bereits erübrigt, da zu dem Zeitpunkt die Entscheidung gefallen war, diese Wand zurückzubauen. Die Fassade war ein wichtiger Baustein zur Stärkung des Platzraums und damit zur Adressbildung des Unternehmens. Mit dem Neubau haben wir den Raum wieder geschlossen und es wäre schön, wenn auf der noch offenen gegenüberliegenden Platzseite eine bauliche Entsprechung entstünde. Natürlich tut es im ersten Moment weh, ein Stück Geschichte dieses Quartiers schwinden zu sehen. Auf der anderen Seite wäre es für uns – unter Berücksichtigung der Vorgaben – keine Option gewesen, das Stück Fassade wiederzubeleben und in die neue Architektur zu

the context of this construction without having the feeling that you need to apologize for it?
CG: Oh yes, I most certainly can. The development of our Nordstern location met with enthusiastic approval among our shareholders. We are collectively proud of this unique building. Everyone who comes to our main headquarters is impressed and positive; this was exactly what I wanted for our new building.

Mr. Jaspert, we spoke just a moment ago about the old, solitary facade of the former boiler house, which was protected by historical listing for a long time; in the end, it was demolished with the agreement of the historical protection office. How do you deal with a question like that as an architect?
FJ: This issue became superfluous during the multiple commission process, since at that time the decision was made to demolish those walls. The facade was an important component in the strengthening of the space and therefore also contributed to the prestige of the

company. Through the new construction, we closed off the space again; it would be nice if, on the other side of the square, which is still empty, an architectural counterpoint could be built. Naturally, initially it's painful to see a piece of local history disappear. On the other hand, considering the conditions of the commission, it would not have been possible for us to incorporate the existing facade into a new building. The urbanistic and architectural clarity would not have been possible if we had preserved the existing boiler house.
It is essentially a question of perspective regarding historical protection as an institution, which is posed to us as a society time and again: How do we deal with history? How do we deal with our roots? Is it not doctrinaire that the bricks themselves are suddenly worth more than their capability?
CG: The goal should be to find a good compromise. We need to preserve an artifact, since it is related to our history, mining in the Ruhr area. The last mine closed in 2018. I think it's just right that we have created so-called "lighthouse projects" here by lending these impressive buildings a new, meaningful use. However, it's important not to become dogmatic. Here at Nordstern, we were able to preserve the majority of the mine buildings, but also to create space for new development in order to look ahead. We need both elements: the historic roots and the future.
FJ: At the moment there is a trend towards using bricks. The re-emergence of building things which are made by hand and "unbreakable" surely plays a role in this trend. After a period with many experiments, we are now seeing a return to tried-and-trusted resources and materials. There are few materials which have as long a lifespan as brick; from this perspective, the re-emergence seems understandable. Coming back to this project,

Zwei Brücken verbinden das Flözgeschoss mit dem Bestand   Two bridges connect the "seam story" with the existing buildings

integrieren. Die stadträumliche und architektonische Klarheit hätte bei Erhalt des Bestands nicht entstehen können.

Im Grunde ist es eine Haltungsfrage, die über den Denkmalschutz als Institution an uns als Gesellschaft immer wieder gestellt wird: Wie gehen wir mit Historie um? Wie gehen wir mit unseren Wurzeln um? Ist es nicht doktrinär, dass uns die Ziegelsteine auf einmal mehr wert sind als eine Leistungsfähigkeit?
CG: Das Ziel sollte es sein, einen guten Mittelweg zu finden. Wir müssen einen Teil erhalten, da er mit unserer Vergangenheit, dem Bergbau im Ruhrgebiet, verbunden ist. 2018 ist das letzte Bergwerk geschlossen worden und ich finde es genau richtig, dass wir hier im Ruhrgebiet Leuchttürme geschaffen haben, indem wir diese beeindruckenden Gebäude wieder einer sinnvollen Nutzung zuführen. Allerdings darf das nicht dogmatisiert werden. Letztendlich haben wir hier auf Nordstern einen Großteil der Zechengebäude erhalten, aber auch Platz für Neues geschaffen, um in die Zukunft blicken zu können. Wir brauchen beide Seiten: den Blick auf unsere Wurzeln und den Blick in Richtung Zukunft.
FJ: Bei diesem Ziegeltrend, den wir aktuell erleben, spielt sicherlich die Rückbesinnung darauf, etwas Handgemachtes und „Unumstößliches" zu bauen, eine Rolle. Nach einer Zeit mit vielen Experimenten findet nun eine Rückkehr zu alten Rohstoffen und Materialien statt, die sich bereits bewährt haben. Es existieren wenige Materialien, die eine derart lange Lebensdauer haben wie Ziegel, insofern ist diese Rückbesinnung verständlich. Tatsächlich haben wir, um auch auf dieses Projekt zurückzukommen, zeitweilig überlegt, ob Ziegel auch hier infrage kommt.

Wir haben uns dann für das zweite den Campus prägende Material entschieden, und das war der Stahl.

Sind es mutige Dinge, die uns manchmal gut zu Gesicht stünden, etwas zu wagen und voranzutreiben?
FJ: Ich glaube, dass Sehgewohnheiten geweitet werden müssen, dass aus einer gewissen Enge ausgebrochen werden muss. Das gelingt nur, indem wir aus Erfahrungen lernen und neue Entwicklungen zulassen. Es ist wichtig, dass wir uns nicht nur erinnern, sondern auch experimentieren. In anderen Ländern geschieht das sicherlich viel stärker und intensiver, in Deutschland haben wir eine starke Bodenhaftung. Jedes architektonische Experiment wird mit Argwohn und Skepsis betrachtet.
CG: Sie haben es sehr gut auf den Punkt gebracht. Ich glaube „mutiger" ist an dieser Stelle das richtige Wort. In Deutschland haben wir kulturell bedingt ein sehr großes Beharrungsvermögen, zudem ist es bequemer, einfach wegzuschauen, anstatt zu handeln.

Bietet Architektur eine Möglichkeit, den Menschen auch solche Themen zu vermitteln und Reibungsfläche zu sein?
FJ: Ich glaube, Architektur ist immer ein Stück weit politisch und soll auch zu Diskussionen anregen. Es gibt keine Kunst, die derart unmittelbar auf das Umfeld und die Gesellschaft Einfluss nimmt. Insofern kann Architektur einen großen Beitrag leisten, aus Gewohnheiten auszubrechen. Durch permanente Wiederholungen entsteht keine Diskussion. Kontrapunkte sind wichtig, um anzuheizen und zu befeuern.

Leicht gekürzte Fassung eines Gesprächs mit Johannes Busmann, erschienen im Magazin polis, *03/2018.*

Luftbild mit dem Neuen Kesselhaus im Vordergrund
Aerial view with the new boiler house in the foreground

we actually considered incorporating bricks into this building for a while. In the end, we settled on the second material which characterizes the campus: steel.

Is it a courageous thing to dare and move things forward? Would that be something that suits us well?
FJ: I think that our way of looking needs to be broadened, that we need to break out of a certain narrowness. That can only happen if we learn from our experiences and allow new developments to happen. It is important that we not only remember, but also experiment. In other countries, that process surely happens much more intensely and to a greater degree; in Germany, we are relatively inflexible. Every architectural experiment is regarded with mistrust and suspicion.
CG: You really got to the heart of the matter. I think "more courageous" is the right phrasing for this situation. In Germany, we have a high degree of inertia as a result of our cultural history. Plus, it is also more comfortable to look away instead of taking action.

Does architecture offer the possibility to convey these topics and potentially also a context in which to approach them?
FJ: I think architecture is always political to some degree and should also encourage discussion. There is no other art form which influences the environment and society in the way that architecture does. In that sense, architecture can make a major contribution to breaking out of old habits. Discussion doesn't come from permanent repetition. Counterpoints are important to stoke and fuel debate.

Slightly shortened version of a discussion with Johannes Busmann, published in the magazine polis, *03/2018.*

Haus der Europäischen Geschichte Brüssel

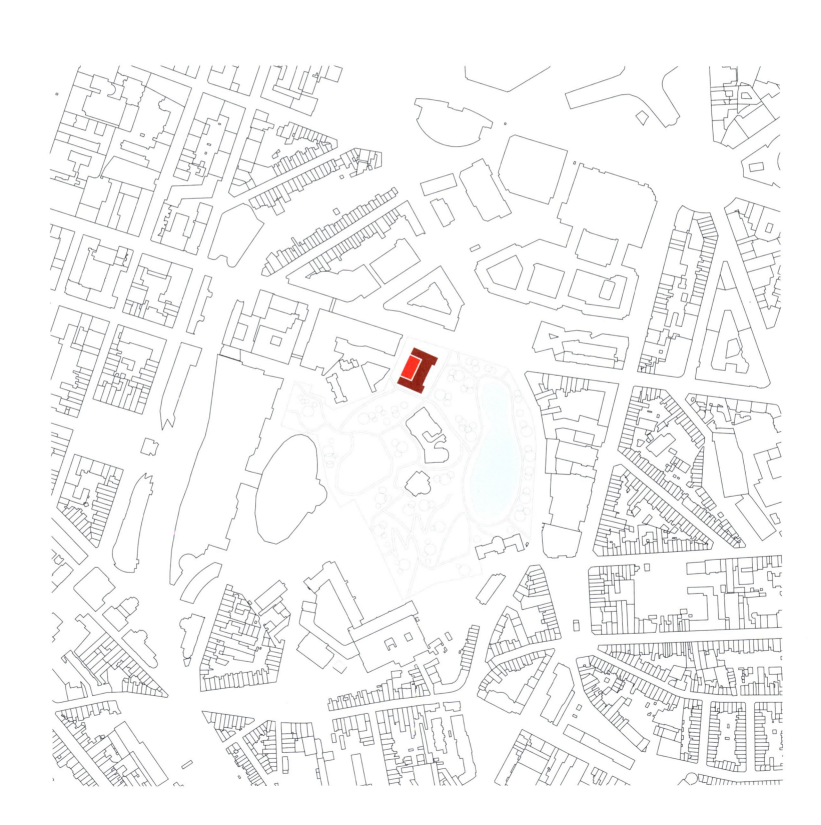

Das Institut Dentaire George Eastman

Wo beginnt die Geschichte Europas? Das Haus der Europäischen Geschichte (Maison de l'histoire européenne) in Brüssel hat überraschenderweise eine transatlantische Vorgeschichte, die mit der Wohltätigkeit des US-amerikanischen Unternehmers George Eastman (1854–1932) beginnt. Eastman hatte mit den Rollfilmen und handlichen Kameras seiner Firma Kodak das Fotografieren erschwinglich gemacht und ein Vermögen verdient. Eastmans Arbeiter profitierten von seinen sozialreformerischen Ideen sowie Schulen, Kliniken und Institute von seiner Spendenbereitschaft. Wie viele Wohlhabende sammelte er Gemälde, doch seine wahre Passion war die Verbesserung der Mund- und Zahnhygiene bei Kindern aus sozialschwachen Familien. Dazu gründete er 1917 in Rochester (NY), dem Sitz von Kodak, ein erstes Institut, in dem eine kostenlose zahnärztliche Behandlung angeboten wurde. Es folgten weitere Einrichtungen in London, Rom, Paris und Stockholm, bis er 1931 eine Million Dollar für die Errichtung eines zahnärztlichen Modellinstituts in Brüssel zur Verfügung stellte. Eastman bestand auf die Beauftragung des Schweizer Architekten Michel Polak (1885–1948) und darauf, dass der Brüsseler Neubau sich an dem Vorbild des Instituts in Rochester orientiere. Ein Grundstück fand sich im Parc Léopold, der durch einen Kranz ebenso renommierter wie repräsentativer Institute zu einem Ort der Wissenschaft und der Erholung geworden war. Dort fügte sich das 1935 eröffnete „Institut Dentaire George Eastman", so die Inschrift auf dem Gesims, ausgezeichnet ein. Über 150 Kinder konnten hier pro Tag behandelt, junge Zahnärzte ausgebildet und Konferenzen abgehalten werden. All dies in einer Atmosphäre, die so wenig wie möglich an eine Klinik erinnern sollte. Stilistisch bewegte sich Polak zwischen Art déco und Neoklassizismus, setzte edle Steine und Hölzer ein und beauftragte den belgischen Maler Camille Barthélémy (1890–1961), den Wartebereich mit Fabelszenen auszumalen.

50 Jahre nach der Eröffnung stellte die Commission d'Assistance Publique de la Ville die Arbeit des Instituts ein. Zunächst vermietete sie das Gebäude an das sich in Brüssel formierende Europäische Parlament, das hier von der Kita bis zur Druckerei und den Chören der Europäischen Gemeinschaft vieles provisorisch unterbrachte und es schließlich 2008 erwarb. Inzwischen hatte sich Europa politisch immer mehr organisiert und mit einem gewaltigen Komplex im Quartier Léopold bauliche Gestalt angenommen, sodass 2009 die Entscheidung fiel, die ehemalige Zahnklinik für das neu zu gründende Haus der Europäischen Geschichte zur Verfügung zu stellen.

Das Haus der Europäischen Geschichte

Für die Transformation der ehemaligen Zahnklinik zum Haus der Europäischen Geschichte und die damit verbundene Sanierung und Erweiterung lobte das Europäische Parlament 2009 einen dreiphasigen internationalen Wettbewerb aus, in dem sich die Arbeitsgemeinschaft JSWD und Chaix & Morel et Associés (Paris) mit dem Versprechen einer transparenten Fortschreibung des Bestandes durchsetzen konnte.

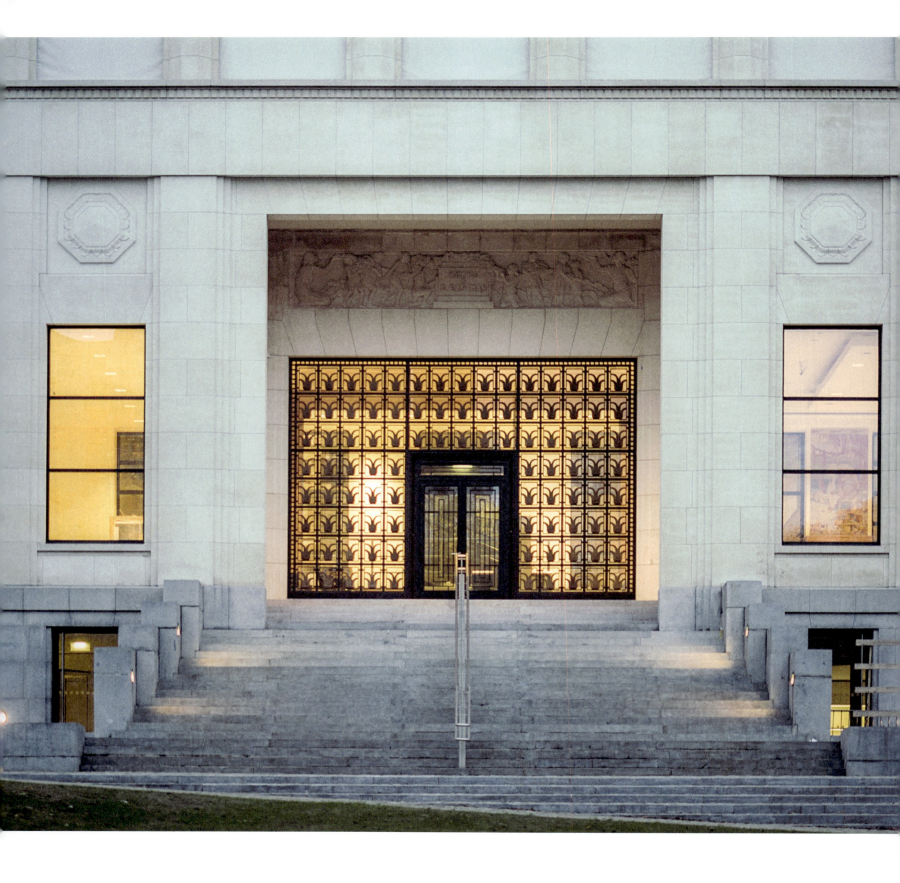

Kaum mehr als ein gläsernes Inlet fügten sie dem steinernen Altbau hinzu. Rückseitig schlossen sie die drei historischen Flügel bündig zum Block, an der dem Parc Léopold zugewandten Schau- und Eingangsseite tritt das Neue als gläserne Krone in der Breite des Mittelbaus in Erscheinung. So bleibt das Gesamtbild weiterhin symmetrisch und axial ausgerichtet, während sich hinter der mit feinen Streifen bedruckten glatten gläsernen Hülle ein scheinbar bewegtes Spiel aus offenen und geschlossenen Flächen abzeichnet. Doch nicht nur die Haut, auch das in Zusammenarbeit mit Werner Sobek entwickelte Tragwerk ist gläsern, sodass die Transparenz der Erweiterung mit der Glasschwertfassade bis aufs Äußerste getrieben wird und die ehemalige Zahnklinik als lichte Europavitrine erscheint.

Schon sehr früh kam das deutsch-französische Architektenteam überein, den Museumsbesuch als einen Spaziergang zu inszenieren, der sich an den Ausblicken auf den Park und das Europaviertel orientieren solle, um die Inhalte des Museums – die Geschichte Europas – direkt mit dem Genius Loci zu verknüpfen. Eine konkrete Museografie gab es zu diesem Zeitpunkt noch nicht und so entwickelten die Architekten ihre Passage um ein lichtes Atrium, in dem die filigrane Treppe zu schweben scheint. Die Treppe, deren sechs Läufe tatsächlich mit Stahlseilen von der Dachkonstruktion abgehängt sind, verbindet nicht nur die Ebenen, sondern wird zu einem Fixpunkt, den die Besucher mit dem Ausstellungsparcours durch Alt- und Neubau immer wieder umrunden. Der Weg führt zum Licht, das durch das Glasdach in die breite Fuge des Atriums fällt und das von dem die Treppe begleitenden Schriftbandkunstwerk *The Vortex of European History* des Künstlers Boris Micka bis herunter zum ersten Antritt gefiltert wird.

Da nur die dem Park zugewandte Ansicht des Altbaus unter Denkmalschutz steht, konnten die Innenräume weitgehend entkernt und mit der Erweiterung neu organisiert und erschlossen sowie die Ausstellungsflächen auf 4000 Quadratmeter verdoppelt werden. Dennoch bleibt der Umgang mit der Substanz respektvoll. Wo immer sich der Neubau dem Bestand annähert, markiert eine Fuge den Wechsel, der immer auch ein Materialwechsel ist.

Im Mai 2017 wurde das Museum eröffnet, aber die Terroranschläge in Paris und Brüssel hatten der Geschichte Europas kurz zuvor ein neues, trauriges Kapitel hinzugefügt. So betreten die Besucher das Haus heute nicht mehr wie seinerzeit die Patienten über die große Freitreppe, sondern werden zunächst durch eine direkt daneben in den Sockel geschnittene Tür nach flughafenartiger Sicherheitskontrolle in die Eingangshalle mit Information, Schließfächern und Shop geschleust, bevor sie die repräsentativen Warte- und Empfangshallen der Klinik in der Etage darüber betreten können. Doch einen vielversprechenden ersten Anblick der aufwendig restaurierten Ausstattung und Fabelmalereien bekommen die Besucher durch die kreisförmigen Deckenausschnitte, die in den unteren Räumen die fehlende Höhe ersetzen. An den ehemaligen Empfangsbereich schließt auf gleichem Niveau im Neubau eine großzügige Fläche für Wechselausstellungen an, in einem Seitenflügel liegt ein Auditorium mit 100 Plätzen, während der andere Flügel von der Verwaltung genutzt wird. Die Dauerausstellung beginnt in der darüber liegenden Etage mit der Frage „Was ist Europa?" und führt die Besucher spiralförmig und thematisch-chronologisch strukturiert in die Höhe – zum Licht. Das Museum versteht sich als ein Ort des informellen Lernens und überlässt es den Besuchern selbst, ihren Weg durch

die zu einem großen Teil multimedialen Installationen und interaktiven Stationen zu finden. Leih-Tablets und -Kopfhörer erläutern die Inhalte und Zusammenhänge in den 24 Amtssprachen der EU.
Die Ausstellungsplaner APD – Acciona Productions and Design aus Sevilla verfolgten mit ihrem introvertierten Konzept einen anderen Ansatz als die Architekten und verwandelten die Ausstellungsräume in Alt- und Neubau in eine große Blackbox. Doch das Haus kann seine Vermittlerrolle jederzeit wieder aufnehmen. Dann vielleicht als „Haus der Europäischen Zukunft"?

The George Eastman Institute of Dentistry Brussels

Where does the history of Europe begin? The House of European History (*Maison de l'histoire européenne*) in Brussels has a surprisingly transatlantic history, beginning with the charity of the US entrepreneur George Eastman (1854–1932). The roll films and smaller cameras that Eastman's Kodak Company developed made taking pictures affordable and earned him a fortune. Eastman's workers benefited from his social reformist ideas as well as from the schools, clinics, and institutes which he donated. Like many wealthy people, he collected paintings, but his true passion was the improvement of children from low-income families' oral and dental hygiene. To do this, he founded an institute offering free dental treatment located in Rochester (NY), the seat of Kodak, in 1917. It was followed by other facilities in London, Rome, Paris, and Stockholm; in 1931, he provided a million dollars for the establishment of a dental model institute in Brussels. Eastman insisted on commissioning the Swiss architect Michel Polak (1885–1948) and that the new building in Brussels follow the example of the institute in Rochester. A plot of land was found in the Parc Léopold, which had become a place of science and recreation through the concentration of renowned and prestigious institutes. There, the "George Eastman Institute of Dentistry," following the inscription on the cornice, opened in 1935 and formed an excellent addition. More than 150 children could be treated here each day; it was also a location where young dentists were trained and conferences were held. All of this in an atmosphere that is as little reminiscent of a clinic as possible. Stylistically, Polak moved
between Art Deco and Neoclassicism, using precious stones and woods; he commissioned the Belgian painter Camille Barthélémy (1890–1961) to paint the waiting area with scenes from nursery rhymes and children's stories.
Fifty years after its opening, the Commission d'Assistance Publique de la Ville discontinued the work of the institute. Initially, it rented the building to the European Parliament, which was forming at that time in Brussels; the Commission used the space for a variety of temporary uses, from a kindergarten to a printing house to the choirs of the European Community. It finally purchased the building in 2008. In the meantime, Europe had become more and more politically organized and transformed into a huge complex in the Léopold district. In 2009, the decision was made to make the former dental clinic available to the newly founded House of European History.

The House of European History
Brussels

For the transformation of the former dental clinic into the House of European History and the related renovation and extension, the European Parliament announced a three-phase international competition in 2009, which was won by a consortium between JSWD and Chaix & Morel et Associés (Paris), who promised a transparent continuation of the existing building.

They added little more than a glass inlet to the historic stone building. At the rear, they extended the three historic wings so that they are now flush with the block. On the side facing Parc Léopold, the new construction's appearance is that of a glass crown over the width of the middle section of the structure. The overall appearance thus remains symmetrical and axially aligned, while a seemingly animated play of open and closed surfaces emerges behind the smooth glass envelope printed with fine stripes. But not only the skin, but also the supporting structure, which was developed in collaboration with Werner Sobek, is made of glass, driving the transparency of the extension with its glass fin facade to the utmost. The former dental clinic has been transformed into a bright European display case.

Very early on, the Franco-German team of architects agreed that the experience of a visit to the museum should focus on the views of the park and the European quarter, in order to link the contents of the museum—the history of Europe—directly with the *genius loci*. A concrete museography did not exist at that time and so the architects developed their passage around a bright atrium in which the delicate staircase seems to float. The staircase, whose six runs are actually suspended from the roof structure with steel cables, not only connects the levels, but also becomes a fixed point with which the visitors circle around the exhibition through the old and new buildings. The path leads to the light that shines through the glass roof into the wide fissure of the atrium and that is filtered down to the first step through artist Boris Micka's sculpture, *The Vortex of European History*, which accompanies the staircase.

Since only the park-facing view of the old building is listed, through the extension the interior could be largely gutted and reorganized and the exhibition space could be doubled to 4,000 square meters. Nevertheless, the handling of the substance remained respectful; wherever the new building connects to the existing one, a joint and a change in material marks the border. The museum opened in May 2017, but the terrorist attacks in Paris and Brussels had recently added a new, sad chapter to Europe's history. Visitors now no longer enter the building like patients once did via the large external staircase, but are first channeled through a door cut directly into the ground floor, where they pass through an airport-like security check and an entrance hall with information, lockers, and a shop before they are permitted to enter the representative waiting area and reception halls of the clinic on the floor above. But visitors can get a promising first glimpse of the elaborately restored fittings and fabulous paintings through the circular ceiling cutouts, which compensate for the lack of height in the lower rooms. The former reception area includes a generous space for temporary exhibitions on the same level in the new building. One wing houses an auditorium with 100 seats, while the other wing is used by

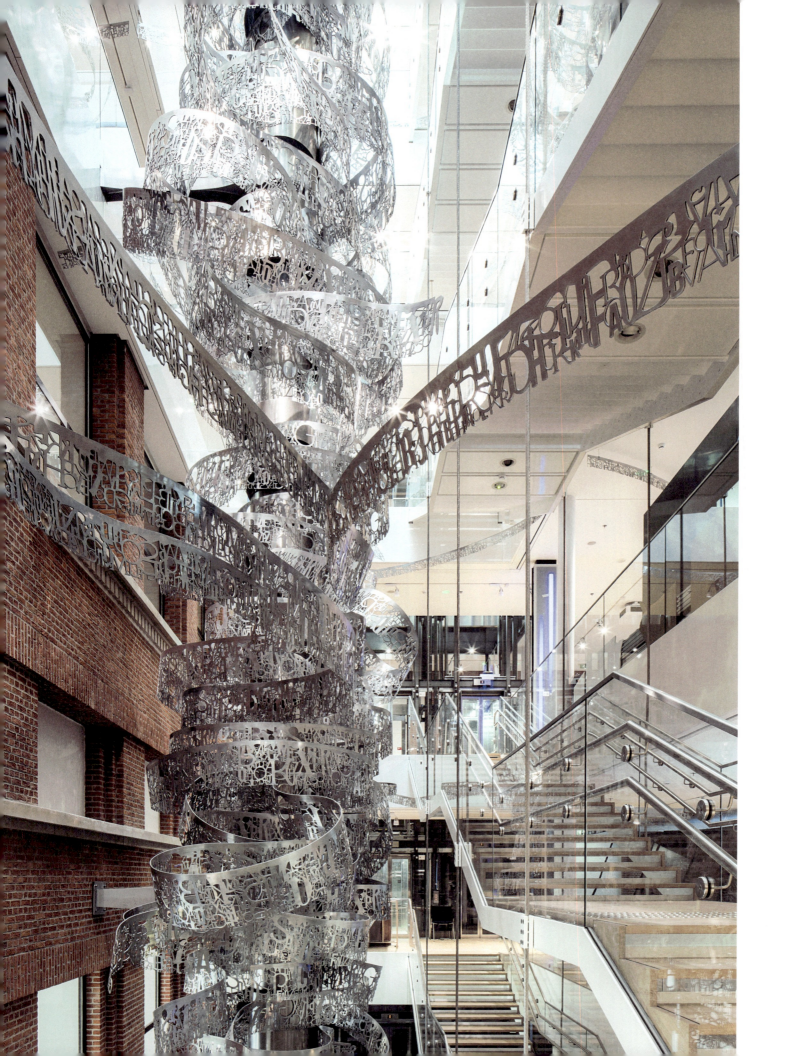

the administration. The permanent exhibition begins on the floor above with the question "What is Europe?" and leads visitors upwards in a spiral and thematic-chronological structure—upwards toward the light. The museum sees itself as a place of informal learning, leaving it up to the visitors themselves to find their way through the exhibition, which is made up of multimedia installations and interactive stations to a large extent. Rental tablets and headphones explain the contents and connections in the 24 official languages of the EU.

The exhibition planners, Seville's APD—Acciona Productions and Design, followed an introverted concept, taking a different approach to the architects: they transformed the exhibition spaces in the old and new buildings into a large black box. But the house can resume its mediating role at any time. Then maybe as the "House of the European Future?"

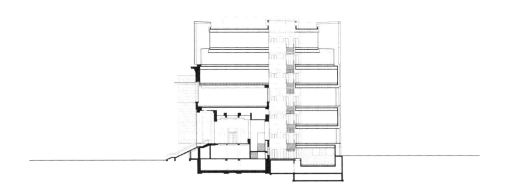

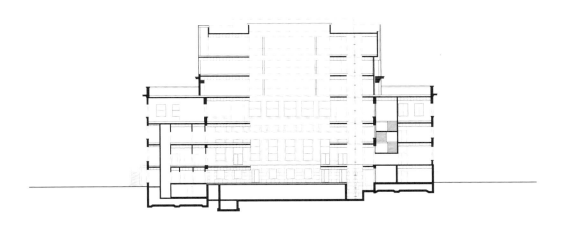

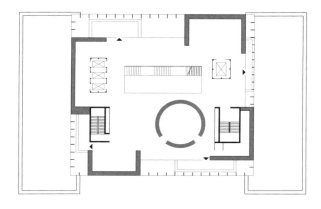

Ebene 6   Level 6

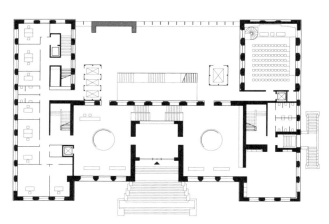

Ebene 1   Level 1

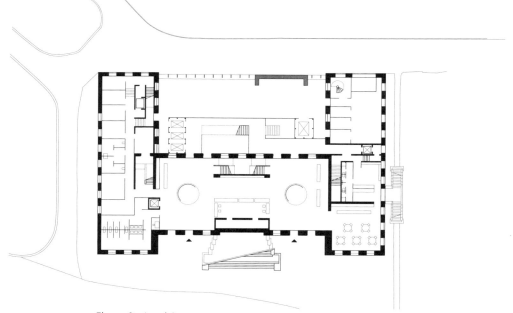

Ebene 0   Level 0

Grenzgänger
Border Crossers

Im intensiven Austausch zwischen Köln und Paris entstand aus einem abstrakten Bild die zeichenhafte Architektur für das Haus der Europäischen Geschichte. Die filigrane Glasfassade und die schwebende Treppe, realisiert mit den Ingenieuren vom Büro Sobek, loten die Grenze des Machbaren neu aus.

In the intensive exchange between Cologne and Paris, the symbolic architecture for the House of European History emerged from an abstract image. The delicate glass facade and the floating staircase, realized with the engineers from the Sobek office, explore the limits of what is feasible.

Dr. Lucio Blandini (Vorstand, Werner Sobek Stuttgart AG) *über die konstruktive Umsetzung der Entwurfsideen*

Dr. Lucio Blandini (CEO, Werner Sobek Stuttgart AG) *about the constructive implementation of the design ideas*

Die Glasfassade

Ausschlaggebend für die hohe Transparenz der äußeren Glasfassade ist die statische Nutzung von horizontalen und vertikalen Glasschwertern. Die vertikalen Glasschwerter haben Spannweiten von 3 bis 14 Metern, die horizontalen Glasschwerter von 1,6 bis 5,6 Metern. Die Breite der Glasschwerter variiert zwischen 52 und 80 Millimetern. Während Breite und Spannweiten der Glasschwerter sehr unterschiedliche Werte aufweisen, ist ihre Tiefe aus gestalterischen Gründen auf zwei Werte begrenzt, und zwar auf 350 Millimeter für Spannweiten von bis zu 10 Metern, und auf 500 Millimeter für Spannweiten von bis zu 14 Metern. Die Glasschwerter bestehen aus laminierten, 12 Millimeter dicken ESG-Weißglasscheiben. Die horizontalen Glasschwerter sind durch eine Bolzenverbindung mit den vertikalen Glasschwertern verbunden;

The Glass Facade

The static use of horizontal and vertical glass fins was decisive for the high transparency of the outer glass facade. The vertical glass fins have lengths between 3 and 14 meters, the horizontal glass fins are 1.6 to 5.6 meters long. The width of the glass fins varies from 52 to 80 millimeters. While the width and length of the glass fins have very different values, their depth is limited to two values for design reasons, namely 350 millimeters for lengths of up to 10 meters, and 500 millimeters for lengths of up to 14 meters.
The glass fins are made of laminated, 12 mm thick white tempered (ESG) glass panes. The horizontal glass fins are joined to the vertical glass fins with bolts; this prevents pressure as a result of temperature variations or settling. A white plastic sleeve, which is hardly visible from the outside,

dadurch werden Zwänge aus Temperaturvariationen oder Auflagersetzungen vermieden. Eine von außen kaum sichtbare weiße Kunststoffhülse verhindert den direkten Kontakt zwischen Glas und Stahl. An dieser Stelle bestehen die Schwerter immer aus sechs Scheiben, von denen drei im Knotenbereich fortgeführt werden. Diese Detaillösung wurde in Anlehnung an vergleichbare Holzbaudetails entwickelt. In den Eckbereichen wurden die 2 x 10 Millimeter starken TVG-Glasscheiben der Vertikalfassade sowie die Dachverglasung als Aussteifungselemente herangezogen, sodass eine dreiseitig steife Ecke entsteht. Die Glasscheiben übernehmen durch Kontakt Druckkräfte; in der horizontalen und vertikalen Fuge verborgene, zugbeanspruchte Edelstahlprofile übernehmen die Zugkräfte.

Wichtigstes Detail der hochtransparenten Fassade ist die Verbindung zwischen Glasschwertern und Glasscheiben. Hierfür wurde von Werner Sobek eine Sonderlösung entwickelt, die ein Zusammenschrauben der zwei Komponenten ermöglicht. Im Werk wurden Edelstahlprofile an die Glaselemente geklebt. Die Verwendung von Langlöchern in den Edelstahlprofilen ermöglicht einerseits den Toleranzausgleich und stellt andererseits sicher, dass Windsoglasten die Verklebung nur senkrecht zur Fuge beanspruchen.

prevents direct contact between the glass and the steel. At this point, the fins always consist of six panes, three of which are continued in the nodal area. This detailed solution was developed on the basis of comparable wooden details. In the corner areas, 2 x 10 millimeter thick semi-tempered (TVG) glass panes on the vertical façade and the roof glazing were used as stiffening elements, creating a three-sided, stiff corner. The glass panes absorb compressive forces through contact; the tensioned stainless steel profiles hidden in the horizontal and vertical joints absorb the tensile forces.

The most important detail of the highly transparent facade is the connection between the glass fins and the glass panes. For this purpose, Werner Sobek developed a special solution that allows the two components to be screwed together. At the factory, stainless steel profiles were glued to the glass elements. The use of elongated holes in the stainless steel profiles allowed tolerance compensation on the one hand and, on the other, ensures that wind suction loads only strain the bond perpendicular to the joint.

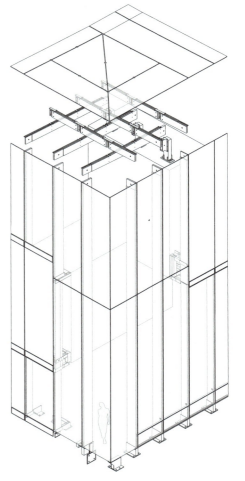

Konstruktion der Glashaut
Construction of the glass skin

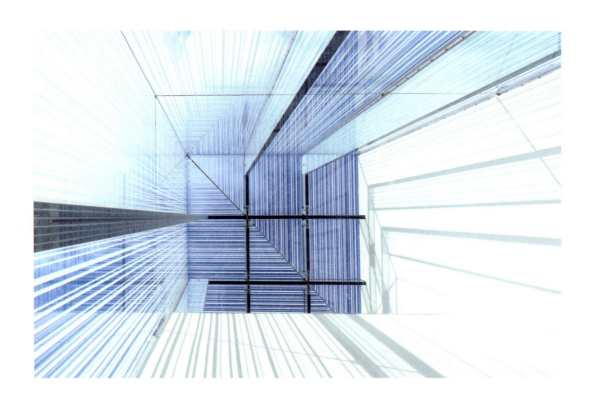

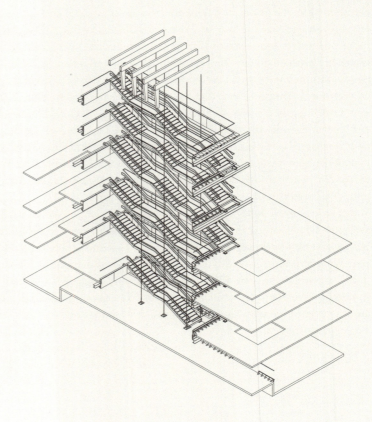

Die Treppe im Atrium

Die stählerne Treppe im Atrium sollte zum einen ein möglichst filigranes Tragwerk aufweisen und zum anderen verschiedene Funktionen in einem Element vereinen. Um dies zu erreichen, wurden 25 Millimeter dicke Stahlbleche als Treppenwangen verwendet. Diese Bleche werden durch die L-förmige Stahlprofile der Stufen seitlich stabilisiert. Um die freien Spannweiten zu reduzieren und um das Schwingungsverhalten der Treppe zu optimieren, wurden die sechs Treppenrampen nicht nur an den jeweiligen oberen und unteren Deckenbereich angeschlossen. Die Rampen werden zusätzlich durch insgesamt sechs Edelstahlseile gehalten und sind seitlich an bestehende Stützen angeschlossen. Die 24 Millimeter dünnen Seile sind nur leicht vorgespannt; sie schließen im Erdgeschoss beziehungsweise am Dachtragwerk des Atriums an. Die Seilklemmen wurden speziell für den Einsatz im Haus der Europäischen Geschichte entwickelt, damit sie sich optisch perfekt in die Wangen integrieren. Auch die Seilfußpunkte sind eine Sonderentwicklung, da für ihre Platzierung nur sehr wenig Platz zur Verfügung stand. Das Atrium wirkt nicht zuletzt dank der leichten Struktur und eleganten Gestaltung der Treppe offen, einladend und hell – durch das Atriumdach kann so diffuses Tageslicht bis in die Ausstellungsräume gelangen.

The Stairs in the Atrium

The steel staircase in the atrium should, on the one hand, have as delicate a structure as possible and, on the other hand, combine different functions in one element. To achieve this, 25 mm thick steel sheets were used as stair stringers. These sheets are laterally stabilized by the steps' L-shaped steel profiles. In order to reduce the free lengths and to optimize the vibration behavior of the stairs, the six stair ramps were not only connected to the respective upper and lower ceiling area; they were additionally affixed by a total of six stainless steel cables and are connected laterally to existing supports. The 24-millimeter thin ropes are only slightly pre-stressed; they are connected on the ground floor or to the roof structure of the atrium, respectively. The rope clamps were specially developed for use in the House of European History so that they optically integrate perfectly with the stair stringers. The cable attachment points are also a special development, as there was very little space available for their placement. Thanks in large part to the light structure and elegant design of the staircase, the atrium is open, inviting, and bright and the atrium roof allows diffused daylight to reach the exhibition rooms.

Konstantin Jaspert (Partner, JSWD)

"The *Maison de l'histoire européenne* is a truly European project. At first, we developed the idea of a glass structure with a simple geometry and a direct relationship to the strict symmetry of the old building. Our French partners reacted to this with the desire for disturbance and inserted glass cabinets in the *facade showcase*, because only building a glass skin was not thrilling enough for them. What followed was an exciting process of converging images and components. The French had the courage to build *everything* out of glass and to ignore technical hurdles; the facade and the delicate staircase could however only be realized with the Stuttgart office Werner Sobek."

"In order for international cooperation to succeed, it is essential to identify an interface at an early stage, so that the roles and tasks are clear and the work is neatly integrated in the end. So that the language barrier does not become a problem, the respective native speaker is always in charge. After the draft was complete, we took over the planning of the facade—both old and new—and everything else, including the overall coordination, was done by the French partner because everything was in French. At the ThyssenKrupp quarter in Essen, things were the other way around: Chaix & Morel developed the facades and we organized everything, integrated the planning, and coordinated the project on site."

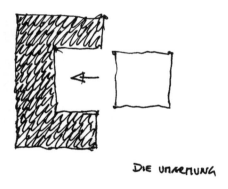
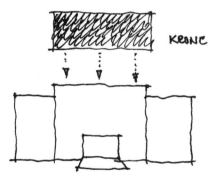
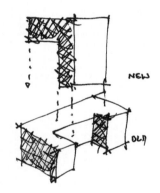

Walter Grasmug (Partner, Chaix & Morel et Associés, Paris)

"We regard the glass insert in the heavy, stone historic building as a kind of showcase. With the transparency from outside to inside and vice versa, we want to highlight the values of the European Union, or more precisely those that we imagine the European Union wants to express through their buildings. This idea was followed to its ultimate expression, as even the structure is made of glass."

"The central staircase in the atrium forms the backbone of the museum. This element allows visitors walking through the building to experience the height of the construction through the light which shines from the top floor into the depths. With each loop and on each floor, it gives orientation, a clear structure in a building full of complex contents."

Koelnmesse 3.0
Köln

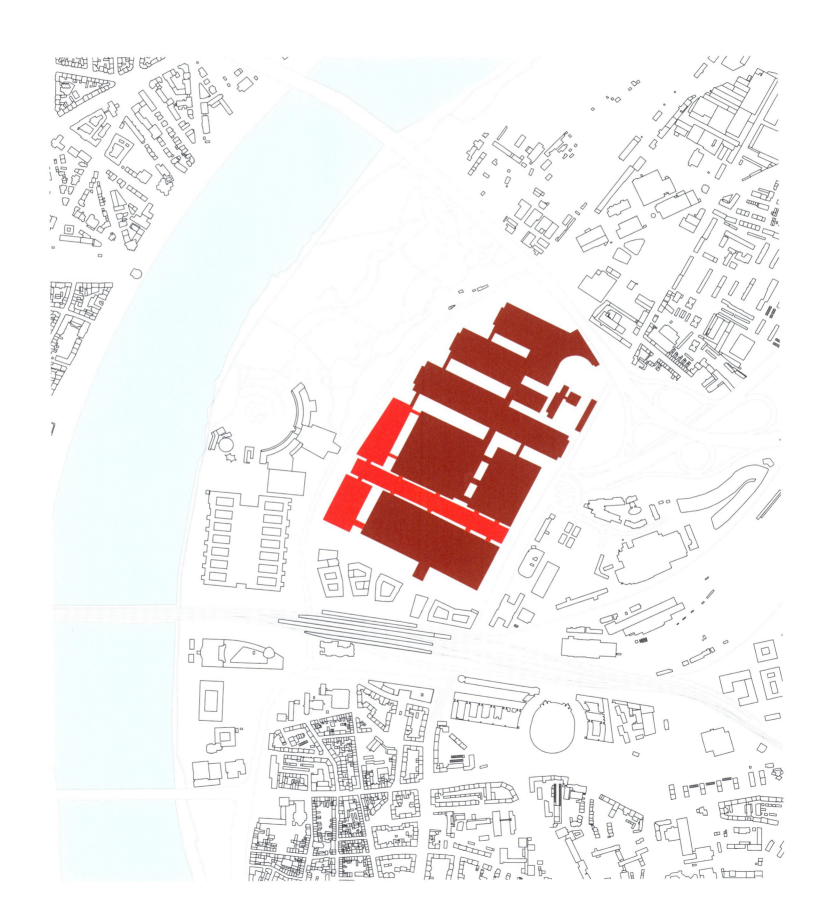

Die Kölner Messe blickt auf eine lange Geschichte als städtischer Handelsplatz zurück, sie lässt sich bis zur Ostermesse im Jahr 967 zurückführen. Einen Meilenstein der Neuzeit bildete die 1914 am Deutzer Ufer veranstaltete Werkbundausstellung; auf deren Gelände ließ der damalige Kölner Oberbürgermeister Konrad Adenauer anschließend Gebäude zu Versammlungs-, Ausstellungs- und Messezwecken bauen. Die dort 1924 veranstaltete Frühjahrsmesse markiert das Gründungsjahr der Messegesellschaft, die heute den Namen Koelnmesse trägt. Bis heute profitiert sie von der innerstädtischen Lage im rechtsrheinischen Stadtteil Deutz, der optimalen Verkehrsanbindung und dem werbewirksamen Domblick – Deutz war für viele Kölner jahrzehntelang gleichbedeutend mit der Messe. Doch so vorteilhaft die zentrale Lage auch ist, das räumliche Wachstum der Messegesellschaft, die mit jährlich über 80 Fachmessen, Ausstellungen, Special Events und Gastveranstaltungen ein wichtiger Wirtschaftsfaktor für Deutz und den Wirtschaftsstandort Köln ist, ist an diesem Ort, wo der Platz begrenzt ist, immer komplizierter zu betreiben. Von großem öffentlichen Interesse ist es außerdem, die Messe, einen in sich hochkomplexen Organismus, schlüssig in den Stadtkörper zu integrieren.

Mit den vier 2006 errichteten Nordhallen verfügt die Koelnmesse über eine Ausstellungsfläche von rund 300000 Quadratmetern in elf zusammenhängenden Hallen; die markanten Rheinhallen aus den 1920er Jahren werden inzwischen anderweitig genutzt. Doch die Gesellschaft expandiert weiter und plant unter dem Titel Koelnmesse 3.0 das umfangreichste Investitionsprogramm in der Geschichte des Unternehmens: Über 700 Millionen Euro sollen von 2015 bis 2030 umgesetzt werden, zahlreiche Modernisierungsmaßnahmen, Neubauten und Verbesserungen der Infrastruktur werden das Messegelände baulich, funktional, aber auch gestalterisch an zukünftige Bedürfnisse anpassen. Die planerische Grundlage für die Expansion der Kölner Messe bildet ein Masterplan aus dem Jahr 2014. Darauf aufbauend lobte die Gesellschaft einen dreiphasigen Hochbauwettbewerb aus, den JSWD Architekten gewannen und für dessen Umsetzung sie nachfolgend als Generalplaner beauftragt wurden. Zwei große Hallenneubauten auf dem Südgelände werden das Messegelände zukünftig auf der Westseite fassen und ihm auf der dem Rheinpark zugewandten Seite ein neues Gesicht geben. Sie werden so dimensioniert sein, dass sie die Flucht der bestehende Gebäudekanten aufnehmen und den Komplex schlüssig fortschreiben. Im Januar 2019 wurde der Grundstein für die Halle 1plus gelegt, einen aufgeständerten Bau, der die Ausstellungsfläche der Messe um rund 10000 stützenfreie Quadratmeter erweitern wird. Genau gegenüber wird das Confex® als multifunktionale Messe-, Kongress- und Event-Location geplant, um damit die Tagungskapazität der Koelnmesse um 5500 Teilnehmer zu erhöhen und zusätzliche Fläche für Messen und Kongresse zu bieten. Über einen angehoben liegenden Vorplatz kann das Confex® von der MesseCity aus direkt erschlossen werden. Herzstück ist die stützenfreie Halle mit einer lichten Höhe von 12,20 Metern, mit den zuschaltbaren Bereichen bietet sie 7500 Quadratmeter Ausstellungsfläche, auf der auch mehrgeschossige Messestände und großformatige Exponate aufgebaut werden können. Angegliedert an diese Halle entstehen Flächen für Konferenz-, Büro- und Gastronomienutzung. Die starke vertikale Gliederung der ziegelroten Bestandsfassaden mit Stützen, Lisenen und stehenden Fensterformaten findet sich in den von JSWD für die Neubauten entworfenen Gebäudehüllen wieder sowie in den neuen

Eingangsbauwerken des Terminals – hier jedoch in einer zeitgemäßen Interpretation: leichter, filigraner und mit weißen Oberflächen.

Eine wichtige Maßnahme, nicht nur zur Verknüpfung der neuen Hallen mit dem Bestand, ist der Bau des 400 Meter langen Ost-West-Terminals. Dieses hochfunktionale, als Magistrale auf mehreren Ebenen großzügig geplante Rückgrat wird in Ergänzung zu dem bereits bestehenden Nord-Süd-Boulevard die Erschließung und die Struktur des gesamten Hallenkomplexes deutlich verbessern. Im Stadtraum wird sich das Terminal mit zwei markanten Köpfen hervorheben. Insbesondere auf der stark frequentierten Ostseite, wo sich filigrane weiße Rundstützen über die gesamte Gebäudehöhe zu einem diaphanen Vorhang verdichten, erhält der Eingang eine großzügige und repräsentative Erscheinung, die auch als freundlich einladende Geste an den Stadtteil Deutz zu lesen ist.

Koelnmesse 3.0
Cologne

The Koelnmesse looks back on a long history as an urban trading venue; its beginnings can be traced back to the Easter Fair in the year 967. A milestone of modern times was the Werkbund Exhibition, which was organized in 1914 on the banks of the Rhine in Deutz; the then mayor of Cologne, Konrad Adenauer, subsequently had buildings constructed for assembly, exhibition, and trade fair purposes at this location. The Spring Fair held there in 1924 marks the founding year of the trade fair company, which today bears the name Koelnmesse. To this day, it benefits from the inner-city location in the district of Deutz on the right bank of the Rhine, optimal transport connections, and an impressive view of the Dom. For many Cologne residents, Deutz has been

synonymous with the trade fair for decades. But as advantageous as the central location is, the spatial growth of the trade fair company, which is an important economic factor for Deutz and Cologne as a business location and hosts more than 80 trade fairs, exhibitions, special events, and guest events every year, has become more and more complicated as a result of the limited space here. It is also of great public interest to coherently integrate the highly complex organism of the Koelnmesse into the body of the city.

With the four northern halls built in 2006, the Koelnmesse has an exhibition space of around 300,000 square meters in eleven contiguous halls; the striking Rheinhallen from the 1920s are now used for other purposes. But the company continues to expand. Under the heading Koelnmesse 3.0, it is planning the most extensive investment program in the history of the company: an expenditure of more than 700 million Euros between 2015 and 2030, numerous modernization measures, new buildings, and infrastructure improvements are intended to adapt the exhibition center structurally, functionally, and aesthetically to future needs. The planning basis for the expansion of the Cologne exhibition center is a masterplan from 2014. Based on this plan, the company announced a three-phase building competition, which was won by JSWD Architects, who were subsequently commissioned with the implementation as the general contractor.

In the future, two large new halls on the southern site will close in the exhibition center to the west and give it a new look on the side facing the Rheinpark. They will be dimensioned so that they continue the alignment of the edges of the existing buildings and the complex in a coherent way. In January 2019, the foundation stone was laid for Hall 1plus, an elevated building which will expand the exhibition area of the fair by approximately 10,000 column-free square meters. Directly opposite, the Confex® is planned as a multifunctional location for trade fairs, congresses, and events; this will increase the conference capacity of the Koelnmesse by 5,500 participants and offer additional space for trade fairs and congresses. The Confex® can be accessed directly from MesseCity via an elevated forecourt. The centerpiece is the column-free hall with a clear height of 12.20 meters; it offers 7,500 square meters of exhibition space across all of the connectable areas, on which even multi-story exhibition stands and large-scale exhibits can be constructed. Conference rooms, offices, and spaces for catering use are attached to this hall. The strong vertical structure of the existing brick-red facades with their columns, pilaster strips, and standing window formats can be found in the building envelopes designed by JSWD for the new buildings, as well as in the new terminal entrance buildings—however, in a contemporary interpretation: lighter, more delicate, and with white surfaces. The construction of the 400-meter-long east-west terminal is an important measure, not only for linking the new halls with the existing buildings. This highly functional backbone, which is generously planned as a multi-level axis, will significantly improve the connection and structure of the entire hall complex and supplement the existing North-South boulevard. The terminal will be highlighted by two distinctive head-end buildings. This is particularly true on the busy eastern side, where filigree round white columns form a diaphanous curtain which stretches the entire height of the building; this design lends the entrance a generous and representative appearance, which can also be read as a friendly inviting gesture to the Deutz district.

Experiment Deutz
The Deutz Experiment

Das Deutzer Rheinufer, an dem auch die Kölner Messe ihren Ursprung hat, ist nicht nur für die Stadt bedeutsam, sondern war auch Schauplatz experimenteller Architektur der Moderne. In der Bürogeschichte von JSWD nimmt das Konglomerat Deutz – Messe einen besonderen Platz ein.

Historisches Luftbild der Kölner Messe, 1928
Historical aerial view of the Cologne trade fair, 1928

The Deutz bank of the Rhine, on which Cologne's trade fair originated, is not only important for the city, but was also the location of experimental modernist architecture. The conglomeration Deutz—Exhibition Center occupies a special place in the office history of JSWD.

Von den Römern wurde Deutz im Jahr 310 als *castrum divitensium* zum Schutz einer Rheinbrücke gegründet, und schon bald entwickelte sich an dem rechtsrheinischen Stützpunkt ein reger Handel mit den Germanen. Wenn man so will, kann man diesen Markt als Keimzelle der heutigen Koelnmesse interpretieren. Besser belegbar beginnt ein solcher Rückblick jedoch mit der *Deutschen Werkbundausstellung Cöln* 1914, für die die Stadt neben finanziellen und administrativen Mitteln auch ein großes Gelände am Deutzer Rheinufer zur Verfügung stellte. Damals war Köln unter den deutschen Großstädten führend bei der Modernisierung und Neugestaltung des Stadtbilds. Namhafte Architekten wurden beauftragt,

Deutz was founded by the Romans in 310 as a *castrum divitensium* to protect a bridge over the Rhine; soon, lively trade with the Germanic tribes developed at the base on the right bank of the Rhine. With a little imagination, one can interpret this market as the nucleus of today's Koelnmesse. The verifiable starting point of the exhibition center on its current location was however the *Deutschen Werkbundausstellung Cöln* 1914, for which the city provided not only financial and administrative funding, but also a large space on the banks of the Deutz Rhine. At that time, Cologne was one of the most progressive German cities in terms of modernizing and redesigning the cityscape. Well-known architects were

Glaspavillon, Bruno Taut, 1914
Glass pavilion, Bruno Taut, 1914

commissioned to design modern exhibition buildings for this first overall exhibition of industrial, artisanal, and artistic production. Walter Gropius' model factory, Bruno Taut's Expressionist glass pavilion, Henry van de Veldes' Werkbund-Theater, and Peter Behrens' Werkbund-Festhalle, among others, were constructed. Although these extraordinary buildings only existed for a few years, their avant-garde attitude paved the way for international modernity. In Deutz, these built theses made the exhibition of architecture and the exhibition center's architecture itself topics which have been repeatedly rethought up until the present day in a comparatively small space.

In the 1920s, Lord Mayor Konrad Adenauer initiated the founding of the trade fair company, which he wanted to use to make Cologne a showcase for Germany. However, the horseshoe-shaped exhibition halls designed by Hans Verbeek and Hans Pieper at the exhibition center grounds in Deutz already reached their capacity during the Spring Exhibition in 1924. For the *Pressa*, which was planned for 1928, Cologne's then director of city planning, Adolf Abel, had the four-year-old Rheinhallen encased in a steel skeleton construction with a suspended Expressionist brick facade to harmonize the irregular design. The colonnades of the complex and the slender tower, which was placed at the northwest corner as a landmark, are striking. With the "Staatenhaus," a gatehouse with two curved wings, Abel set a strong counterpart to the Rheinhallen, thus not only shaping the image of the exhibition center, but also the image of the city, which was then multiplied by the more than five million visitors to the *Pressa*.

After the war, the largely destroyed exhibition center was quickly rebuilt and use was resumed. In 1950, the first *photokina* took place there. During the post-war economic boom, the Cologne trade fair expanded across the railway tracks to the east for the first time through the construction of several new halls; it soon surpassed its prewar size. In the immediate vicinity, the river banks, which were now a landscape of gently rolling rubble hills, were formed into a long missing space for leisure and recreation. A further architectural highlight was the 1957 BUGA, for whose main entrance directly at the Messeturm Frei Otto designed a steel arch covered with a sail made of glass silk—a constructive and technical sensation which Otto still outdid with the star-shaped tent of the Tanzbrunnen. The second

moderne Ausstellungsbauten für diese erste Gesamtschau industrieller, handwerklicher und künstlerischer Produktion zu entwerfen. Gebaut wurden unter anderem die Musterfabrik von Walter Gropius, der expressionistische Glaspavillon von Bruno Taut, Henry van de Veldes Werkbund-Theater und die Werkbund-Festhalle von Peter Behrens. Diese außergewöhnlichen Bauten standen zwar nur wenige Jahre, ihre avantgardistische Haltung bereitete allerdings den Weg für die internationale Moderne. In Deutz haben diese gebauten Thesen das Ausstellen von Architektur und die Ausstellungsarchitektur selbst zu Themen gemacht, die bis heute auf einer vergleichsweise kleinen Fläche immer wieder neu erdacht werden.

In den 1920er Jahren initiierte der Oberbürgermeister Konrad Adenauer die Gründung der Messegesellschaft, mit der er Köln zu einem Schaufenster für Deutschland machen wollte. Die von Hans Verbeek und Hans Pieper auf dem Deutzer Messegelände hufeisenförmig angeordneten Messehallen erreichten ihre Kapazitätsgrenze aber schon mit der Frühjahrsmesse 1924. Für die 1928 geplante *Pressa* ließ Adolf Abel, damals Stadtbaudirektor in Köln, die erst vier Jahre bestehenden Rheinhallen mit einer Stahlskelettkonstruktion und vorgehängter expressionistischer Ziegelfassade ummanteln, um die uneinheitliche Gestaltung zu harmonisieren. Markant sind die Kolonnaden des Komplexes sowie der an der Nordwestecke als Landmarke eingefügte schlanke Turm. Mit dem Staatenhaus, einem Torbau mit zwei geschwungenen Flügeln, setzte Abel den Rheinhallen ein starkes Gegenstück zur Seite und prägte damit nicht nur das Bild der Messe, sondern auch das Bild der Stadt, das nicht zuletzt von den über fünf Millionen Besuchern der *Pressa* multipliziert wurde.

Nach dem Krieg wurde das weitgehend zerstörte Messegelände rasch wieder aufgebaut und in Betrieb genommen, 1950 fand dort die erste *photokina* statt. Während der Wirtschaftswunderjahre wuchs die Kölner Messe mit mehreren neuen Hallen erstmals über die Bahngleise hinweg nach Osten und überstieg bald die Größe der Vorkriegszeit. In direkter Nachbarschaft entstand aus der durch Trümmerberge modellierten Uferlandschaft der in der Stadt lange vermisste Raum für Freizeit und Erholung. Einen weiteren baulichen Höhepunkt markierte die BUGA 1957, für deren direkt am Messeturm gelegenen Haupteingang Frei Otto einen mit einem Segel aus Glasseide überspannten Stahlbogen entwarf –

Tanzbrunnen mit Sternwellenzelt, Frei Otto, 1957
Tanzbrunnen with star-shaped tent, Frei Otto, 1957

Messeturm und Randbebauung um die Rheinhallen, Adolf Abel, 1928
Messeturm and peripheral construction around the Rheinhallen, Adolf Abel, 1928

eine konstruktive und technische Sensation, die Otto mit dem Sternwellenzelt des Tanzbrunnens noch überbot. Die zweite BUGA, 1971, nahm die gestalterischen Spuren wieder auf und modernisierte den Rheinpark. Der 2015 eröffnete Rheinboulevard mit Ufertreppe (planorama) schloss an den Park an und führte zu einer deutlichen Aufwertung des öffentlichen Raums in Deutz.

Die Koelnmesse wuchs auf dem Areal östlich der Bahn zu einem komplexen Organismus heran und trennte sich von den denkmalgeschützten Abel-Bauten. Durch ihre Lage profitierte sie zum einen vom Strukturwandel in Mülheim und Deutz, der große Industrieareale verfügbar machte, zum anderen von der für eine Messe ungewöhnlichen Nähe zum Stadtzentrum. Das urbane Umfeld der Messe erhielt 1995 mit dem Technischen Rathaus und der Kölnarena (Peter Böhm) zwei neue großmaßstäbliche Magneten. Um dieser Dynamik gerecht zu werden, lobten die Deutsche Bahn AG, die Stadt Köln und die Koelnmesse im Jahr 2000 einen städtebaulichen Ideenwettbewerb für den Ausbau des Bahnhofs

BUGA 1971 took up this design language again and modernized the Rheinpark. The Rhine boulevard and shoreline stairs (planorama), which opened in 2015, acted as a continuation of the park and led to a significant improvement of the public spaces in Deutz.

The Koelnmesse to the east of the train tracks developed into a complex organism and separated itself from the listed Abel buildings. Thanks to its location, it profited on the one hand from the structural changes in Mülheim and Deutz, which made large industrial areas available, and, on the other hand, from the close proximity to the city center, unusual for an exhibition center. Two new large-scale magnets were constructed near the exhibition center in 1995: the Technical City Hall and the Cologne Arena (Peter Böhm). In order to do justice to this dynamic, Deutsche Bahn AG, the city of Cologne, and Koelnmesse announced an urban design competition in 2000 for the conversion of the Deutz railway station into an ICE terminal. The competition was won by a consortium between two young offices: Jaspert & Steffens Architects (Jürgen Steffens and Konstantin Jas-

ICE-Terminal Köln Messe/Deutz, 1. Preis 2000 | Kongresszentrum Köln-Deutz, 1. Preis 2002 | MesseCity Süd, Köln-Deutz, 1. Preis 2006
ICE Terminal Köln Messe/Deutz, 1st prize 2000 | Cologne-Deutz Congress Center, 1st prize 2002 | MesseCity South, Cologne-Deutz, 1st prize 2006

Deutz zum ICE-Terminal aus. Den Wettbewerb gewann die Arbeitsgemeinschaft der beiden noch jungen Büros Jaspert & Steffens Architekten (Jürgen Steffens und Konstantin Jaspert) und WJD Architekten (Rolf Watrin, Frederik Jaspert, Olaf Drehsen). In ihrem zeichenhaften Entwurf überspannt eine gläserne Dachkonstruktion in Quadratform sämtliche Gleise und wird mit einem Hotelhochhaus zu einer prägnanten Großform ergänzt. Basierend auf diesem Erfolg fusionierten die beiden Büros und firmierten bereits unter dem Namen JSWD Architekten, als sie 2002 den nächsten großen Wettbewerb in unmittelbarer Nachbarschaft der Koelnmesse gewannen. Ihr signifikanter amorpher Baukörper war als Mittelpunkt eines Kongresszentrums gedacht, das, flankiert von zwei Hochhäusern und ergänzt um eine siebengeschossige Kammstruktur, als Bindeglied zwischen die Messehallen und den Bahnhof hätte gesetzt werden sollen. Beide Entwürfe von JSWD sind in dieser Form nicht realisiert worden, sie haben jedoch, ebenso wie zentrale, in dem 2006 durchgeführten Werkstattverfahren „Städtebauliche Entwicklung Umfeld Bahnhof Köln Messe/Deutz" entwickelten Elemente, die nachfolgenden Planungen der Koelnmesse und der MesseCity maßgeblich beeinflusst. So hat die jahrelange intensive Beschäftigung mit dem Ort und seiner Nutzung dazu geführt, dass sich JSWD in dem 2015 ausgelobten dreiphasigen Wettbewerb zur Koelnmesse 3.0 durchsetzen konnten und nun einen wichtigen Beitrag dazu leisten, die Messe der Zukunft zu gestalten. Ganz unabhängig von den Planungen der Koelnmesse realisierte JSWD vis-à-vis 2006 die Constantin Höfe. Das mäanderförmig über das schmale Grundstück gelegte Büro-, Wohn- und Geschäftshaus liegt als Schirm und Filter zwischen dem historischen Zentrum von Deutz und dem Entwicklungsgebiet von Messe und ICE-Terminal, einer in Tempo und Maßstab so ungleichen Nachbarschaft.

pert) and WJD Architects (Rolf Watrin, Frederik Jaspert, Olaf Drehsen). In their emblematic design, the tracks are spanned by a square glass roof construction, which is supplemented by a high-rise hotel to form a striking, large structure. Based on this success, the two offices merged; they had already begun operating under the name JSWD Architects when they won the next major competition in the immediate vicinity of the Koelnmesse in 2002. Its significant, amorphous structure was intended to be the centerpiece of a convention center. Flanked by two skyscrapers and supplemented by a seven-story comb structure, it was envisioned as a link between the exhibition halls and the train station. Both of these designs were not able to be realized in this form; however, they and elements of the workshop process "Urban Development of the Train Station Surroundings Cologne Exhibition Center/Deutz," which was conducted in 2006, have both significantly influenced the subsequent planning of Koelnmesse and MesseCity.

The years of intensive study of the location and its use resulted in JSWD's success in the three-phase competition for Koelnmesse 3.0 in 2015, in which they will now make an important contribution to shaping the future of the exhibition center.

Independent of the Koelnmesse planning, JSWD also realized the nearby Constantin Höfe project in 2006. The office, residential, and commercial building, which meanders across a narrow plot of land, serves as a screen and filter between the historic center of Deutz and the area where the much larger and more hectic exhibition center and ICE-Terminal are located.

Constantin Höfe, Köln-Deutz, 2006   Constantin Höfe, Cologne-Deutz, 2006

Fragen an Gerald Böse
(Vorsitzender der Geschäftsführung, Koelnmesse GmbH):

Mit der Maßnahme Koelnmesse 3.0 ändert sich auch das Gesicht der Messe. Wie möchten Sie in der Stadt wahrgenommen werden?
Gerald Böse: Ich bin sicher, dass die Koelnmesse auch bisher schon als treibende Kraft für die Stadt und die Region wahrgenommen wird: durch Millionen hochkarätiger Gäste, die wir hierher bringen, durch positive Botschaften zum Messe- und Wirtschaftsstandort Köln in aller Welt, durch aktive Vernetzung mit gleichgesinnten engagierten Institutionen in unserem Umfeld.
Um diesem Anspruch auch in Zukunft gerecht zu werden, müssen wir im Wettbewerb der Messeplätze ganz vorne mitspielen und für die Branchen, die uns ihr Vertrauen schenken, attraktiv bleiben. Deshalb investieren wir unsere Ideen und Ressourcen in den Standort und setzen unsere Vision Koelnmesse 3.0 um. Jeder zufriedene Messeteilnehmer, den wir mit der Flexibilität unserer Hallen – beispielsweise im neuen Confex® –, mit den Möglichkeiten des Geländes, Events und emotionale Live-Kommunikation zu inszenieren, überzeugt haben, tut auch der Stadt und der Region gut. Ich würde mich freuen, wenn auch die Kölner, genau wie wir bei der Koelnmesse, auf das zukünftige neue Gesicht blicken und wissen: Hier ist eine Institution, die unserer Stadt Impulse gibt und ihren Platz im internationalen Wirtschaftsgeschehen entscheidend mitbestimmt.

Die reine Größe betreffend erreicht die Koelnmesse in Deutz sicher bald ihre Grenzen – wie planen Sie weiter, wenn die Quantität ausgereizt ist?

Zukünftige Messe-, Kongress- und Eventhalle Confex®
Future trade fair, congress and event hall Confex®

GB: Wir haben für die absehbare Zukunft geplant, soweit wir sie überhaupt absehen können. Wir setzen auf ein modernes Gelände, auf seine Flexibilität und seine Anziehungskraft. Es geht nicht um Flächenerweiterung oder Kapazitätsausbau. Mit unserem Gelände, wie es sich nach Abschluss des Projekts Koelnmesse 3.0 darstellen wird, können wir einige Jahrzehnte hervorragend arbeiten. Wir werden uns in Deutz und im rechtsrheinischen Köln, dessen Umfeld seinerseits immer attraktiver wird, sicher noch sehr lange wohlfühlen.

„Deutz ist unser Schicksal"

Im Gespräch mit Jürgen Steffens (Partner, JSWD) über die Koelnmesse 3.0 und den Stadtbezirk Deutz:

Die Koelnmesse ist ein komplexer, über Jahrzehnte gewachsener Organismus. An welchen baulichen Fixpunkten orientieren Sie sich, um das Areal zur Koelnmesse 3.0 weiterzuentwickeln?
Jürgen Steffens: Die jüngste Erweiterung der Koelnmesse sind

Questions to Gerald Böse (CEO, Koelnmesse GmbH):

Koelnmesse 3.0 will also change the face of the exhibition center. How would you like to be perceived in the city?
Gerald Böse: I am sure that the Koelnmesse is already perceived as a driving force for the city and the region today: through the millions of high-caliber guests that we bring here, through worldwide positive messages about Cologne as a trade fair and business location, and through active networking with like-minded institutions.
In order to live up to this claim in the future, we have to play a leading role in the competition between exhibition centers and remain attractive for the industries that trust us. That is why we are investing our ideas and resources in this location and implementing our vision, Koelnmesse 3.0. Every satisfied trade fair participant whom we have won over with the flexibility of our halls—for example in the new Confex®—and with the possibilities of our exhibition space to house both events and emotional live communication, is also good for the city and the region.
I would be delighted if the people of Cologne, just like us at the Koelnmesse, look to the future new face of the exhibition center and know that this is an institution that gives our city impetus and has a decisive influence on its place in international economic affairs.

In terms of sheer size, the Koelnmesse in Deutz will soon reach its limits—how do you plan further when the quantity is exhausted?
GB: We have planned for the foreseeable future as far as we can anticipate. We rely on a modern space, on its flexibility and its appeal. It is not about the simple expansion of area or capacity. After the completion of the Koelnmesse 3.0 project, we will be able to work optimally for several decades. I am certain that we will feel at home in Deutz and in Cologne, on the ever more attractive right bank of the Rhine, for a long time.

"Deutz is our destiny"

A conversation with Jürgen Steffens (Partner, JSWD) about Koelnmesse 3.0 and the Deutz district:

The Koelnmesse is a complex organism that has grown over decades. Which structural fixed points have you oriented on to develop the site into the Koelnmesse 3.0?
Jürgen Steffens: The latest extension of the Koelnmesse was the northern halls. We, however, began with the southern halls, in order to complete their structure from the perspective of urban design. To do this, we oriented the new buildings, Hall 1plus and Confex®, on the existing buildings in order to create an overall sense of order. This creates a new, strong east-west axis that complements the existing north-south axis. This improves both the

die Nordhallen. Wir setzen jedoch bei den Südhallen an, um ihre Struktur mit einem städtebaulichen Anspruch zu arrondieren. Dazu nehmen wir die Kanten der Bestandshallen auf und binden die Neubauten, Halle 1plus und Confex®, in die Ordnung ein. Dadurch entsteht eine neue, starke Ost-West-Achse, die die bestehende Nord-Süd-Achse ergänzt. Sowohl die Orientierung als auch die Funktionalität verbessern sich in hohem Maße.

Viele Kölner, insbesondere die Deutzer, haben die Sorge, dass das Messegelände sich zu einer Stadt in der Stadt entwickelt.
JS: Ich weiß gar nicht, woher diese Sorge kommt, denn die Messe gibt es an diesem Standort schon seit ihrer Gründung. Diese Form der Nutzung ist damit historisch begründet. Die Kölner können froh sein, dass die Messe diesen Standort hat und nicht vor den Toren der Stadt liegt. Ein innerstädtisches Messegelände mit einer Ausstellungsfläche von fast 300000 Quadratmetern betrachte ich durchaus als eine Qualität. Denken Sie zum Beispiel an die Zeit, wenn die 370000 Besucher der *gamescom* nach Deutz strömen – lebendiger kann es hier kaum werden! Die Messe ist ein Organismus, ein pulsierender Ort, der Menschen in Bewegung setzt und verbindet. Dass sie nicht mit der Stadt verwoben sei, ist eine Ansicht, die ich nicht teile.

Wie nimmt die Koelnmesse 3.0 Kontakt mit der Außenwelt auf?
JS: Zugegeben, die Eingänge im Osten und Westen der Messe waren bisher nicht gut wahrnehmbar und wirkten wenig einladend. Mit den nun markanteren neuen Eingängen dort und dem Confex® sendet die Messe deutliche Zeichen der Öffnung zur Stadt. Ähnlich wirkt auch der Stadtbalkon, der aus unserem Wettbewerbsbeitrag zur MesseCity in das städtebauliche Konzept aufgenommen wurde. Schon damals haben wir es uns als eine sehr urbane Situation vorgestellt, wie die Besucher geschmeidig aus dem Deutzer Bahnhof kommen und über den Messebalkon durch die MesseCity in die Messe flanieren.

Immer wieder in der Geschichte Ihres Büros spielt sich Entscheidendes in Deutz ab. Das kann doch kein Zufall sein!
JS: Deutz ist unser Schicksal – seit dem Jahr 2000 beschäftigen wir uns fast durchgehend mit diesem Terrain. Damals haben wir den internationalen Wettbewerb „Köln Messe/Deutz" gewonnen, sind durch die von der UNESCO gestartete Debatte über den Hochhauskranz mitgegangen und konnten schließlich ein Werkstattverfahren für einen Bürostandort mit großem Kongresszentrum für uns entscheiden. Die benachbarten Constantin Höfe waren schließlich ein interessantes Nebenprodukt, für das sich Hochtief-Projektentwicklung mit uns engagiert hat. Dieses Gebäude mit Wohnungen, Büros und Flächen für Gastronomie ist ein Stück wertiger Architektur, durch seine mäandrierende Form ist es aber auch eine städtebauliche Geste, mit der wir die Deutzer Wohnquartiere von der Bahntrasse abschirmen. So konnten wir das Verständnis von Architektur und Stadt mit diesem Projekt sehr deutlich zum Ausdruck bringen.

orientation and the functionality to a great extent.

Many Cologne residents, especially those in Deutz, are worried that the exhibition center is developing into a city within the city.
JS: I really do not know where this concern comes from, because the exhibition center has been located on this spot since its foundation. This form of use is therefore historically justified. The people of Cologne should be happy that the exhibition center is located here and not just outside the city. An inner-city exhibition center with an exhibition area of almost 300,000 square meters is, in my opinion, a real boon. For example, think back to when nearly 370,000 visitors to the *gamescom* flocked to Deutz—it can hardly get any livelier here! The exhibition center is an organism, a pulsating place that sets people in motion and connects them. I do not share the opinion that it should be set apart from the city.

How does the Koelnmesse 3.0 get in contact with the outside world?
JS: Admittedly, the entrances to the east and west of the exhibition center were not very legible and seemed uninviting up until now. The new, more distinctive entrances and the Confex® open the exhibition center toward the city. The city balcony, which was included in the urban design concept and originally came from our competition entry to MesseCity, has a similar effect. Already back then, we envisioned it as a very urban situation, in which the visitors emerge from the Deutz train station and stroll across the exhibition center balcony through the MesseCity and into the exhibition center itself.

Time and again in the history of your office, important events have taken place in Deutz. That cannot be a coincidence!
JS: Deutz is our destiny—since 2000, we have been working on this area almost without interruption. Back then, we won the international competition "Cologne Exhibition Center/Deutz". We became involved in the discussion from the debates begun by UNESCO about a circle of high-rises and finally, in a workshop procedure, our idea for an office location with a large congress center was chosen. The neighboring Constantin Höfe was an interesting side effect of this process, for which Hochtief Project Development collaborated with us. This building with apartments, offices, and areas for dining and food outlets is a piece of significant architecture; due to its meandering form, it is also an urban gesture with which we shielded the Deutz residential neighborhoods from the train tracks. In this way, we were able to clearly articulate our understanding of architecture and urban design through this project.

Baustelle der Halle 1plus, Koelnmesse 2019
Construction site of Hall 1plus, Koelnmesse 2019

The Icon Vienna
Wien

In vielen europäischen Metropolen wurde der Eisenbahnverkehr lange Zeit über Kopfbahnhöfe an das Stadtzentrum herangeführt. Mit den oft prachtvollen Empfangsgebäuden war der Anspruch verknüpft, dass die Großstadt der Ausgangspunkt oder das Ziel der Reisenden zu sein hat. Umstiege zur Weiterfahrt in andere Richtungen spielten in dieser Logik eine untergeordnete Rolle. Transitpassagiere mussten mehr oder weniger umständlich vom einen zum anderen Endbahnhof gelangen.

Ab den 1870er Jahren gab es in Wien Überlegungen für einen zentralen Bahnhof, der aber erst 2004 mit dem Masterplan zur Umgestaltung des Areals um den Südbahnhof Gestalt annahm. Der neue Hauptbahnhof existiert offiziell seit 2014 und ersetzt den Südbahnhof, der für die Neuorganisation des Wiener Bahnknotens aufgegeben wurde. Von den 109 Hektar des alten Bahnhofsareals belegt der Hauptbahnhof samt Infrastruktur nur noch etwa 50 Hektar. Auf den frei gewordenen Flächen befinden sich neue Stadtquartiere im Bau: das Quartier Belvedere (etwa 25 Hektar) und das Sonnwendviertel (etwa 34 Hektar).

Das Quartier Belvedere, benannt nach dem nicht weit entfernten Schloss, schließt nordöstlich an den Hauptbahnhof an. Angesichts der prognostizierten 150000 Fahrgäste und Besucher pro Tag ist eine große bauliche Dichte dem Ort angemessen. Mit dem dreiteiligen Hochhausensemble The Icon Vienna entstand eine urbane Landmarke, die als Bindeglied zwischen dem Hauptbahnhof und dem neuen Quartier dient. JSWD hatten 2013 den internationalen Wettbewerb für dieses prominent gelegene Dreiecksgrundstück in einer Arbeitsgemeinschaft mit BEHF Architects (Wien) gewonnen. Die Jury würdigte vor allem die Formulierung der drei Baukörper, ihre Durchlässigkeit im Erdgeschoss sowie die Klarheit ihrer Orientierung. Sowohl in ihrer Organisation zueinander als auch in der Öffnung zur Stadt seien sie überzeugend. Gelobt wurde nicht zuletzt die Differenziertheit in der Ausformulierung der Fassade, die das städtebauliche Konzept unterstütze.

Der Wettbewerbserfolg hatte sicher auch mit einer überzeugenden Metapher zu tun, der sich die Architekten bedienten. Die abgerundete Form der drei unterschiedlich hohen Türme (88, 66 und 38,5 Meter) vergleichen sie mit Felsen, die von einer Strömung geschliffen worden sind. Tatsächlich sind an diesem Ort die Verkehrsströme beträchtlich. Der Wiedner Gürtel weitet sich für den Individualverkehr auf bis zu acht Spuren, und fast 1100 Züge ziehen jeden Tag im dichten Takt unter dem expressiv gefalteten Bahnhofsdach vorbei. Diese dynamischen Strömungskräfte prägen den Ort und stellen die rautenförmigen *footprints* der drei Türme in einen weithin sichtbaren und nachvollziehbaren Zusammenhang. Durch ihre Setzung an den drei Spitzen des Grundstücks geben sie selbstverständlich und organisch drei Passagen frei, die den Übergang zwischen Stadt und Bahnhof erlauben. Das dreigeschossige Sockelgeschoss bündelt diese Wege zu einer öffentlichen Mall, in der sich Einzelhandel und Begegnungszonen mischen.

Jeder der Türme wird im Erdgeschoss über eine eigene Lobby erreicht. Turm A besteht aus 24 Obergeschossen und ist für eine Maximalbelegung von ca. 3120 Mitarbeitern ausgelegt. Im Turm B mit 17 Obergeschossen können bis zu 1760 Mitarbeiterplätze untergebracht werden, im Turm C mit neun Obergeschossen bis zu 880 Mitarbeiter. Jede Büroetage kann in vier Mieteinheiten unterteilt und sowohl in einer Open-Space-Variante als auch in Zellenstruktur organisiert werden. Der Kern der Türme nimmt jeweils die Vertikalerschließung, Besprechungsräume, Coffee Points, Sanitärräume und weitere Nebenfunktionen auf. Die Fassaden wirken, entsprechend dem Bild vom geschliffenen Felsen, bei Tageslicht glatt und makellos, zeigen aber bei Dunkelheit und Kunstlicht eine gewisse Tiefe. In Kooperation mit dem Ingenieurbüro Werner Sobek (Stuttgart) entwickelten JSWD und BEHF eine geschosshohe zweischalige Glaskonstruktion, die aus einer äußeren festverglasten Prallscheibe und einer inneren Dreifach-Isolierverglasung besteht. Feine Farbunterschiede der Fassadenprofile erzeugen eine differenzierte Optik, der Farbkanon aus Anthrazit, Platin und Bronze unterstützt die hochwertige Anmutung. Indem das Fassadenraster alle zwei, drei oder vier Geschosse um eine Achse verspringt, werden die Etagen visuell zu „Paketen" zusammengefasst. Der Wechsel belebt nicht nur das Fassadenbild, sondern illustriert auch das Konzept des Bauherrn, der mit dem Icon Vienna nicht nur einen einzigen, sondern unterschiedliche Mieter ansprechen möchte.

The Icon Vienna

In many European cities, rail traffic historically reached the city center by way of a terminus station. The frequently impressive station buildings were connected to the claim that this city should be either the travelers' destination or point of departure. Changing trains in order to travel onward in other directions played a subordinate role in this logic.

Passengers in transit therefore had an awkward time getting from their point of departure to their final destination. Since the 1870s, Vienna has considered building a central railway station; these considerations finally took form in 2004 with the master plan for the restructuring of the area around the South Station. The new main station has been officially open since 2014 and replaces the South Station, which was abandoned as a result of the new organization of Vienna's railway network. The new central railway station and its infrastructure only use 50 of the 109 available hectares, however. A new city district is therefore being constructed on the remaining area: the Belvedere Quarter (approximately 25 hectares) and the Sonnwendviertel (approximately 34 hectares).

The Belvedere Quarter, named for the nearby palace, borders on the new railway station to the northeast. In light of the predicted 150,000 travelers and visitors daily, high urban density at this location is appropriate. The three-part high-rise ensemble The Icon Vienna has created an urban landmark which serves as a connecting element between the railway station and the new district. JSWD, in a joint venture with BEHF Architects (Vienna), won the international competition for this prominently located triangular site in 2013. In their decision, the jury praised the design relationship of the three buildings, the permeability of their ground floors and the clarity of their orientation. Both the buildings' organization relative to one another and the opening towards the city played a role in the positive outcome. The jury also complimented the sophistication in the formulation of the facade, which actively supports the urban design concept.

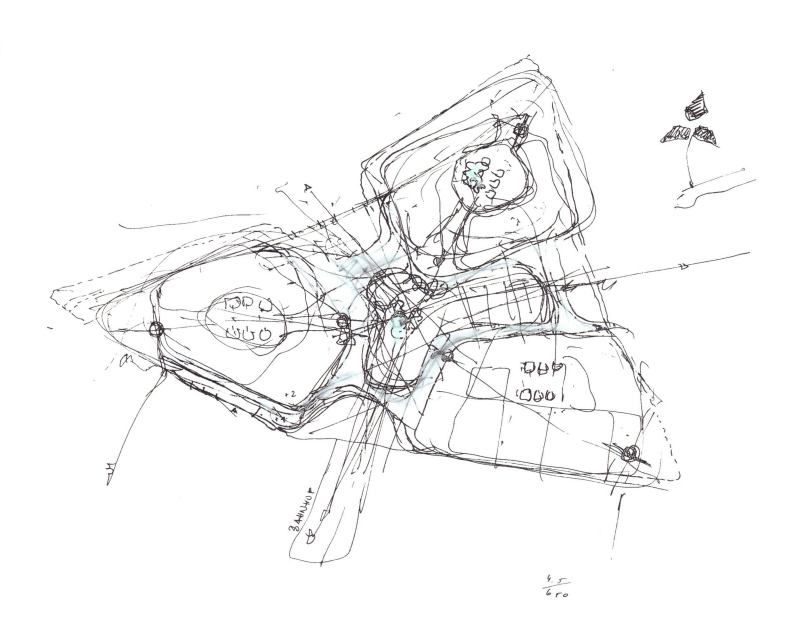

The competition success was surely also in part the result of a convincing metaphor which the architects made use of. The rounded edges of the three towers, each of which has a different height (88, 66, and 38.5 meters), are reminiscent of stones which have been worn smooth by water currents. The traffic currents at this location are indeed considerable. The Wiedner Gürtel widens to up to eight lanes for cars, and nearly 1,100 trains pass daily and at frequent intervals under the expressively folded station roof. These dynamic flow forces characterize this location and put the rhombic footprints of the three buildings into a visible and comprehensible context which can be seen from quite some distance. Through their placement at the three points of the building lot, three passageways between the city and the train station have been naturally and organically created. The three-story base level bundles these pathways into a public mall, in which retail and areas for socializing mix.

Each of the towers is accessed on the ground floor through its own lobby. Tower A has a total of 24 floors and offers space for up to 3,120 employees. Tower B, which has 17 floors, has space for up to 1,760 employees. Tower C, with just 9 floors, can accommodate up to 880 employees. Each office story can be divided into four rental units and can be organized either following open spatial concepts or traditional office structures. The cores of the towers house the vertical access, conference rooms, coffee points, sanitary facilities and additional ancillary functions.

In conformity with the image of polished stones, in natural light, the facades seem smooth and pristine; in the dark and under artificial light, however, they demonstrate a certain depth. In collaboration with the engineering offices of Werner Sobek (Stuttgart), JSWD and BEHF developed a floor-to-ceiling two-shell glass construction made up of an exterior impact pane and an interior triple insulated pane. Subtle color variations in the facade profile create a nuanced visual appearance; the color palette of anthracite, platinum and bronze underpins the high-quality impression. The facade grid shifts around the axis every two, three, or four stories, visually creating "packages" of floors. This variation not only makes the facade more lively, it also illustrates the concept of the construction client, who wants to attract a number of smaller tenants, not only one large one.

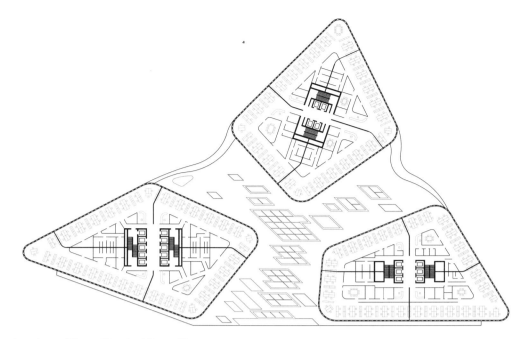

Regelgeschosse Büros   Standard floor offices

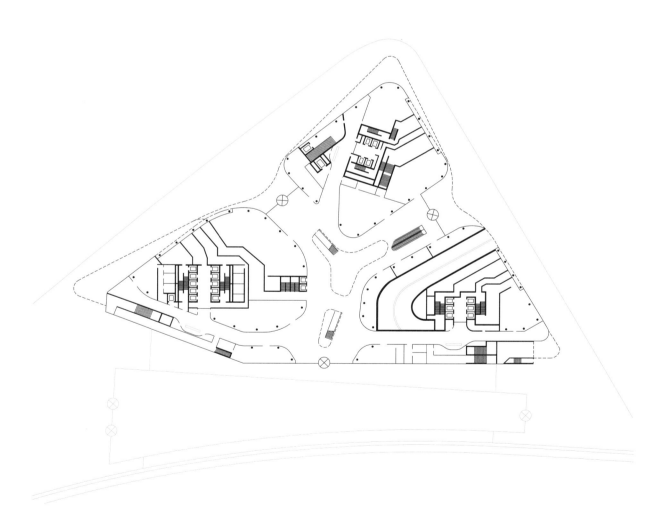

Ebene 0   Level 0

Hochhäuser in der Stadt
High-rises in the City

Ein Gespräch mit Frederik Jaspert (Partner, JSWD) und Tobias Unterberg (Associate Partner, JSWD) über gescheiterte Hochhausprojekte, das gelungene Icon Vienna und den Versuch, Regeln für ein gutes Hochhaus zu finden.

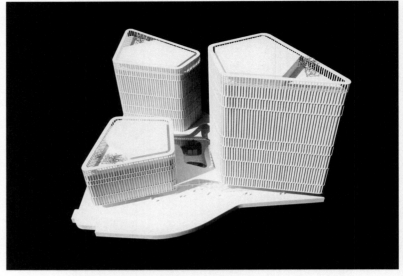

Modell des Icon Vienna Model of the Icon Vienna

A conversation with Frederik Jaspert (Partner, JSWD) and Tobias Unterberg (Associate Partner, JSWD) about failed high-rise projects, the successful Icon Vienna and the search for rules for a good high-rise.

Frederik Jaspert, wieso löst das Hochhaus nach über einem Jahrhundert der Moderne noch immer erbitterte Diskussionen aus – zumindest in europäischen Städten?
Frederik Jaspert: Hochhäuser verändern die Silhouette einer Stadt. Sie treten meist in Konkurrenz zum Kirchturm, der jahrhundertelang die städtebauliche Dominante war. Für jede gewachsene Stadt ist es eine große Herausforderung, den richtigen Weg im Umgang mit Gebäuden zu finden, die alles andere überragen.

Gibt es dafür inzwischen Rezepte?
FJ: Die Regeln sind kaum zu verallgemeinern, jede Stadt hat ihren eigenen Grundriss und ihre spezifischen Rahmenbedingungen. Wir haben seit Gründung unseres Büros sehr unterschiedliche Erfahrungen mit Hochhausprojekten gemacht.

Wann haben Sie sich zum ersten Mal mit dieser Bauaufgabe beschäftigt?
FJ: Der erste Wettbewerb von JSWD war der „ICE-Terminal Köln-Deutz/Messe" im Jahr 2000. Um den Bahnhof herum hatten wir ein Hochhausensemble entworfen – eine rechtsrheinische „Corona" als Pendant zur historischen Stadtkrone des Doms auf der gegenüberliegenden Rheinseite. Das Ensemble sollte den Stadtteil Deutz stärken und eine Initialzündung sein für weitere Entwicklungen auf der „schäl

Frederik Jaspert, why does the high-rise still trigger bitter discussions—at least in European cities—after more than a century of modernism?
Frederik Jaspert: High-rises change the silhouette of a city. They usually compete with the church tower, which was the highest feature for centuries. Organically developed cities all face the enormous challenge of finding the right way to deal with buildings that are higher than everything else.

Have any recipes been developed?
FJ: The rules are hard to generalize; each city has its own layout and specific conditions. We have had very different experiences with high-rise projects.

When did you first start working on this topic?
FJ: JSWD's first competition was the ICE terminal Cologne-Deutz/Exhibition Center in 2000. We designed a high-rise ensemble around the station—a "corona" on the right bank of the Rhine as counterpart to the historic city and the cathedral on the opposite side of the river. The ensemble was intended to strengthen the district of Deutz and be a catalyst for further developments on the "schäl Sick," the traditionally less reputable right bank.

What happened after you won the competition?
FJ: At that time, the ministries of urban development and business were controlled by one party; the

Sick", dem traditionell schlecht beleumundeten rechten Ufer.

Was geschah nach dem Wettbewerbsgewinn?
FJ: Damals lagen die Ressorts Stadtentwicklung und Wirtschaft in einer Hand, die politischen Entscheidungsträger neigten dazu, die zulässige Bauhöhe immer weiter nach oben zu schrauben. Die UNESCO sah schließlich die Wirkung des Doms durch die bis zu 120 Meter hohen Häuser beeinträchtigt und drohte mit Entzug des Welterbestatus. Nach langen Verhandlungen einigte man sich schließlich auf eine annähernd halbierte Gebäudehöhe.

Wenig später wiederholte sich diese Debatte in München.
FJ: Was der Dom für Köln, ist die Frauenkirche für München. 2004 entwarfen wir im Zuge eines Wettbewerbs das Stadtquartier Isar Süd für Siemens, zu dem auch drei hohe Häuser gehörten. Nach zwei Jahren Planung wurde das Projekt in den – noch andauernden – Diskussionen um geeignete Hochhausstandorte und -höhen zerrieben und letztlich aufgegeben.

Dauerte es deswegen fast zehn Jahre, bis sich JSWD in Wien wieder mit dem Thema Hochhaus beschäftigte?
FJ: In Wien hatte man aus diesen Diskussionen gelernt. Dort entsteht am neuen Hauptbahnhof seit einigen Jahren ein hochverdichtetes Stadtquartier. Die Stadt hat offensiv Hochhausstandorte ausgewiesen, deren Lage und vertretbare Höhen im Vorfeld über Sichtfeldanalysen geprüft und in einem „Fachkonzept Hochhäuser" festgeschrieben. Dieser Prozess war eingebettet in ein umfassendes Stadtentwicklungskonzept, das Sicherheit für die Verwaltung, die Investoren und die Planer schafft. Unser Ensemble Icon Vienna konnte als einer von mehreren Bausteinen dieser Entwicklung in sehr kurzer Zeit geplant und realisiert werden.

Tobias Unterberg, als Associate Partner bei JSWD und Projektleiter waren Sie mit der Realisierung des Wettbewerbsentwurfs betraut. Hat Ihnen die gründliche Vorarbeit des Wiener Hochhauskonzepts die Arbeit erleichtert?

Kongresszentrum am ICE-Terminal Köln Messe/Deutz, 1. Preis 2002
Congress center at the Köln Messe/Deutz train station, 1st prize 2002

political decision-makers were inclined to set the permissible height ever higher. UNESCO was of the opinion that the new buildings, which were up to 120 meters high, adversely affected the visual effect of the cathedral and threatened to withdraw the cathedral's World Heritage status. After lengthy negotiations, they finally agreed on a maximum height approximately half the height of the cathedral.

A little later this debate was repeated in Munich.
FJ: The parallel to the Cathedral in Cologne is the Frauenkirche in Munich. In 2004, in the course of a competition, we designed the urban neighborhood "Isar Süd" for Siemens, which also included three tall buildings. After two years of planning, the project was crushed in the—still ongoing—discussions about suitable high-rise locations and heights and ultimately abandoned.

Was that why it took nearly ten years before JSWD dealt with the topic of high-rise buildings again, this time in Vienna?

FJ: In Vienna, they had learned from these discussions. Around the new central station there, a dense urban neighborhood has been under development for several years. The city has actively identified high-rise sites, checked their locations and heights in advance with field of view analysis, and incorporated them into a "high rise concept." This process was embedded in a comprehensive urban development concept which provides security for the administration, investors, and planners. Our ensemble Icon Vienna was conceived and realized in a very short time as one of several components of this development.

Tobias Unterberg, as associate partner at JSWD and project manager, you were entrusted with the realization of the competition design. Did the thorough preparation of the Viennese high-rise concept make your work easier?
Tobias Unterberg: Of course, the binding nature of the planning was an advantage for everyone involved. In such a project, unrest often arises

Siemens Campus Isar Süd, München, 1. Preis 2001
Siemens Campus Isar South, Munich, 1st prize 2001

Baugrund am neuen Wiener Hauptbahnhof Construction site at the new Vienna Central Station

Tobias Unterberg: Sicher war die stadtplanerische Verbindlichkeit für alle Beteiligten von Vorteil. Unruhe entsteht in einem solchen Projekt ja oft, wenn auf politischer Ebene über Ästhetik diskutiert wird oder Investoren im laufenden Prozess versuchen, von der Politik Zugeständnisse zu erlangen, um Flächen zu maximieren. Bei solchen Kraftproben können die Architekten und Planer oft nur vom Rand aus zuschauen.

Wie ist es als deutsches Büro, in Österreich zu bauen?
TU: In das Baurecht und die Standards mussten wir uns erst einarbeiten, das hatte aber den Vorteil, dass unser angeeignetes Wissen in manchen Bereichen frischer war als bei unserem österreichischen Partner. Das ergab hin und wieder Anlässe, um augenzwinkernd die üblichen Klischees vom „Piefke" und dem „Ösi" zu pflegen. Mit der Zeit entstand ein sehr angenehmes zwischenmenschliches Verhältnis, und – für mich der entscheidende Faktor – Vertrauen! Erst wenn alle Beteiligten einander vertrauen, kann ein derartiges Projekt gelingen.

Das klingt nach einem reibungslosen Arbeiten.
TU: Nicht von Beginn an, das war ein Prozess. Das Vertrauen auf Bauherrenseite mussten wir uns hart erarbeiten. Danach verlief alles reibungsloser. Geholfen hat sicherlich, dass die Schnittstellen eindeutig waren. Unser Wiener Partnerbüro BEHF Architects war zuständig für den Sockel, wir für die drei Türme und die Fassadenplanung, die wir bei uns inhouse erstellt haben. Damit Innen und Außen dieselbe Sprache sprechen, gab es intensive Abstimmungsrunden – zuerst mit unserem Partnerbüro und dann mit dem Bauherrn –, die zu dem „Ergebnis aus einem Guss" geführt haben.

Hätten Sie die Ausführungsplanung nicht gerne selbst gemacht?
TU: Doch, selbstverständlich. Mit der Übergabe der Leitdetails war unsere Aufgabe hier aber erfüllt. So etwas kann heikel sein, weil wir als when aesthetics are discussed at the political level or when investors try to gain concessions from politicians in the middle of the process in order to maximize space. In showdowns like that, architects and planners can often only watch from the sidelines.

What is it like to build in Austria as a German office?
TU: We had to familiarize ourselves with the local construction law and standards, but that had the advantage that our acquired knowledge was sometimes fresher than our Austrian partners'. This occasionally offered the chance to wink at the usual stereotypes the Germans and Austrians have about one another. Over time, a very pleasant interpersonal relationship emerged, and—for me, the deciding factor— trust! A project like this can only succeed when all parties trust one another.

That sounds like an effortless process.
TU: Not from the outset; it was a process. We had to work hard to gain the client's confidence. After that everything went more smoothly. It certainly helped that the tasks were clearly divided. Our Vienna partner office BEHF Architects was responsible for the foundation; we were responsible for the three towers and the facade planning, which we created in-house. There were intensive rounds of coordination—first with our partner office and then with the client—to make sure that the same design language was spoken inside and out. This led to a well-rounded result which feels like it was designed all in one go.

Would you have liked to have done the execution planning yourself?

Schloss Belvedere, Wien Belvedere Palace, Vienna

Bonner Skyline mit Montage des neuen Hochpunkts am Kanzlerplatz
Bonn skyline with installation of the new high point at Kanzlerplatz

Architekten dann keine wirkliche Kontrolle mehr über die Qualität haben. Hier hat das allerdings hervorragend funktioniert, weil wir mit den Leitdetails bereits viele Bereiche vorgedacht hatten und das Wiener Büro HNP Architects unsere Vorgaben sehr gut umgesetzt hat. Hinzu kommt, dass die Projektleitung und -steuerung ebenfalls sehr engagiert war und zusammen mit den ausführenden Architekten und Baufirmen vielfach Lösungen gefunden hat, mit denen wir mehr als zufrieden sind.

Gute Gründe für JSWD, sich weiterhin mit dem Hochhaus zu beschäftigen…
FJ: Schon allein deswegen, weil es jeweils andere Rahmenbedingungen gibt, mit denen wir umgehen müssen, wenn der Baugrund knapp und der Flächenbedarf groß ist. Aus unserer Erfahrung muss ein Hochhaus zuallererst an der richtigen Stelle stehen und es muss Ratio und Emotion gleichermaßen ansprechen. Im selbstverständlichen Zusammenspiel der Parameter Wirtschaftlichkeit, Langlebigkeit, sinnfällige Konstruktion und Technik, Proportion und Fassadengestalt entsteht im Idealfall ein Haus, das positiv ausstrahlt und einen Mehrwert für die Stadt hat.

Beweisen Sie es!
FJ: Bei unserem Projekt Neuer Kanzlerplatz in Bonn war es unstrittig, dass ein neues Hochhaus die alte Hochhausscheibe des Bonn-Centers von 1969 ersetzt – es ist einfach die richtige Stelle. Zwischen Bahn- und Pkw-Trassen und am Übergang von der Altstadt zum Bundesviertel gelegen, markiert der Neubau weithin sichtbar den Auftakt in die Museumsmeile. Hier ist das Hochhaus, auch auf Anregung der Stadtverwaltung, im Verlauf des Planungsprozesses sogar noch in die Höhe gewachsen. Die gewonnene Höhe tut nicht nur der Proportion gut, sondern schließt den Neubau auch in den Ring der Bestandsgebäude Langer Eugen, Post Tower und WCC-Turm ein. Nach Fertigstellung können wir uns gerne dort treffen und dies alles überprüfen.

TU: Yes, of course. Once we handed over our specifications, our task was fulfilled. It can be tricky, because as architects we then have no real control over the quality. In this case, however, it worked very well, because we had already given some thought to many areas in the specifications and the Viennese office HNP Architects implemented everything very well. In addition, the project management and control were also very committed; together with the executing architects and construction companies, they often found solutions with which we are more than satisfied.

Good reasons for JSWD to continue to work on high-rises.
FJ: Yes, if only for the reason that there are different framework conditions that we have to deal with when building ground is scarce and spatial needs are high. In our experience, a high-rise must be located in the right place first and foremost and it must address ratio and emotion equally. In the natural interaction of the parameters cost-effectiveness, longevity, sensible construction and technology, proportion, and facade shape, ideally a building emerges which has a positive resonance and added value for the city.

Prove it!
FJ: In our project New Chancellor Square in Bonn, it was undisputed that a new high-rise would replace the old high-rise of the 1969 Bonn Center—it's just a good location. Located between the train tracks and the highway and at the transition from the historic city center to the federal district, the new building visibly marks the beginning of the Museum Mile, even from afar. At this location the high-rise even grew in height over the course of the planning process at the suggestion of the city administration. The increase in height is not only good for the proportions, but also incorporates the new building in the ring of the existing buildings Langer Eugen, Post Tower and WCC Tower. After it is completed, we can meet there and see for ourselves.

Neue Mitte Porz
Köln

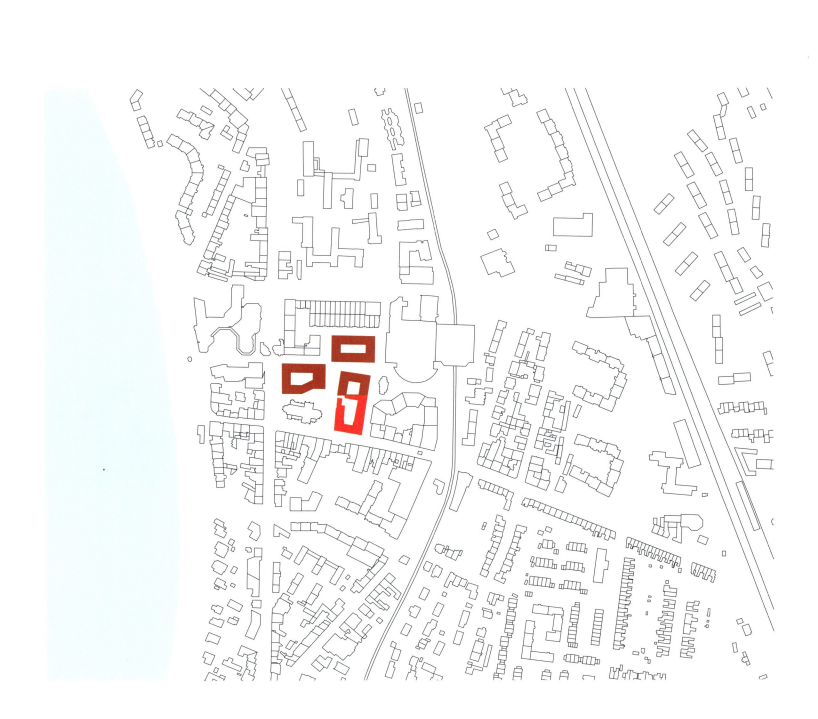

Porz als Nebenmitte hat es schwer, denn schon der dem Begriff innewohnende Widerspruch der Positionen „neben" und „Mitte" zeigt, wie unmöglich eine derartige Existenz ist. Dieser von Fritz Schumacher (1869–1947) verwandte Begriff ist inzwischen unüblich, heute spricht man von Bezirkszentren, wenn man die zweite Ebene der städtebaulichen Hierarchie meint. Dabei ist es genau dieser Widerspruch, an dem Porz sich seit Jahrzehnten abarbeitet. Rechtsrheinisch, etwa 15 Kilometer südlich der Kölner Innenstadt gelegen, gibt die ehemals selbstständige Kleinstadt seit ihrer Eingemeindung 1975 dem Stadtbezirk seinen Namen. Meint man heute das alte Zentrum, heißt es außerhalb der Behörden PORZity.

Die in den 1970er Jahren umgesetzte Neuordnung war, obwohl modern gedacht, nur kurzlebig. Kleinteilige Substanz wurde abgerissen und von einem monolithischen Warenhaus (damals Karstadt, zuletzt Hertie) plus überdimensioniertem Marktplatz ersetzt. Nicht nur das urbane Konzept, auch der Maßstabssprung wurden bald zum Problem. Der große, introvertierte Klotz verstellte Wege und Blicke, erzeugte Angsträume an seinen Rändern, der Handel litt und mit ihm das städtische Leben. Fünf Jahre stand das große Warenhaus leer, bis die Stadt Köln es 2014 erwarb und ihre Stadtentwicklungsgesellschaft moderne stadt mit einer Machbarkeitsstudie beauftragte, die sie zusammen mit JSWD durchführte. Zwei Alternativen – Umnutzung versus Abriss und Neubau – wurden in mehreren Varianten untersucht, die schließlich favorisierte Lösung in einer Planwerkstatt mit Bürgerbeteiligung diskutiert.

Ein wirkliches Zentrum, ein Markt soll im Herzen der städtebaulichen Neuordnung entstehen, das war der Wunsch vieler Bürger. Möglich wird dies durch den Abriss des als Fremdkörper wahrgenommenen Warenhauses und weiterer Bauten, die Wege und Sichtachsen verstellen. Die gewaltige Baugrube erscheint Anfang 2019 als großmaßstäbliche Tabula rasa, doch die Neue Mitte Porz soll die Fehler der Vergangenheit nicht wiederholen. Mit drei kleineren Baublöcken entwickelten JSWD eine neue, wesentlich schärfer gezeichnete Ordnung, die bestehende Wegebeziehungen und Sichtachsen zwischen Rathaus, Rhein und City Center schlüssig zusammenführt. Der neue Kirch- und Marktplatz ist deutlich kleiner dimensioniert als zuvor, was seiner Lesbarkeit und Nutzungsvielfalt sehr zugute kommen wird. Auch funktional wird die Stadt an dieser Stelle nicht neu erfunden, sondern weitergedacht. Der ruhende Verkehr findet Platz in der zweigeschossigen Tiefgarage; Einzelhandel, Gastronomie und ein Supermarkt beleben die Erdgeschosse. Der erhöht liegende Gemeindesaal bietet einen Anknüpfungspunkt für die Pfarrei St. Josef. In den Obergeschossen entstehen 130 Wohnungen, von denen rund 30 Prozent öffentlich gefördert sind. Städtisches Leben – auch nach Ladenschluss und am Wochenende – soll die große Leere in Porz füllen und der Neuen Mitte eine eigene Identität verleihen.

Das von JSWD geplante Haus 1 bildet das westliche Portal zur Neuen Mitte. An seinen Stirnseiten zitieren Spitzgiebel das Bild altstädtischer Kleinteiligkeit, während darunter 50 Wohnungen und ein Vollsortimenter Platz finden. Haus 2 und 3 werden nach Qualifizierungsverfahren von Molestina Architekten und Kaspar Kraemer Architekten mit unterschiedlichen Bauherren geplant und variieren im Sinne der Ensemblebildung in Duktus und Materialität der von JSWD mit Haus 1 gesetzten Parameter.

Porz' New City Center

Porz has a hard time as a secondary city center (*Nebenmitte*), as the contradiction in the terminology "secondary" and "city center" demonstrates; it seems impossible that this type of place should exist. This term, which was coined by Fritz Schumacher (1869–1947), has meanwhile fallen out of fashion; today, the term district center is common when talking about the second tier of urban spatial hierarchies. However, Porz has had to deal with precisely this contradiction for decades. Porz lies on the right bank of the Rhine, about 15 kilometers south of Cologne's inner city. The formerly independent small town has lent the district its name since its incorporation in 1975. The old center of the town is commonly referred to as PORZity.

The spatial restructuring of the area which took place in the 1970s followed modern principles but was unfortunately short-lived. The small-grained existing urban fabric was demolished and replaced with a monolithic department store (formerly Karstadt, most recently Hertie) and an oversized market square. Both the urban concept and the change in scale soon became a problem. The large, introverted building blocked pathways and visual connections and created trouble spots at its edges. Retail suffered and, as a result, so did the urban liveliness. The enormous department store stood empty for five years, until the city of Cologne bought it in 2014 and tasked the city-run development company *moderne stadt* with a feasibility study, which they completed together with JSWD. Two alternatives—repurposing or demolition and new construction—were examined in a range of variations. The favored version was discussed in a planning workshop with citizens.

The desire voiced by many citizens was a real city center and a market square at the heart of the urban restructuring. This was made possible through the demolition of the shopping center, which felt like a foreign body, and additional buildings which obscured pathways and visual connections. At the beginning of 2019, the enormous construction pit appears to be a large-scale tabula rasa; however, Porz' New Center should not repeat the mistakes of the past. Through three, smaller buildings, JSWD created a new, much clearer spatial order, which coherently combines existing pathways and visual connections between the city hall, Rhine, and the City Center. The new church and market square is much smaller than its predecessor, which will certainly benefit its legibility and the diversity of its future uses. Functionally, the city will not be reinvented at this location, but rather developed further. There is a new space for parking cars in the two-story underground parking garage; retail, up-market food outlets, and a supermarket enliven the ground floors. The church hall, which is elevated, offers a link to the parish of St. Joseph. The upper stories will house 130 apartments, of which approximately 30 percent are publicly subsidized. Urban life—even after closing time and on the weekends—will fill the yawning emptiness in Porz and lend the New Center its own identity.

House 1, which was planned by JSWD, forms the western gate to the New Center. On its end faces, pointed gables invoke the image of historic small-scale construction; 50 apartments and one full-range provider find space in this building. Houses 2 and 3 were planned with different clients; a qualification procedure awarded the design of these two buildings to Molestina Architects und Kaspar Kraemer Architects. The buildings use a similar design language and materiality to House 1, in line with the goal of creating a coherent ensemble.

Die große Sehnsucht nach Kleinteiligkeit
Longing for Small Scale

Im Gespräch mit Andreas Röhrig (Geschäftsführer, moderne stadt, Gesellschaft zur Förderung des Städtebaues und der Gemeindeentwicklung mbH) und Konstantin Jaspert (Partner, JSWD) über die Neue Mitte Porz

A conversation with Andreas Röhrig (managing director, moderne stadt, Gesellschaft zur Förderung des Städtebaues und der Gemeindeentwicklung mbH) and Konstantin Jaspert (Partner, JSWD) about Porz' New Center.

Mit der Neuen Mitte Porz ergibt sich die seltene Gelegenheit, eine großmaßstäbliche Entscheidung der Vergangenheit zu korrigieren. Warum hat das städtebauliche Leitbild irgendwann nicht mehr funktioniert?
Konstantin Jaspert: Das große Hertie-Kaufhaus zerschnitt den ursprünglich einmal sehr präsenten Friedrich-Ebert-Platz in ein Vorne und ein Hinten. Aber erst das 2003 eröffnete City Center höhlte das einstige städtebauliche Konzept vollkommen aus, denn es machte die eigentliche Rückseite zur belebten Seite. Der große Platz an der Vorderseite hingegen verwaiste. Nachdem das Kaufhaus geschlossen wurde, weil sich der Typus des Warenhauses überlebt hatte, war bald der gesamte Kernbereich ausgestorben, die Geschäfte standen leer. Das gab den Anstoß, die Situation gründlich zu überdenken.
Andreas Röhrig: Strukturen wie die, die wir in Porz vorfanden, sind schlichtweg an ihrer Größe gescheitert, zumal sie auch an ihren Rändern und Schnittstellen viele intransparente und dunkle Räume erzeugten.

Was macht die Neue Mitte Porz besser – oder anders?
AR: Die erste Grundsatzentscheidung war, dass die Neue Mitte Porz keine neue Mall sein darf. Unser Ziel ist es, eine gute Balance zwischen Städtebau und Handels-

Porz' New Center offers the rare opportunity to change a past large-scale decision. Why did this urban model stop working?
Konstantin Jaspert: The large Hertie shopping center divided the once very prominent Friedrich Ebert Square into a back and a front. But it was actually the City Center, which opened in 2003, which completely undermined the urban concept behind the construction, since it made the back side into the animated one. The large square at the front, on the other hand, was abandoned. After the shopping center was closed because this type of department store was outlived, the entire core area became deserted. The shops were all empty. And this was the impetus for a comprehensive reassessment.
Andreas Röhrig: Structures like the ones we found in Porz failed simply as a result of their size. In addition, they created a number of opaque and dark spaces at their edges and interfaces.

What makes the New Center better—or different?
AR: The first basic decision was that Porz' New Center should not be a new mall. Our goal was to strike a good balance between urban design and retail. We have achieved that through an urban design that combines permanence and flexibility in order to be able

wirkung zu erzeugen. Das erreichen wir mit einem Städtebau, der Dauerhaftigkeit und Flexibilität vereint, um auch auf die für den Handel so typischen kurzfristigen Veränderungen reagieren zu können. Außerdem binden wir eine Vielzahl von Akteuren in die Gesamtentwicklung ein, damit keine Monostruktur entsteht, sondern eine identitätsstiftende Maßstäblichkeit, die der des alten Porz sehr ähnlich ist.

Wie kann sie sich als Nebenmitte in Köln behaupten?
AR: Ich sehe Porz nicht als Konkurrenz zur Kölner Innenstadt. Lieber ist mir der Vergleich mit den mittelgroßen Städten im Westfälischen, Lippstadt oder Paderborn. Die funktionieren, weil ihre Maßstäblichkeit stimmt und sie den täglichen Bedarf bedienen. Wenn Porz sich auf die Menschen konzentriert, die dort leben, hat es als Zentrum durchaus eine Berechtigung. Die sensationelle Rheinlage tut ein Übriges.

Welches war – oder ist – das dringendste Anliegen, das Sie mit dem Projekt verfolgen?
AR: Wir möchten vor Ort glaubwürdig erscheinen, wir möchten den Menschen vermitteln, dass wir ihre Wahrnehmung, in Porz passiere nichts, ernst nehmen und sie widerlegen. Wir haben Vertrauen zurückgewonnen, sehr genau zugehört und in der Machbarkeitsstudie fünf Varianten untersuchen lassen, um alle Belange ernst zu nehmen und damit eine solide Basis für unser Handeln zu schaffen.
Es ging nicht darum, in einem Schritt etwas Großes zu entwickeln, sondern einen Prozess in Gang zu bringen. Darum wird zeitgleich zu der Neuen Mitte Porz mit ihren drei neuen Häusern an einem integrierten Stadtentwicklungskonzept gearbeitet, das uns noch zwei oder drei Jahrzehnte beschäftigen wird.

Sind Sie die Machbarkeitsstudie ergebnisoffen angegangen? Insbesondere die Frage, ob und wie man das Kaufhaus umnutzen kann, stelle ich mir sehr interessant vor.
KJ: Wir haben festgestellt, dass eine reine Nutzungsänderung des ehemaligen Kaufhauses, zum Beispiel als Rathaus, die städtebaulichen Defizite – die Barrierewirkung, die unangemessene Platzgröße – nicht behoben hätte. Aus Gesprächen erfuhren wir, dass Porz mit Hertie einen Teil seiner Identität verloren hatte, gleichzeitig war aber eine große Sehnsucht nach Kleinteiligkeit zu spüren. Ganz abgesehen davon, dass das Kaufhaus neben einer enormen Gebäudetiefe auch technische Probleme mitbrachte, zeigte unsere Studie, dass der Erhalt der Großstruktur keine Aufbruchsstimmung vermittelt hätte.

Wie ermittelten Sie schließlich den angemessenen Maßstab für Gebäude und öffentliche Räume?
KJ: Im Wesentlichen haben wir uns hier am Wesen der europäischen Stadt, dem steten Wechsel zwischen Gasse und Platz, orientiert, der eine gewisse Dichte erzeugt. Das adäquate Verhältnis von Gebäudehöhe und Gassenbreite konnten wir aus der Umgebung des Kaufhauses ableiten, sie gibt eine gewisse Körnung vor: Die Gebäude sind drei bis fünf Geschosse hoch und haben überwiegend geneigte Dächer.
AR: An einer Stelle kamen wir eher per Zufall auf die richtige Lösung. Lange Zeit war unklar, ob das an die Kirche St. Josef angebaute Dechant-Scheben-Haus erhalten bleibt. Um dort eine Engstelle zu vermeiden, ließen JSWD Haus 1, in dessen Erdgeschoss eine große Handelsfläche geplant ist, an jener Ecke zurückspringen. Dieser Knick blieb, obwohl das Pfarrzentrum schließlich abgerissen wurde. Diese

Abbruch Hertie-Kaufhaus
Demolition of the Hertie department store

to react to the short-notice changes typical of retail. In addition, we involved a large number of actors in the overall development so that a mono-structure could not develop. We were striving for a scale which would help promote an individual identity and was similar to that of historical Porz.

How can Porz assert itself as a secondary city center?
AR: I don't see Porz as being in competition with the Cologne inner city. I much prefer a comparison with mid-sized cities in Westphalia like Lippstadt or Paderborn. They function well because their scale is appropriate and serves daily needs. If Porz concentrates on the people living here, then the center is certainly justified. Its sensational location on the Rhine does the rest.

What was—or is—the most important task that you are trying to achieve with this project?
AR: We want to appear believable on the ground. We want to communicate to local residents that we take their impression that nothing happens in Porz seriously and are working to change that. We have won back trust, listened very closely, and examined five variants in the feasibility study in order to take all interests seriously and create a solid basis for the next steps. It wasn't about developing something big in one step, but rather about starting a process. For this reason, an integrated urban development concept is being developed simultaneously to Porz' New Center with its three new buildings; this concept will keep us busy for the next two to three decades.

Did you approach the feasibility study without a fixed end point in mind? I would be particularly interested to know whether and how the shopping center could have been repurposed.
KJ: We realized that simply introducing a new use to the former shopping center, for example

kleine Störung im Gefüge ist ganz wunderbar, weil sie an St. Josef einen Platz mit einer einzigartigen Mikroatmosphäre ausformt, die man kaum besser entwerfen könnte.

Welche Bilder hatten Sie dabei im Kopf?
KJ: Was wir an gewachsenen Städten so lieben, sind eben solche Unregelmäßigkeiten. Wir wollten deswegen auch kein Implantat auf dem Reißbrett konstruieren. In Köln, Rodenkirchen, Nippes, Ehrenfeld oder im Belgischen Viertel, überall dort, wo es Quartiersidentität gibt, haben wir ähnliche bauliche Strukturen entdeckt: kleinere und mittelgroße dichte Gassen, die sich auf kompakte Plätze öffnen. Allzu weit muss man also gar nicht gehen, um Vorbilder für die Neue Mitte Porz zu finden. Im nächsten Schritt haben wir nach einer zeitgemäßen Formensprache für diese vertrauten Stadträume gesucht. Mit Abstraktion und Reduktion lassen wir nun das Altstädtische nicht als Zitat, sondern als etwas Zeitgemäßes entstehen.

Die verbaute Mitte Porz: zentral das Kaufhaus, rechts das Dechant-Scheben-Haus
The fully built-out center of Porz: the department store is in the center and the Dechant-Scheben building is on the right

Sie setzen auf Durchmischung. Welche Rolle spielt das Wohnen in der Neuen Mitte Porz? Welche die Gemeinde St. Josef?
AR: Das Wohnen spielt eine zentrale Rolle, denn darüber lässt sich Aufenthaltsqualität und Stabilität erzeugen – sofern die Durchmischung stimmt. Von zentraler Bedeutung sind die Vielfalt und die Vielzahl der Akteure. Jedes Haus hat einen eigenen Investor, und jeder von ihnen spricht eine eigene Nutzergruppe an. Die Aachener Siedlungs- und Wohnungsgesellschaft baut in Haus 3 ein neues kirchliches Gemeindezentrum mit angeschlossenen Wohngruppen. In Haus 2 wird das Wohnungsunternehmen Sahle Wohnen das Kooperative Baulandmodell Köln abbilden und 30 Prozent geförderten Wohnungsbau anbieten. In Haus 1 werden Mietwohnungen in unterschiedlicher Größe entstehen.
KJ: Ganz wichtig ist, dass dort auch nach Geschäftsschluss noch Leben ist, denn eine solche Kernzone darf nachts nicht sozial verwaisen.
AR: Das stimmt, bevor wir dort anfingen, gab es in den Dunkelzo-

converting it into the city hall, would not have solved the urban design problems—the barrier effect, the inappropriate size of the square. We learned from discussions that when Hertie left, Porz lost part of its identity; at the same time, there was a palpable desire for small-scale development. Independent of the fact that the shopping center had technical problems in addition to its enormous size, our study showed that the preservation of the building did not inspire a feeling of renewal and change.

How did you determine the appropriate scale for the buildings and open spaces?
KJ: Essentially, we oriented ourselves on the underlying concept of the European city, a constant alternation of street and square which lends a certain density. We were able to derive the appropriate relationship between building height and street width from the surroundings. They determine a certain grain size: the existing buildings are three to five stories high and the majority of them have pitched roofs.
AR: At one location, we actually reached the correct answer by accident. For a long time it was unclear whether the Dechant Scheben House, which is built onto the Church of St. Joseph, would be preserved or not. In order to prevent a narrow point there, JSWD modified the respective corner of House 1; a large retail space is planned for the ground floor. This recess remained even though the parish center was in fact demolished. This little disturbance in the structure is really wonderful; it forms a unique micro-atmosphere at St. Joseph's which one could not have planned better.

What images did you have in your head while designing?
KJ: What we love about organically evolved cities are just these irregularities. We didn't want to create an

implant on the drawing board. In Cologne, Rodenkirchen, Nippes, Ehrenfeld or the Belgian Quarter, everywhere we have a district identity, we have also discovered similar built structures: small and medium-sized dense streets which open onto compact squares. You don't have to go very far to find models for Porz' New Center. In the next step, we looked for a contemporary design language for these familiar urban spaces. Through abstraction and reduction, we were able to create a historical feel not as an imitation, but rather as something contemporary.

You stress mixed use. What role does housing play in Porz' New Center? And what role does St. Joseph's parish play?
AR: Housing plays a central role, since it is a key component in creating a high-quality space and stability—as long as the mix is correct. The variety and number of actors are also important. Each building has its own investor, and each of them addresses a different user group. The Aachener Siedlungs- und Wohnungsgesellschaft is building a new parish center with attached housing groups in House 3. In House 2, the residential construction company Sahle Wohnen is going to illustrate Cologne's cooperative building land model and offer 30 percent subsidized housing. In House 1, rental apartments of various sizes will be constructed.
KJ: It's very important that there is life on the streets after the shops close; a central zone like this cannot be allowed to be deserted at night.
AR: Yes, that's true. Before we started working here, there were problems with drug dealing and violence in the dark areas. The situation improved dramatically through the demolition of the shopping center and the creation of the construction site because the space became clearer. We assume

nen Probleme mit Drogenhandel und Gewalt. Schon durch den Hertie-Abbruch und die Einrichtung der Baustelle hat sich die Situation erheblich verbessert, weil sie überschaubar geworden ist. Wir gehen davon aus, dass das Quartier mit drei bewohnten Häusern und belebten Erdgeschosszonen auch Sicherheit ausstrahlen wird.

Stichwort Nachhaltigkeit: Warum könnte der Neuen Mitte Porz eine längere Lebensdauer beschieden sein als der Vorgängerstruktur?
AR: Nachhaltig sind zum Beispiel die breit gefächerten Eigentumsverhältnisse, denn statt einer Großstruktur haben wir demnächst drei separat bewirtschaftete Gebäude. Dass alle Akteure eine Bindung zu Porz haben und sich die Kölner Architekturbüros in den Wettbewerben durchsetzen konnten, schafft eine Verbindlichkeit. Mit diesen Planungen tragen wir eine große Verantwortung für die Zukunft unserer Stadtgesellschaft. Auch deshalb haben wir uns, losgelöst von den Gesetzmäßigkeiten des Kapitalmarktes, dazu entschieden, die aufwendigste und nachhaltigste Lösung der fünf in der Machbarkeitsstudie untersuchten Varianten zu realisieren. Ich bin zuversichtlich, dass die Porzer diesen Wert einmal schätzen werden.
KJ: Neben der Nutzungsvielfalt wird auch der Städtebau ein Faktor für die Langlebigkeit sein, denn er greift auf ein seit Jahrhunderten gut funktionierendes Modell zurück. Weil er Räume verbindet und Wege verknüpft, wird er als selbstverständlich wahrgenommen werden. Und wir wissen ja: Da, wo sich Wege kreuzen, entwickelt sich Handel ganz organisch.

Baugrube, 2019   Construction site, 2019

that the new neighborhood with three inhabited buildings and lively ground floors will also contribute to safety here.

Now a question about sustainability: why could Porz' New Center enjoy a longer life than its predecessor?
AR: The widely distributed ownership structures are sustainable, for example. Instead of one large structure, we have three, separately-managed buildings. All three actors also have a connection to Porz, and all three competitions were won by architectural offices from Cologne; that helps to create commitment. Through this planning, we took on a lot of responsibility for the future of our urban society. This is also the reason why we chose the most complex and sustainable solution of the five that we examined in the feasibility study instead of simply basing the decision on the usual market tenets. I am confident that the residents of Porz will appreciate this value.
KJ: In addition to the variety of uses, the urban design itself will be a factor in the longevity of this project; it falls back on a model that has worked well for hundreds of years. Because it connects spaces and pathways, it is perceived as self-evident. And we know well: where pathways cross, trade develops organically.

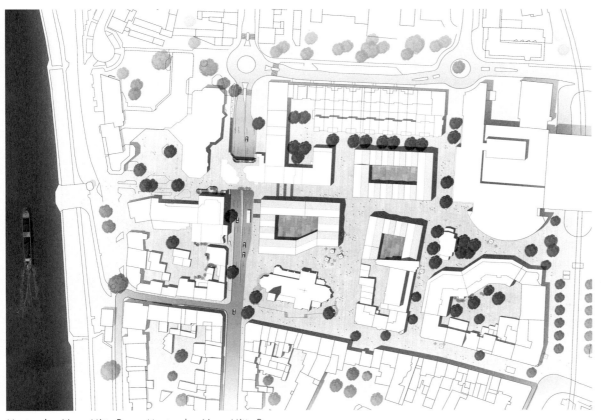

Masterplan Neue Mitte Porz   Masterplan Neue Mitte Porz

Universitätsklinikum UKSH Schleswig-Holstein

CAMPUS KIEL CAMPUS KIEL

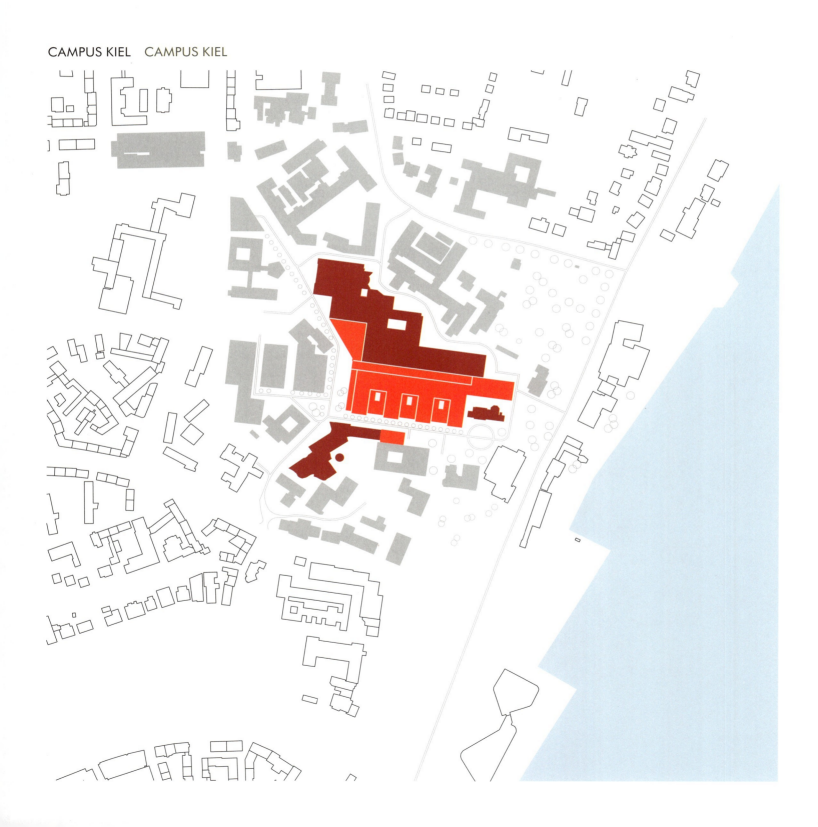

CAMPUS LÜBECK CAMPUS LÜBECK

Das Universitätsklinikum Schleswig-Holstein (UKSH) ist seit der Fusion der Universitätskliniken Kiel und Lübeck eine der größten Universitätskliniken in Europa. An seinen beiden Standorten stellt das UKSH insgesamt 2500 Betten bereit und beschäftigt rund 14200 Mitarbeiter, davon mehr als 2000 Ärzte. Damit stellt es die medizinische Maximalversorgung in Schleswig-Holstein sicher, ist also insbesondere für die Behandlung der am schwersten Erkrankten und Verletzten verantwortlich.

Die schleswig-holsteinische Landesregierung beschloss 2009 den *Baulichen Masterplan der Universitätsmedizin der Zukunft in Schleswig-Holstein*, um den zunehmend komplexeren Ansprüchen an Krankenversorgung, Forschung und Lehre auch weiterhin gerecht werden zu können. Grundlage für die bauliche Gestaltung bildeten Prognosen und Kapazitätsberechnungen, die den demografischen Wandel ebenso berücksichtigen wie den medizinischen Fortschritt. Über eine europaweite Ausschreibung fand das Land mit dem Bieterkonsortium aus BAM PPP Deutschland GmbH und VAMED Health Project GmbH 2014 einen privaten Partner für ein innovatives Finanzierungsmodell. Es übertrug ihm Planung, Bau und Betrieb der Immobilie, die weiterhin im Besitz der öffentlichen Hand bleibt, für 30 Jahre und ein Investitionsvolumen von 1,7 Milliarden Euro. Für die architektonische Planung der Neubauten und Sanierungsmaßnahmen zeichnet die Arbeitsgemeinschaft PG Architekten UKSH – bestehend aus JSWD Architekten, HDR TMK Architekten, tsj architekten und sander.hofrichter architekten – verantwortlich. Sie wird von Olaf Drehsen, JSWD, in allen Belangen vertreten.

An beiden Standorten wird der Bestand umfassend saniert und erweitert, um mit interdisziplinär ausgerichteten Gebäuden in einer hochfunktionalen Infrastruktur die Wirtschaftlichkeit und Wettbewerbsfähigkeit des UKSH zu verbessern. Der Grundgedanke ist, im Rahmen der Maßnahme an beiden Standorten mit dem Bau einer angemessen dimensionierten und sensibel platzierten Großform Nutzungen zu zentralisieren und Funktionen durchgehend horizontal zu schichten. Damit sollen Wege verkürzt, Arbeitsabläufe effizienter gestaltet und die Orientierung erleichtert werden. JSWD waren außerdem für die Erarbeitung gestalterischer Grundsätze einer Corporate Architecture für die Marke UKSH zuständig.

Die Sockelzonen der Neubauten sind an beiden Standorten regionaltypisch mit rotem Ziegel verblendet, die darüber liegenden Bettenstationen werden so mit weißen Faserzementplatten verkleidet, dass die Fugen mit den Fensteröffnungen korrespondieren. Einen schönen Kontrast dazu bilden die feststehenden Sonnenschutzelemente aus goldfarbenem Streckmetall. So nehmen die Campi eine zeitgemäße Haltung ein, greifen aber auf vertraute Materialien, Oberflächen und Formen zurück, um einen hohen Wiedererkennungswert der Bauten zu erzeugen. Bei der Planung der Patientenzimmer spielt das Wohlbefinden der Patienten eine große Rolle. Große Fenster, niedrige Brüstungen, die den Ausblick nach draußen auch aus dem Krankenbett erlauben, freundliche Farben und warme Holztöne schaffen dort bei höchster Funktionalität und Einhaltung aller hygienischen Standards eine angemessene Behaglichkeit.

University Medical Center UKSH Schleswig-Holstein

Since the merger of the university hospitals Kiel and Lübeck, the University Hospital Schleswig-Holstein (UKSH) has been one of the largest university hospitals in Europe. At its two locations, the UKSH provides a total of 2,500 beds and employs around 14,200 people, including more than 2,000 doctors. It ensures a maximum level of medical care in Schleswig-Holstein and is responsible in particular for the treatment of the most seriously ill and injured patients.

In 2009, the state government of Schleswig-Holstein decided to develop a structural master plan for the state's university medical center of the future in order to be able to continue to meet the increasingly complex demands of patient care, research, and teaching. The design was based on forecasts and capacity calculations which considered both demographic change and medical progress.

Through a Europe-wide tendering process in 2014, the state found a private partner for an innovative financing model: the bidder consortium comprising BAM PPP Deutschland GmbH and VAMED Health Project GmbH. The state transferred the planning, construction, and operation of the property, which remains in the hands of the public sector, to the consortium for 30 years and entrusted it with an investment of 1.7 billion euros.

The working group PG Architects UKSH—which is made up of JSWD architects, HDR TMK architects, tsj architects and sander.hofrichter architects—is responsible for the architectural planning of the new buildings and the renovation. Olaf Drehsen is the working group's representative.

At both locations, the existing buildings will be comprehensively refurbished and expanded; the intention is to improve the profitability and competitiveness of the UKSH through interdisciplinary buildings embedded in a highly functional infrastructure. The basic idea is to centralize usage and organize functions horizontally at both locations with the construction of an appropriately dimensioned and sensitively placed large-scale building. This should shorten paths, make workflows more efficient, and facilitate orientation. JSWD was also responsible for developing the design principles behind the corporate architecture for the UKSH brand.

The ground floors of the new buildings will be faced with locally-typical red brick at both locations; the floors above, which house the inpatient units, are clad with white fiber-cement slabs in such a way that the joints correspond with the window openings. The fixed sun protection elements made of gold-colored expanded metal form a nice contrast to these elements. In this way, the campuses take a contemporary approach, while still relying on familiar materials, surfaces, and shapes to create a high recognition value for the buildings. The well-being of the patients played a major role in the planning of the patient rooms. Large windows and low balustrades, which also allow views out from the hospital bed, friendly colors and warm wood tones promote an atmosphere of comfort while still incorporating maximum functionality and compliance with all hygiene standards.

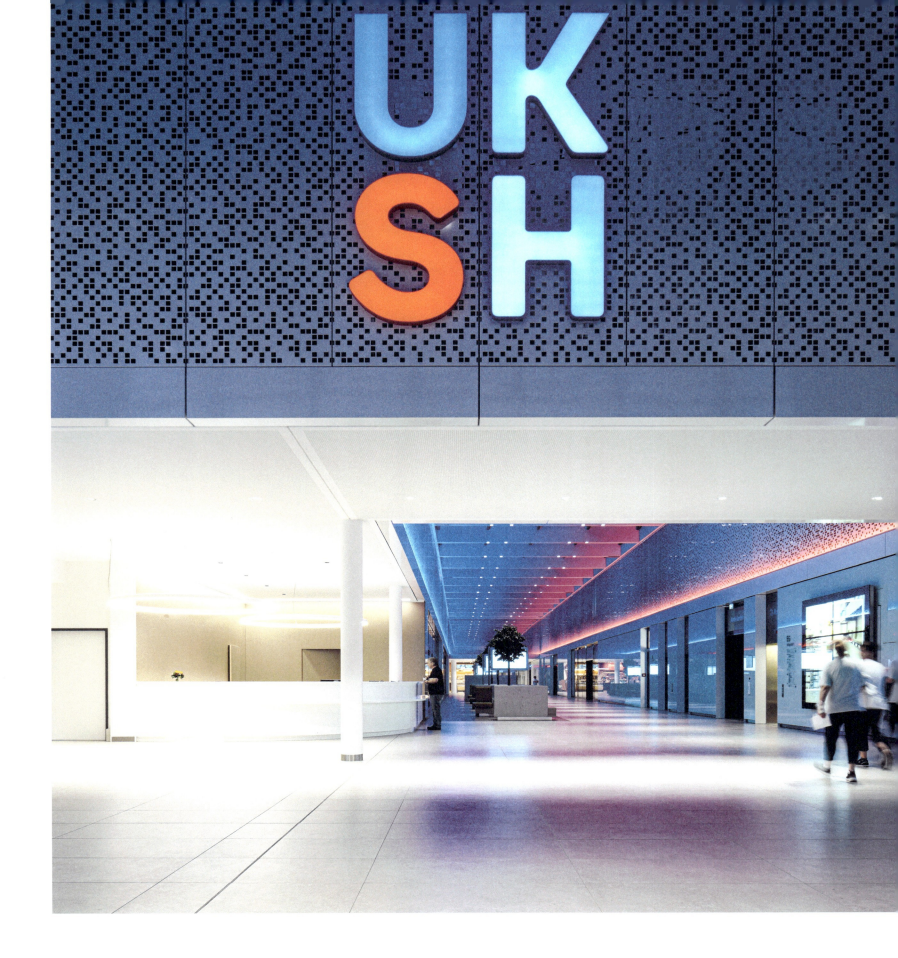

Campus Kiel

Im Frühjahr 2016 wurde in Kiel der Grundstein für das neue „Klinikum der Zukunft" gelegt. Im neuen Zentralklinikum Kiel werden die Nutzungen der 21 Kliniken in einer städtebaulichen Großform zentralisiert, in der Neubau und Bestand ebenso funktional wie sensibel miteinander verzahnt sind. Flankiert von der neuen Cafeteria und dem denkmalgeschützten Gebäude der HNO-Klinik erhält der Campus einen präsenten Vorplatz als neue Mitte und Verteiler für die Besucher, Patienten und Mitarbeiter des gesamten Klinikums. An dem von Bäumen flankierten und mit Außengastronomie bespielten Roten Platz erscheint der Haupteingang als gläserne Fuge im Sockelbau und bildet den Kopf der Ost-West-Magistrale, die Alt- und Neubau miteinander verbindet. Im zweigeschossigen Sockelbau des Neubaus sind die Ambulanzen und neu entstehenden Kompetenzzentren auf kurzem Wege zu erreichen. Darauf liegen – in einer viergeschossigen, nach Süden offenen Kammstruktur organisiert – die Bettenstationen, die über Aufzüge direkt an die Magistrale angeschlossen sind. Auch das Kopfzentrum für HNO-, Augen- und Zahnmedizin bekommt mit dem neuen Vorplatz eine neue Adresse. Der größtenteils denkmalgeschützte Bestandsbau der HNO-Klinik wird umgebaut und den neuen Anforderungen entsprechend erweitert.
Ein schmaler Annex an der Ostseite des großen Komplexes beherbergt das neue Mutter-Kind-Zentrum, das über den botanischen Garten auf die Förde blickt. Der Altbau der gegenüberliegenden Frauenklinik, die zu ihrer Ursprungsform zurückgebaut wurde, erhielt mit dem Neubau einen wirkungsvollen Rahmen.

Campus Kiel

The cornerstone for the hospital of the future was laid in Kiel in the spring of 2016. In Kiel's new central hospital, the uses of the 21 clinics will be centralized in a large-scale urban design in which new construction and existing buildings are sensitively and functionally integrated. The campus will be given a prominent forecourt as a new center and distributor for visitors, patients, and staff which will be flanked by the new cafeteria and the listed ENT clinic building. On the Red Square, which is lined with trees and houses outdoor eating offerings, the main entrance appears as a glass gap in the ground floor and forms the head of the east-west corridor connecting the old and new buildings. The ambulances and newly developed competence centers can be reached quickly in the two-story ground floor construction of the new building. The inpatient units are located in a four-story comb-shaped building which is built on top of this structure and opens to the south; the units are directly connected to the main corridor by elevators. The main center for ENT, ophthalmology, and dentistry will also be given a new address with the new forecourt. The largely listed ENT clinic building will be rebuilt and expanded to meet new requirements.
A narrow annex on the east side of the large complex houses the new Mother and Child Center, which overlooks the botanical garden on the Förde. The new construction also offers the historical building of the gynecological clinic opposite, which was restored to its original form, new, impressive surroundings.

Campus Lübeck

Bereits im Herbst 2015 wurde mit den Rohbauarbeiten für den Erweiterungsbau des Campus Lübeck begonnen. Im Rahmen der Maßnahme werden städtebauliche Bestandsstrukturen vervollständigt und als Ringschluss neu organisiert. 20 Kliniken, die teilweise in Provisorien untergebracht waren, werden nun in den Zentralkomplex integriert.
Eine baumbestandene Achse führt Patienten, Mitarbeiter und Besucher von der Ratzeburger Allee über einen eingeschobenen, leicht abgesenkten Vorplatz zu den am Ostkopf des vielgliedrigen Gebäudekomplexes gelegenen Haupteingang. Die mehrgeschossige Eingangshalle zeigt sich als neue Adresse des Klinikums offen und freundlich mit verglaster Front und Oberlichtbändern – eine Atmosphäre, die auch die auf den Vorplatz ausgerichtete Cafeteria ausstrahlt. Im viergeschossigen Sockel des direkt daran anschließenden Neubaus befinden sich nun der Zentral-OP für das gesamte Klinikum, die von der Südflanke angefahrene interdisziplinäre Notaufnahme und weitere klinische Funktionsbereiche sowie ein Seminarraumzentrum. Die darauf ruhende H-förmige Struktur kragt mit ihren zweigeschossigen Köpfen leicht darüber hinaus und bildet mit einer konsequenten Lochfassade die kleinteiligeren Pflegebereiche ab. Auf dem Dach erhält der Neubau einen Hubschrauberlandeplatz mit direkter Anbindung an alle relevanten Einrichtungen.

Campus Lübeck

The structural work for the expansion of the Lübeck campus began in autumn 2015. In this construction process, the existing built structure will be completed and reorganized in the form of a ring. Twenty clinics, some of which were housed in temporary structures, are now being integrated into the central complex.
An axis lined with mature trees leads patients, employees, and visitors from Ratzeburger Allee via an inserted, slightly lowered forecourt to the main entrance at the eastern end of the multi-unit building complex. The multi-story entrance hall offers a new visual appearance to the hospital: open and friendly as a result of the glass front and skylight belts—an atmosphere that also extends to the adjacent cafeteria.
The four-story pedestal of the adjoining new building now houses the central operating room for the entire hospital, the interdisciplinary emergency department, which is approached from the southern flank, other clinical functional areas, and a seminar room center. The H-shaped structure above it, with its two-story head ends, extends slightly beyond the pedestal construction; the perforated facade sets off the smaller-sized care areas. A heliport with direct access to all relevant facilities will be constructed on the roof of the new building.

Klinik der Zukunft
Clinic of the Future

Prof. Dr. Jens Scholz (Vorstandsvorsitzender, UKSH)
„Der Schlüssel zu einer erfolgreichen Zukunft des Universitätsklinikums Schleswig-Holstein liegt in seiner Identität. Dazu leisten JSWD als Architekten gemeinsam mit dem Konsortium, dem sie vorstehen, einen großen Beitrag. Die „Klinik des Lichts" wurde im Laufe der Planungen zu einer einprägsamen Beschreibung für die helle und freundliche Architektur der Neubauten, die unseren Patienten Zuversicht gibt und zu ihrer Genesung beiträgt. Gleichzeitig unterstützen das wertige Ambiente und die hocheffiziente räumliche Organisation die Attraktivität der 14200 Arbeitsplätze des UKSH. Für uns ist das auch im Wettbewerb um die besten Mitarbeiter in der Krankenversorgung, Forschung und Lehre ein entscheidender Faktor."

Prof. Dr. Jens Scholz (CEO, UKSH)
"The key to a successful future for the University Medical Center Schleswig-Holstein lies in its identity. JSWD and the consortium they lead have made a major contribution to this in their role as architects. In the course of planning, the 'Clinic of Light' became a memorable description for the bright and friendly architecture of the new buildings, which gives our patients optimism and helps contribute to their recovery. At the same time, the high-quality ambience and the highly efficient spatial organization increase the attractiveness of the 14,200 workplaces at the UKSH. For us, this is also a decisive factor in the competition for the best employees in health care, research, and teaching."

CEO Prof. Jens Scholz bei der Einweihung des Campus Kiel, 2019
CEO Prof. Jens Scholz at the inauguration of the Kiel campus, 2019

Magistrale im Bestand des Campus Lübeck
Main promenade through the existing Lübeck campus buildings

A conversation with Olaf Drehsen (Partner, JSWD) about the importance of architecture for the identity and success of a university hospital that wants to heal, teach, research, and learn to work economically, conducted in the summer of 2019, shortly before the opening of the renovated and expanded UKSH locations in Kiel and Lübeck.

The clinic is a place for diagnosis, therapy, research, and teaching, all highly technical, highly efficient, but with the claim that people should feel comfortable there. Asked provocatively: is the hospital of the future a medical factory with a hotel atmosphere?

Olaf Drehsen: The specialization of the clinics is crucial so that as many patients as possible can heal. The processes and spatial requirements are highly complex and require intensive cooperation with specialized planners. However, this does not mean that there is no room for us as architects to incorporate design elements into the public areas or in the patient rooms. It is a crucial factor in recovery that patients feel comfortable, so the term "hotel atmosphere" is not completely wrong.

What was the architects' special achievement?
OD: We are proud of the fact that we have constantly improved the architecture even after the competition procedure. From the design, which was relatively vague at first, we were able to develop an individual leitmotif for the locations Kiel and Lübeck and thus for the UKSH as a whole; we achieved this by using regional materials such as brick and making a reference to the location. For example, in Kiel, we have opened the campus to the *Förde*, so that the patients know where they are and do not feel like they are stuck deep in the belly of

Campus Lübeck vor der Erweiterung   Campus Lübeck before the expansion

a medicine machine. They should think: I am in my UKSH.

But patients do not come to the hospital because of the beautiful surroundings…
OD: Probably not, but people who need medical help want to be sure that they get the best possible care—and we have incorporated

Ein Gespräch mit Olaf Drehsen (Partner, JSWD) über die Bedeutung der Architektur für die Identität und den Erfolg einer Universitätsklinik, die heilen, lehren, forschen und wirtschaftlich arbeiten möchte, geführt im Sommer 2019, kurz vor der Eröffnung der sanierten und erweiterten UKSH-Standorte in Kiel und Lübeck.

Das Klinikum ist ein Ort für Diagnose, Therapie, Forschung und Lehre, all das hochtechnisiert, hocheffizient, wohl aber mit dem Anspruch, dass die Menschen sich dort wohlfühlen sollen. Provokant gefragt: Ist das Krankenhaus der Zukunft eine Medizinfabrik mit Hotelatmosphäre?

Olaf Drehsen: Die Spezialisierung der Kliniken ist entscheidend dafür, dass möglichst jeder Patient dort einen Heilungsprozess erfahren kann. Die Abläufe und räumlichen Anforderungen sind hochkomplex und erfordern eine intensive Zusammenarbeit mit den Fachplanern. Das heißt aber nicht, dass es für uns Architekten in den öffentlichen Bereichen oder in den Patientenzimmern keine Gestaltungsspielräume gäbe. Es ist ein entscheidender Faktor für die Gesundung, dass die Patienten sich wohlfühlen, daher ist der Begriff der Hotelatmosphäre nicht ganz verkehrt.

Worin besteht die besondere Leistung der Architekten?
OD: Stolz sind wir darauf, dass wir die Architektur auch nach dem konkurrierenden Verfahren stetig verbessert haben. So konnten wir aus der Gestaltung, die anfangs noch relativ vage war, ein individuelles Leitbild für die Standorte Kiel und Lübeck und damit für das UKSH entwickeln, indem wir auf regionale Materialien wie den Ziegel zurückgreifen und einen Bezug zum Ort herstellen; oder zum Beispiel in Kiel, wo wir den Campus zur Förde geöffnet haben, damit die Patienten wissen, wo sie sich befinden, und nicht das Gefühl haben, tief im Bauch einer Medizinmaschine festzustecken. Sie sollen denken: Ich bin in meinem UKSH.

Neubau am Campus Kiel   New construction on the Kiel campus

Aber die Patienten kommen doch nicht wegen der schönen Umgebung in ein Krankenhaus…
OD: Das wohl nicht, aber wer medizinische Hilfe benötigt, möchte sicher sein, die bestmögliche Versorgung zu erhalten – und dieser Qualitätsanspruch bezieht die bauliche Umgebung mit ein. Für die Wahrnehmung der Patienten und Besucher ist es wesentlich, dass die Gestaltung außen wie innen eine Qualität hat, die in der besten medizinischen Versorgung ihre Entsprechung findet.

Was bedeutet Corporate Architecture im Krankenhausbau?
OD: Bei einem Universitätsklinikum ist die Außendarstellung deutlich wichtiger als bei einem „gewöhnlichen" Krankenhaus. Für das UKSH spielt die Architektur aber auch deswegen eine große Rolle, weil seine Häuser in Kiel und in Lübeck durchaus stadtbildprägend wirken. Corporate Architecture bedeutet in diesem Fall, dass die beiden Standorte über eine gemeinsame Architektursprache zu einem Klinikum vereint werden. Großen Wert this commitment to quality into the built environment. For the perception of patients and visitors, it is essential that the design has a high quality both outside and inside which finds its equivalent in the quality of the medical care.

What does corporate architecture mean in hospital construction?
OD: In a university hospital, the external presentation is much more important than in a "normal" hospital. For the UKSH, however, architecture also plays an important role because its buildings in Kiel and in Lübeck have a strong influence on the cityscape. In this case, corporate architecture means that the two sites have been united into a single hospital using a common architectural language. Great emphasis has been placed on developing a homologous architecture, with similar attributes, materials, and shapes at both locations. Although both campuses, due to their locations and positions, bring different requirements, we have created trademarks with high recognition value through the bright entrance halls and spacious patient rooms. As an employer, UKSH has also made it a core goal to provide its employees with outstanding working conditions.

Let's talk about phase zero. Can architects still rely on tried-and-true solutions in hospital construction today? Or does the typology have to be continuously redeveloped in view of technical and medical progress?
OD: It depends on which client a clinic is planned for. There are operators who have exactly defined what they need. There is no room

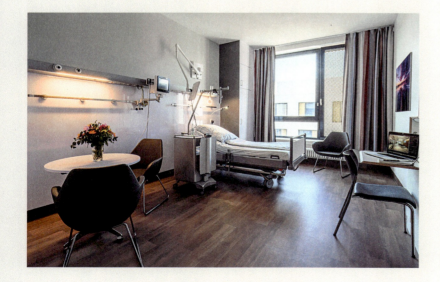

haben wir darauf gelegt, für beide eine gleichwertige Architektur, mit ähnlichen Attributen, Materialien und Formen, zu entwickeln. Auch wenn beide Campi, dem Ort und der Lage geschuldet, unterschiedliche Voraussetzungen mitbringen, haben wir mit den lichten Eingangshallen und den großzügigen Patientenzimmern Markenzeichen mit hohem Wiedererkennungswert geschaffen. Als Arbeitgeber ist es dem UKSH ein zentrales Anliegen, seinen Mitarbeitern herausragende Arbeitsbedingungen zu bieten.

Zur Phase Null: Können Architekten beim Krankenhausbau heute noch auf Bewährtes zurückgreifen? Oder muss der Typus angesichts des technischen und medizinischen Fortschritts kontinuierlich neu entwickelt werden?
OD: Es kommt darauf an, für welchen Auftraggeber eine Klinik geplant wird. Es gibt Betreiber, die ganz genau definiert haben, was sie benötigen. Da besteht keinerlei Spielraum für Neues. Bei Universitätskliniken wie dem UKSH hingegen können wir Typen entwickeln, denn da werden in der Phase Null wichtige Entscheidungen getroffen, wird ein Masterplan erstellt. In jedem Fall aber wird das Raumprogramm, die Belegungsplanung, parallel mit Fachplanern entwickelt, die zum Beispiel die Bettenkapazität aufgrund der lokalen Altersstruktur ermitteln. Will man für jeden Standort einen „Maßanzug" entwickeln, ist eine längere Phase Null erforderlich. Aber natürlich: Was sich bewährt hat, kommt immer wieder vor – auch die Römer haben schon sehr gute Heilanstalten gebaut.

for new things. At university clinics such as the UKSH, on the other hand, we can develop typologies, because important decisions are made in phase zero and a master plan is drawn up. In any case, the room program and occupancy planning are developed together with specialized planners who, for example, determine the necessary bed capacity based on the local age structure. If you want to develop a "tailor-made" solution for each location, a longer phase zero is required. But of course: elements which have proven themselves will always be included—after all, even the Romans built very good hospitals.

Haus und Platz

Building and Square

KÖLN-RODENKIRCHEN   COLOGNE RODENKIRCHEN

BRÜHL   CITY OF BRÜHL

Bezirksrathaus Rodenkirchen

Nur wenige Minuten geht man vom JSWD-Büro am Maternusplatz bis zum Vorplatz des Bezirksrathauses Rodenkirchen. Ungleich weiter voneinander entfernt sind die städtebaulichen Leitbilder, die diese beiden Orte geprägt haben. 1967, als der Rathausvorplatz fertiggestellt wurde, galt es als das Ideal des modernen Menschen, mit seinem Pkw zum Einkaufen in die Stadt fahren und es direkt vor dem Ladengeschäft parken zu können. Diese Vorstellung war 2009, als der umgestaltete Maternusplatz übergeben wurde, längst obsolet. Innerhalb der gut vier Jahrzehnte hat sich erwiesen, dass Städte besser funktionieren, wenn sie den Menschen nicht Parkplätze, sondern Orte zur Begegnung anbieten, formelle wie informelle. Allerdings waren und sind trotz des guten ÖPNV-Angebots in Rodenkirchen größere Eingriffe notwendig, um das noch immer bestehende Problem des ruhenden Autoverkehrs zu lösen. Solange der eigene Pkw emotional als unverzichtbar gilt, müssen Parkplätze in ausreichender Zahl vorgehalten werden, weil sonst insbesondere die Einzelhändler befürchten, dass ihr Standort an Attraktivität verlieren könnte. Heute gelingt dies mit Tiefgaragen zumindest stadtverträglicher als früher.

Der Anlass für die Neubewertung des Rathausplatzes in Rodenkirchen war aber nicht in erster Linie der Zustand des öffentlichen Raums, sondern das Rathausgebäude selbst. Der achtstöckige Bau (Walther Ruoff, 1967), der den kleinen Platz nach Nordosten begrenzt, ist ein starker Vertreter der brutalistischen

Betonbaukunst, der sich jedoch zusammen mit seinem direkten Umfeld durch jahrzehntelange Vernachlässigung in einem traurigen Zustand befindet; seine gestalterischen Qualitäten sind heute kaum mehr ablesbar. Nachdem der Stadtkonservator es 2005 abgelehnt hatte, das Rathaus unter Denkmalschutz zu stellen, und zudem Schadstoffe in der Substanz nachgewiesen wurden, stand eine Sanierung, die ja einer städtebaulichen Neuordnung nicht grundsätzlich entgegengestanden hätte, nicht länger zur Debatte. Abriss und Neubau wurden 2008 beschlossen, die städtebauliche Neuordnung wurde über eine Mehrfachbeauftragung bestimmt. Doch wie in Köln leider nicht unüblich vergingen weitere neun Jahre, ehe ein Wettbewerb ausgelobt wurde.

JSWD, deren Entwurf im März 2018 mit dem ersten Preis ausgezeichnet und zur Umsetzung empfohlen wurde, präsentierten das neue Bezirksrathaus als eine Stadtloggia, die Stadt und Stadtleben abbildet. Der Platz vor dem Rathaus, heute noch namenlos und zugeparkt, soll zu einer offenen Bühne werden, die Ansicht des neuen Rathauses ihr Prospekt. Doch tritt der Neubau nicht als stolzer Solitär auf, sondern lässt sich auf die Verflechtung mit dem Stadtgefüge ein – grün auf der Rheinseite, urban seine Front. Das Erdgeschoss wird großzügig geöffnet, wodurch das Rathaus schlüssig und schwellenlos sowohl an die bestehenden wie an die ergänzten Platzränder anschließt. Die filigranen Natursteinelemente der vorgehängten Fassade erlauben einen hohen Glasanteil, sodass die im Erdgeschoss gelegene Meldehalle und das Bürgeramt der Institution Stadt eine unerwartet transparente Erscheinung verleihen.

Diese Idee transportiert auch die dem Stadtplatz zugewandte Loggia der Beletage. Das Foyer des Sitzungssaals öffnet sich mit großzügiger Geste und bietet ein Szenario, um besondere Anlässe gemeinsam zu feiern. Die gegenüberliegende Gartenterrasse dient auch dem Luftholen in den Sitzungspausen. Die Stadt möge sich öffnen, so kann man diese Formen interpretieren, die auch in den Fraktionsräumen der Bezirksvertretung auf gleicher Ebene und den Ämtern in den darüber liegenden Geschossen eine Entsprechung finden. Niemand soll hier im dunklen Kämmerchen sitzen, im Gegenteil: Wenn es um Kommunales geht, ist die Stadt im Fokus.

JSWD überzeugten die Jury mit dem ebenso starken wie heiter-offenen Charakter von Haus und Platz. Doch hier geht es um weit mehr als um Bilder und Ansichten: Es ist ein Stück Stadt, das verhandelt wird. Heute zeigt die Betrachtung des nahegelegenen Maternusplatzes, welches Potenzial in einem – vermeintlich unverzichtbaren – Parkplatz schlummert. Dass sich das im Zusammenspiel mit einem offenen und öffentlichen Gebäude noch weiter steigern lässt, spricht für die Umsetzung des neuen Bezirksrathauses Rodenkirchen.

Rodenkirchen District Town Hall

It is just a short walk from the JSWD office at Maternusplatz to the square in front of the Rodenkirchen district town hall. The urban design concepts which have shaped these two locations are, however, much further apart. In 1967, when the district town hall's square was completed, the dominant paradigm was that of the modern person who drives into the city with his or her car to go shopping and parks directly in front of the shops. This concept had long been obsolete when the redesign of Maternusplatz was completed in 2009. Within the intervening four decades, it had been shown that cities function better when they offer people spaces for formal and informal communication instead of parking. However, larger interventions are and have been necessary in Rodenkirchen to address persistent parking issues, despite the good public transport connection. As long as people still have an emotional connection to owning their own cars, a sufficient number of parking spots needs to be provided, otherwise the location could become less attractive; retailers in particular worry about this point. Today, underground parking garages make the situation more compatible with current concepts than in the past.

The motivation for the redesign of the town hall square in Rodenkirchen was, however, not first and foremost the condition of the public space, but rather the town hall building itself. The eight-story building (Walther Ruoff, 1967), which frames the small square to the northeast, was a strong example of brutalist concrete architecture, which, together with its surroundings, was however in a sad state after years of neglect. Its high-quality design was hardly recognizable anymore. After the city administration rejected an application to place the town hall under historical protection and contaminants were discovered in the building materials, a renovation, which would not have fundamentally stood in the way of an urban reorganization, was no longer on the table. The decision to demolish the old town hall and build a new one in its place was made in 2008; the urban reorganization was awarded in a multiple commission. However, as is not unheard of for Cologne, nine years passed before a competition was announced.

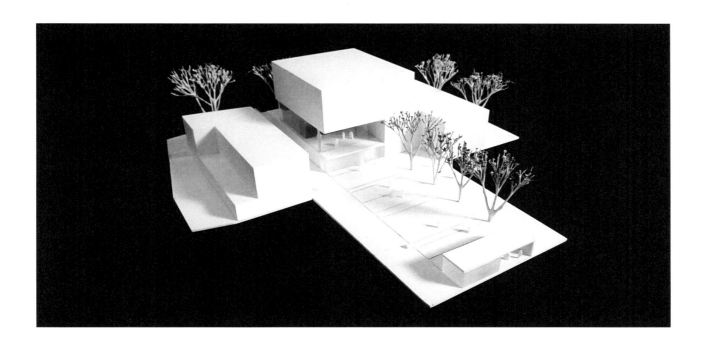

JSWD, whose design was awarded first prize in March of 2018 and recommended for construction, presents the new district town hall as a municipal loggia, which depicts the city and urban life. The square in front of the city hall, today still nameless and full of parked cars, should become an open stage with the view of the new city hall as its backdrop. However, the new construction is not playing the part as a stand-alone intervention, but rather integrates itself into the surrounding buildings—green towards the Rhine, urban to its front. The ground floor boasts a generously open profile which connects the town hall logically and threshold-free to the edges of the existing and future sections of the square. The delicate natural stone elements of the suspended facade permit a high proportion of glass, so that the reception area on the ground floor and the municipal offices offer an unexpectedly transparent appearance.

The loggia on the mezzanine level, which faces the square, also communicates this idea. The foyer of the assembly room opens itself through a generous spatial gesture and offers a space to celebrate special events. The garden terrace opposite is well suited for getting a breath of fresh air during breaks between sessions. One can interpret these forms, which have their counterparts in the parliamentary offices of the district administration on the same floor and the administrative offices on the floors above, as suggesting that the city should open itself. No one should hide behind the curtain, on the contrary: when municipal matters are discussed, the city should be clearly visible.

JSWD won over the jury with the simultaneously strong and cheerfully open character of the building and the square. But it's about much more than pictures and aspects: it is a piece of the city which is being decided. Today, a view to nearby Maternusplatz shows what kind of potential can slumber under a—supposedly indispensable—parking lot. The fact that this potential can be further increased in conjunction with an open and public building speaks for the implementation of the new Rodenkirchen district town hall.

Erweiterung Rathaus Brühl und Neugestaltung Janshof

Auch in der Nachbarkommune Brühl wurde etwa zeitgleich die Konstellation Rathaus – Platz diskutiert. Hier jedoch waren die Teilnehmer des Wettbewerbs aufgefordert, das denkmalgeschützte Rathaus am Steinweg mit einer Erweiterung als Ersatz für einen Anbau aus den 1960er Jahren zu einem modernen, bürgerfreundlichen Haus auszubauen und den angrenzenden Janshof als Stadtplatz zu gestalten. Während die historische Front des Rathauses am Marktplatz liegt, soll die Erweiterung mit der Stadtbibliothek zum Steinweg und insbesondere zum Janshof, der ein zentrales Thema der Brühler Innenstadtentwicklung ist, Präsenz zeigen.

JSWD gewannen den Wettbewerb mit einem Rathausneubau, der die Kubatur des Denkmals fortführt und daraus ein ortstypisches, gleichsam eigenständiges Gebäudevolumen aus drei ineinander verzahnten Baukörpern entwickelt. Der Entwurf nimmt das Spiel differenzierter Stadträume in der Brühler Altstadt auf, indem er die Eingänge Markt, Steinweg und Janshof im Erdgeschoss des Rathauses zusammentreffen lässt. Trauzimmer, Servicezentrum, Multifunktionssaal, Bibliothek und Verwaltung sind so angeordnet, dass sie den unterschiedlich hohen Besucherfrequenzen und Öffnungszeiten entsprechend autark erschlossen werden.

Interessant ist die giebelständige Ansicht des gestaffelten Kopfbaus, die die altstädtischen Proportionen jener Gasse widerspiegelt, die den Janshof anbindet. Die Art und Ordnung der Öffnungen in der Gebäudehülle aus sandfarbenem geschlämmtem Ziegel verleihen dem Erweiterungsbau eine gute Lesbarkeit: Große Einschnitte markieren die Eingänge, Lochfassaden die Büroetagen, während Filtermauerwerk die Bibliothek abschirmt.

Bauliche Nachverdichtungen stärken den Stadtraum und lösen den Charakter des zufällig entstandenen Hinterhofes auf. Der neue Janshof wird hochwertiger Platzraum mit repräsentativen Adressen und Aufenthaltsqualität – dies jedoch in einer Dimension, die nicht mit dem unmittelbar angrenzenden Markt in Konkurrenz tritt.

Extension of the Brühl City Hall and Redesign of the Janshof

In the neighboring town of Brühl, the constellation of city hall and square was being discussed at almost the same time. Here, however, the competition participants were required to build an extension for the existing, protected town hall at Steinweg as a replacement for the 1960s' annex; the result is intended to be a modern, citizen-friendly building and the adjoining Janshof is intended to be redesigned into a public square. While the historical front of the town hall faces the market square, the new extension, which will also house the town library, will face Steinweg and in particular Janshof, which is of central importance in Brühl's interior development.

JSWD won the competition with a new building which acts as a spatial extension of the protected town hall and is made up of three intersecting sections, thus forming a building which is simultaneously locally typical and idiosyncratic. The design incorporates the interplay between differentiated urban spaces in Brühl's historic city center by bringing together the three entrances from the market, Steinweg, and Janshof in the ground floor of the town hall. The wedding room, service center, multi-function assembly room, library, and administration have different visitor numbers and opening hours; they have therefore been arranged so that they are individually accessible.

The view from the gable side of the staggered head-end building, which reflects the historical proportions of the lane which connects it to the Janshof, is particularly interesting. The type and organization of the openings in the building envelope of sand-colored, elutriated bricks lend the extension building a high degree of legibility; large openings mark the entrances, punctuated facades show the office levels, and filter walls screen the library. New construction in the area strengthens the urban quality and gives the back courtyard a more intentional feeling. The new Janshof will be a welcoming, representative, high-quality square and a desirable address—however, to a degree that does not compete with the immediately adjacent market square.

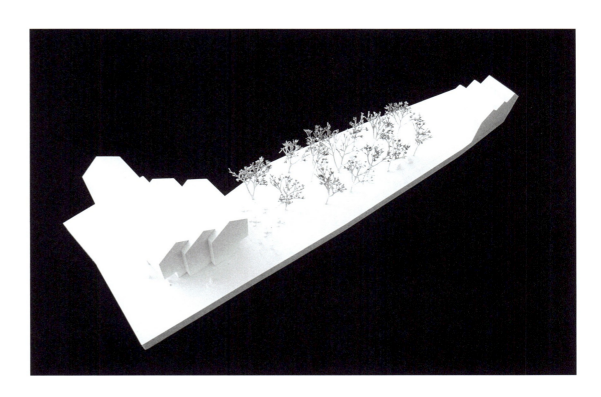

Zehn Jahre Maternusplatz
Ten Years Maternusplatz

Ansichtskarte vom Maternusplatz aus den 1960er Jahren   Postcard of Maternusplatz from the 1960s

Haus und Platz, das Vertikale und das Horizontale sind die Elementarteilchen der Stadt. Richtig platziert und angemessen proportioniert können sie auch auf erodierten Flächen wieder Leben entstehen lassen. So zeigt es das Beispiel Maternusplatz, den JSWD seit zehn Jahren täglich im Blick haben.

Building and square: the vertical and horizontal are the elementary building blocks of the city. Properly placed and appropriately sized, they have the ability to bring life back to eroded spaces. The example of Maternusplatz, which JSWD has seen every day for the last ten years, demonstrates this well.

Pläne zur Veränderung bekannter Strukturen machen vielen Menschen Angst. Sie fürchten den Verlust des Gewohnten, sind verunsichert, ob sie auch in dem (noch) unbekannten Neuen heimisch sein werden. Der Maternusplatz hatte sich, obwohl er nie als Platz angelegt worden war, zu einem, wie man es heute nennt, urbanen Mittelpunkt des Kölner Stadtteils Rodenkirchen entwickelt. Durch seine zentrale Lage bot er sich an für Märkte und Kirmes, für Kundgebungen und Versammlungen. Doch an den meisten Tagen im Jahr wurde der Platz zum Abstellen von Autos genutzt. Im Sinne einer Stadtentwicklung, deren übergeordnetes Ziel es ist, die Identität, aber auch die Wirtschaftskraft der Nebenzentren zu stärken, war das zu wenig. Um mit der rasanten Entwicklung des Stadtzentrums und dem immer attraktiver werdenden Umland Schritt halten zu können, lobte die Stadt Köln 2001 einen städtebaulichen Realisierungswettbewerb zur Umgestaltung der Fläche in eine „neue Mitte" aus, den JSWD gewannen. Aus dem stadtbildlichen Kontext entwickelten sie eine Bebauung an der Westseite des Platzes und eine Tiefgarage unter der gesamten Fläche. Damit stießen sie zunächst auf Widerstände gegen eine Veränderung des – offensichtlich mangelhaften – Status quo. Fünf Jahre lang wurde diskutiert und geplant, 2009 war der Platz fertiggestellt und die neuen Gebäude konnten bezogen werden. Zehn Jahre danach lässt sich eine erste Bilanz ziehen.

Baugrube an der bis dahin offenen Platzkante
Construction site on the previously open edge of the square

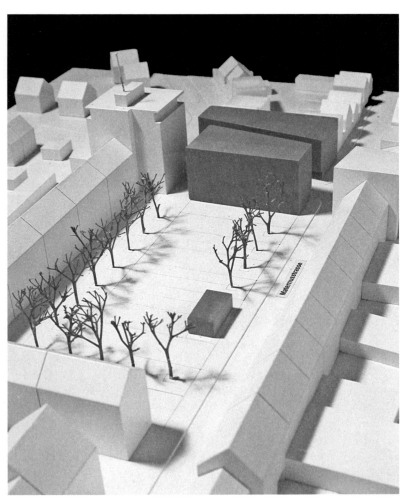

Modellstudie Model study

Plans to change well-known structures often make people anxious. They worry about losing the things they are familiar with and whether they will be able to get used to the (still) unknown. Maternusplatz, although it was never conceived or designed as a square, had become an urban center, as one calls it today, of the Cologne district of Rodenkirchen. As a result of its central location, it was an ideal place for markets and fairs, protests and assemblies. However, most days the square was used for parking. For an urban development strategy whose overarching goal is to strengthen the identity and the economic potential of secondary centers, this was inadequate. In order to keep up with the rapid development of the city center and the ever more attractive suburbs, in 2001 the city of Cologne announced an urban design competition for the redesign of the space into a "new center" which was won by JSWD. Based on the surrounding cityscape, they developed construction on the western side of the square and an underground parking garage underneath the entire area. At first, they were confronted with resistance to a change of the—obviously deficient—status quo. Discussion and planning took five years; in 2009, the square was complete and the new buildings could be moved into. Ten years on, it's possible to make a first assessment.

Although it wasn't planned this way in the beginning: it was a perfect fit that JSWD, whose nearly 60 employees were scattered across four locations at the time, could move into the four upper stories of the head-end building on the western side of the square. In the meantime, the office has grown to 150 employees, so that every table in the open-concept space is filled. The partners' offices are located on the top floor. When they look out of the window, they can observe the lively hustle and bustle on the newly designed square, which is now completely free of cars; these are all parked in the two-story parking garage beneath. The entrance to the parking garage is located at the rear of the buildings at a new roundabout

Der ehemalige Parkplatz wurde zum Marktplatz, Spielplatz und Treffpunkt.
The former parking lot has become a market square, playground and meeting point.

Auch wenn es anfangs nicht geplant war: Es fügte sich perfekt, dass JSWD, deren damals gut 60 Mitarbeiter an vier verschiedenen Standorten saßen, die vier Obergeschosse des Kopfbaus an der Westseite des Platzes beziehen konnten. Inzwischen ist das Büro auf 150 Mitarbeiter angewachsen, sodass heute jeder Tisch in den offen gestalteten Etagen besetzt ist. In der obersten befinden sich die Büros der Partner. Wenn ihr Blick aus dem Fenster schweift, können sie das rege Treiben auf dem neu gestalteten Platz beobachten. Der ist nun vollkommen frei von Autos, da diese in der zweigeschossigen Tiefgarage unter der Platzfläche parken. Die Zufahrt befindet sich auf der Rückseite der Gebäude an einem neuen Kreisverkehr, um die Platzsituation nicht zu stören. Einzig die Fahrzeuge der Marktbeschicker, die an drei Tagen in der Woche hier ihre Stände für Obst, Gemüse, Fisch und Haushaltswaren aufbauen, verkehren noch dort. Nicht nur an den Markttagen, sondern auch an den übrigen Tagen des Jahres finden die Rodenkirchener genügend Gründe, sich auf dem großzügig dimensionierten Platz zu treffen: Stadtfest, Karneval, sei es auf ein Eis, ein Schwätzchen, zum Rollschuhlaufen, um im Schatten oder in der Sonne zu sitzen.

Mit dem Neubau des zweiteiligen Büro- und Geschäftshauses erhielt die Westseite des Platzes einen sinnfälligen Abschluss. Im Erdgeschoss öffnet sich die Gastronomie in den öffentlichen Raum und bewirtschaftet einen Teil der Platzfläche. Der Neubau überragt die traufständigen Nachkriegsbauten der übrigen Platzkanten um ein Geschoss. Den über die Jahrzehnte in bunten Farben gestrichen Fassaden des Bestands setzten JSWD eine weiß geputzte Ansicht entgegen, deren bodentiefe Fenster – fast ist man verführt, sie Schaufenster zu nennen – mit anthrazitfarbenen, metallischen Leibungen plastisch aus der glatten Fassade hervortreten. Sie folgen ihrem eigenen Rhythmus, ohne Dissonanzen in order not to disturb the spatial situation. Only the cars of the market stand operators, who sell fruit, vegetables, fish and household goods here three times a week, are still permitted to drive on the square. There are many reasons for the residents of Rodenkirchen to meet in this attractive setting outside of market days: city festival, carnival, for ice cream, to chat, to roller skate, or to sit in the sun or the shade.

The new construction of the two-part office and retail building lent the western side of the square a sensible closure. On the ground floor, food and dining outlets open out into the public space and use part of the square. The new construction is one story taller than the lengthwise postwar construction on the other edges of the square. The buildings, which have been painted a range of colorful hues over the years, contrast with the clean white facade of the JSWD building. Its full-length windows—one is almost tempted to call them display windows—emerge sculpturally from the smooth facade in anthracite-colored, metal reveals. They follow their own rhythm without creating dissonance with the existing built space. On the ground floor of the second building, which is positioned parallel to the first, there are two shops and a police station; the offices and apartments on the three upper floors and their open spaces are oriented toward the quiet interior of the block.

The long northern flank of the square is bordered by the busy Maternusstraße. Honey locusts located in large planters contain the space without closing it off; the seating attached to the planters extends the invitation to sit and enjoy the space. It has become a characteristic of the square that the use of reduced design elements enables many of the variations of Cologne's *Veedels* (districts) to take place, both formal and informal, for children and adults and in particular for seniors, and facilitates chance and planned meetings.

mit dem Bestand zu erzeugen. Im Erdgeschoss des zweiten, parallel angeordneten Baukörpers befindet sich außer zwei Ladenlokalen auch eine Polizeidienststelle; die Büros und Wohnungen der drei Obergeschosse orientieren sich mit ihren Freiflächen zum ruhigen Blockinneren.
Die lange Nordflanke des Platzes wird von der belebten Maternusstraße flankiert und eingesehen. In Kübeln gepflanzte Gleditschien fassen die Fläche, ohne sie abzuschließen, die daran angebrachten Sitzgelegenheiten lesen sich als eine freundliche Einladung zum Bleiben. Es ist zu einem Charakteristikum des Platzes geworden, dass er mit reduzierten Gestaltungsmitteln viele Spielarten des kölschen *Veedels* zulässt, formell oder informell, für Kinder wie Erwachsene und insbesondere auch Senioren, in zufälligen wie antizipierten Begegnungen.

Neubau an der westlichen Platzkante, seit 2009 das Büro von JSWD Architekten
New building on the western edge of the square, since 2009 the office of JSWD Architects

Ecole Centrale Clausen
Luxemburg

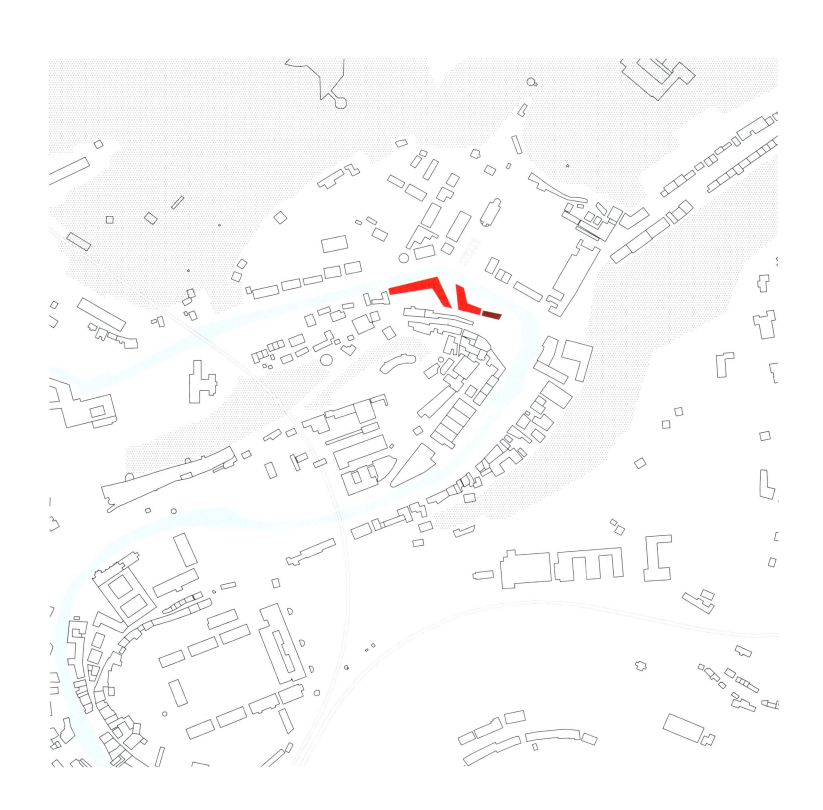

Der Stadtteil Clausen liegt im Tal der Alzette in der Luxemburger Unterstadt. Hoch darüber thronen, umringt von der mittelalterlichen Festungsanlage, auf der einen Seite die Oberstadt und auf dem schroffen Fels gegenüber die Überreste des Fort Thüngen. Dahinter, auf dem Kirchberg-Plateau, expandiert die supermoderne Europa-Stadt. So malerisch und für die Geschichte Europas so bedeutend ist dieser Ort, dass die UNESCO die Luxemburger Altstadt und die Festung zum Weltkulturerbe erklärte. Wer dort bauen möchte, dem wird es nicht leicht gemacht, doch ein einzigartiger Rahmen ist bereits gesetzt: Die Stadt Luxemburg schrieb 2007 einen internationalen Wettbewerb für den Neubau einer Vor- und Grundschule mit Sporthalle in Clausen aus. Diese sollte direkt am Ufer der Alzette auf einer Industriebrache errichtet werden und so geplant sein, dass die neue Struktur harmonisch in den an dieser Stelle schadhaften Bereich des historischen Siedlungsmusters eingewebt wird. JSWD überzeugten hier mit dem Entwurf eines ebenso komplexen wie schlüssigen Stadtteilchens. Es überträgt das charakteristische Orts- und Landschaftsbild auf einen kleineren Maßstab, den sich Kinder ganz intuitiv erschließen.

Das Schulgelände liegt am Hang des Altmuster-Plateaus. Den tiefsten Bereich bildet die neu befestigte Uferkante der Alzette, der höchsten Punkt liegt an der steil ansteigenden Straße, die von einer Reihe historischer Wohnhäuser abgeschirmt wird. Von allen Seiten ist das Gelände zugänglich, es gibt eine neue und eine alte Brücke, die das Flüsschen überqueren, sowie historische und neu angelegte Treppen, die den kleinen Campus mit dem Bestand vernetzen. Die beiden bumerangförmigen Schulbauten – ein zweigeschossiger für die *école maternelle* mit sechs Klassenräumen und ein dreigeschossiger für die *école fondamentale* mit 16 Klassen – sind so angeordnet, dass ihre Schenkel jeweils einen eigenen Spielbereich einfassen. Erschlossen werden die beiden Schulen über einen geschützt im Innenbereich liegenden Platz. Die Architekten haben sich die bewegte Topografie zunutze gemacht, indem sie die Zweifeld-Sporthalle direkt an den Hang gestellt haben. Das große Volumen tritt so auf der Alzette-Seite nur als sandsteinfarbener Sockel in Erscheinung. Gefasst von der straßenseitigen Bebauung und dem langen Schenkel der Grundschule entsteht zudem auf dem Hallendach ein Spielplateau für die größeren Kinder. Die Stufen der über die gesamte Breite gezogenen Treppe laden zum Sitzen ein und verwandeln den Eingangsbereich auf dem unteren Niveau auf informelle Weise zu einer Bühne.

Fast scheint es, als hätten sich die Architekten mit der sensiblen Modellage und Verknüpfung des Geländes eine gewisse Freiheit für die Gestaltung der Ansichten erkämpft. Denn diese sind – ganz ortsbilduntypisch – weitgehend gläsern und mit weißen Bändern horizontal gegliedert. Dadurch fällt viel Tageslicht in die Klassenräume und Flure der einhüftig organisierten Schulgebäude. Aus- und Einblicke verbinden die Kleinen und die Großen, das Draußen mit dem Drinnen.

Ecole Centrale Clausen
Luxembourg

The district of Clausen is located in the valley of the Alzette in Luxembourg's lower city. High above it lay the remains of Fort Thüngen embedded in the rugged rock on one side with the upper town opposite; the medieval fortress surrounds both of them. Behind it, on the Kirchberg Plateau, the super-modern Europa City is growing. This location is so picturesque and so important to the history of Europe that UNESCO declared Luxembourg's old town and fortress a World Heritage Site. Those who want to build here face a range of challenges; however, a unique framework has already been created. In 2007, the City of Luxembourg announced an international competition for the construction of a new nursery and elementary school with a sports hall in Clausen. This complex was to be erected directly on the bank of the Alzette on an industrial brownfield site and planned in such a way that the new structure would be harmoniously integrated into this rift in the historical urban fabric. JSWD's winning design develops a mini-neighborhood that is as complex as it is coherent. It translates the characteristic local and landscape identities to a smaller scale which children intuitively understand.

The school grounds are located on the slope of the Altmuster plateau. The lowest area is the newly fortified bank of the Alzette, the highest point is on the steeply sloping road, which is shielded by a series of historic residential buildings. The site is accessible from all sides; there is a new and an old bridge crossing the river, as well as historic and newly built staircases linking the small campus to the existing buildings. The two boomerang-shaped school buildings—a two-story one for the école maternelle with six classrooms and a three-story one for the école fondamentale with 16 classes—are arranged in such a way that their flanks each enclose an area to play in. The two schools are accessed via a sheltered indoor area. The architects took advantage of the varied topography by placing the two-field sports hall underground. In this way, from the Alzette side, the large volume appears only as a sandstone-colored foundation. Bordered by the street-side development and the long leg of the elementary school, a play plateau for the older children has, moreover, been created on the roof of the hall. The steps of the full-width staircase invite one to sit and informally transform the entrance area at the lower level into a stage.

It almost seems as if the architects, with the sensitive modeling and linking of the site, have struggled to maintain a certain freedom in shaping their facades. Because these are—atypical for the rest of the neighborhood—predominantly made of glass and horizontally structured with white bands. As a result, plenty of natural light shines into the classrooms and corridors of the school building. Viewing possibilities in both directions connect the younger students with the older ones and the outside with the inside.

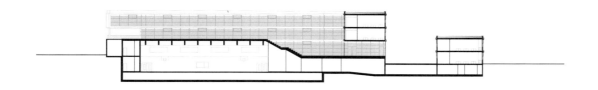

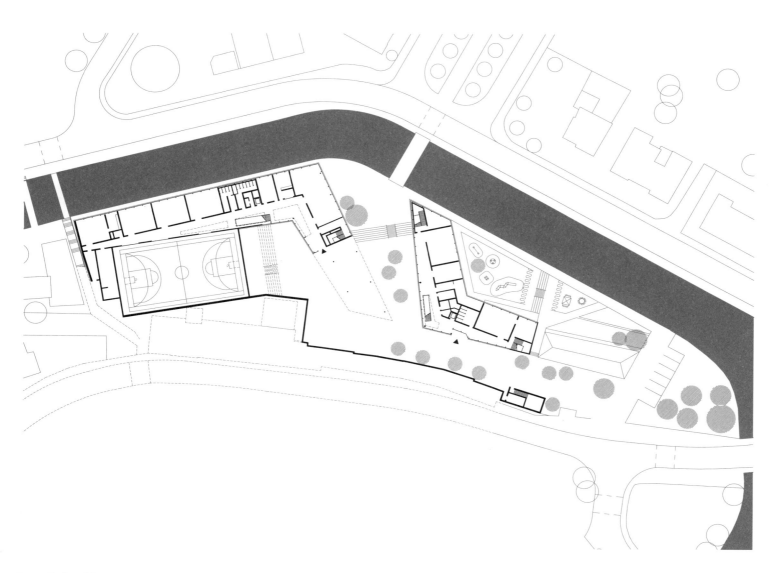

Ebene 0   Level 0

Ebene 1 Level 1

Gebaute Bilder
Built Images

Dass Bauen für Kinder nicht kindisch sein muss, um kindgerecht zu sein, zeigen Architektur und Außenanlagen der Ecole Centrale Clausen im Kleinen wie im Großen.

The fact that building for children does not have to be childish in order to be child-friendly is demonstrated by the architecture and outdoor facilities of the Ecole Centrale Clausen on a small and a large scale.

Präsenz am Ufer der Alzette
Presence on the banks of the Alzette

Patrick Jaenke (Associate Partner, JSWD)
„Mit unserer Architektur liefern wir Räume, die zunächst sehr neutral sind. Das bleiben sie aber nur solange, bis die Kinder sie mit ihrem Spiel, ihrem Dasein, ihren mitgebrachten oder gebastelten Dingen in Besitz genommen haben und auf ihre Weise nutzen. Wir wünschen uns, dass die Kinder die Schule ganz intuitiv zu ihrer Schule machen."
„Das Schöne an gebauten Bildern ist, dass man sie sehen kann aber nicht muss. Vielleicht ist es für den einen oder anderen nur eine neue Schule, ein cooler Spielplatz. Doch wer sich darauf einlässt, wer Bekanntes und Vertrautes aus dem üblichen Kontext löst, der entdeckt dort den Dorfplatz, das Forum, die Vorhänge und den Spielteppich. Die Bilder im Gebauten nehmen Gestalt an. Und vielleicht prägt sich das ein oder andere Bild so bei den Kindern ein, dass der nächste Fransenteppich an einem anderen Ort sie an den Spielplatz der neuen Schule erinnern wird."

Patrick Jaenke (Associate Partner, JSWD)
"With our architecture, we deliver spaces which are initially very neutral. But they only stay that way until the children have taken possession of them with their play, their existence, and the things they have brought or made. We want the children to turn the school into their school."
"The beauty of built images is that you can see them or not. For some, it's just a new school or a cool playground. But those who get involved, those who remove well-known and familiar things from their usual context, will discover the village square, the forum, the curtains, and the play mat. The beauty of it is that children do this intuitively by using the place daily in their own way. And maybe the image of the playground becomes so memorable for them that the next fringed carpet reminds them of it."

Der Campus als Stadt im Kleinen

Es ist die Lage im Tal der Alzette, die allein schon viel Bewegung in den Campus bringt. Die Uferkante des Flüsschens verläuft in einer Kurve, zu beiden Seiten steigt das Gelände steil an. Der Campus der Ecole Centrale liegt mitten in Clausen, soll dort einwachsen. Helles Kunststeinpflaster kennzeichnet den Campus, mal ist es offen verlegt, meist jedoch bildet es eine geschlossene Decke, die an der dem Flüsschen zugewandten Seite einen soliden Sockel ausformt. Als Teil des Dorfkerns ist der Campus auf allen Seiten offen, die Durchwegung ist einladend, zitiert einen Dorfplatz, markiert ihn mit einem großen Baum mit Sitzbank. Innerhalb des Geländes bewegen die Kinder sich frei; geschützt vor den Gefahren, die die Straße und die Uferkante mit sich bringen, flanieren sie durch Gassen und über Plätze.

The Campus as a City on a Small Scale

The location in the Alzette Valley alone brings a lot of movement to the campus. The bank of the river runs in a curve, on both sides the terrain rises steeply. The campus of the Ecole Centrale is located in the middle of Clausen; the school should become part of it. Light-colored artificial stone paving characterises the campus; sometimes it is laid spaced, but usually it forms a closed surface, and forms a solid foundation on the side facing the river. As part of the village center, the campus is open on all sides; the pathways are inviting and reference the form of a village square, marked with a large tree and bench. Within the grounds, the children move freely. Protected from the dangers of the road and the water's edge, they stroll through the campus' alleys and squares.

Die Schule als „Stadtteilchen" mit Häusern, Durchwegung und Plätzen   The school as a "district" with houses, passageways and squares

  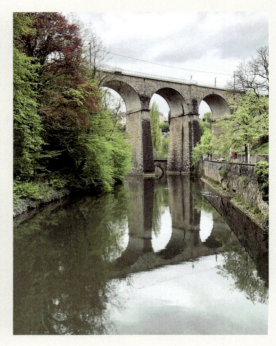

Brücken und Treppen

Häuser und Außenräume der Schule reagieren nicht nur auf das, was die Topografie fordert, sie überzeichnen und thematisieren die Höhensprünge. Auf dem Dach der eingegrabenen Turnhalle entsteht ein Plateau zum Spielen. Der Vorplatz unten wird zum Forum, wenn das Schülerpublikum auf den Sitzstufen der breite Treppe Platz genommen hat. Auch die Brücke gehört zum Schulbau, sie erst macht die Öffnung und den Anschluss möglich. Nicht aus Stein sollte sie sein, wie die Nachbarbrücke flussabwärts oder das hohe Viadukt in der anderen Richtung, sondern deutlich lesbar als zeitgemäßes Bauwerk. Die dichten dunklen Stahlstreben des Geländers imitieren den Saum des Waldes auf dem Bergrücken. Und sollte ein Hochwasser es bedingen, hebt eine Hydraulik die Brücke aus der grob gemauerten Befestigung empor, sodass sie dem anschwellenden Fluss keinen Widerstand bietet.

Einblicke und Durchblicke

Die Schulgebäude sind schmal, rücken dicht an die Nachbarn heran. Die beiden „Bumerangs" formen zwei geschützte Plätze, einen großen konischen Zwischenraum und kleinere Gassen an den Rändern. Diese Art der altstädtischen Wegeführung erscheint bekannt, in diesem Kontext kitzelt sie die Sehgewohnheiten allerdings ein wenig. Die Blicke aus den Fenstern sind gerichtet: Während die Kleinen auf ihren Spielplatz schauen, haben die Größeren die neutrale Landschaft als Kulisse vor den Fenstern ihres Klassenraumes. Aus den Fluren schauen sie alle aufeinander, dort ist die Interaktion erwünscht, die Ablenkung, die Verbindung schafft. Wer war zuerst auf dem Klettergerüst? Sind die anderen schon draußen? Was habt ihr gebastelt? Zeigt uns, was ihr geübt habt! Im nächsten Jahr bin ich auch bei den Großen dort drüben! Und auch die Turnhalle hat ein Fenster, nicht nach draußen, denn sie liegt ja unter der Erde, sondern in den Flur – dies also eher ein Einblick in das sportliche Treiben dort unten als ein Ausblick.

Bridges and Stairs

The school's buildings and outdoor spaces not only react to the topography, they exaggerate and highlight the height differences. A plateau for outdoor play has been created on the roof of the buried gymnasium. The forecourt below becomes a forum when the student audience has taken a seat on the steps of the wide staircase.

The bridge is also part of the school; it makes the opening and the connection possible. It was not made of stone, as the neighboring bridge downstream or the high viaduct in the other direction, but is rather clearly legible as a contemporary piece of construction. The dense dark steel struts of the railing imitate the edge of the forest on the ridge. And in the event of a flood, a hydraulic system lifts the bridge out of the roughly bricked fortification so that it will offer no resistance to the swelling river.

Insights and Views

The school buildings are narrow and constructed close to the neighboring buildings. The two boomerangs form two sheltered spaces, a large conical space, and smaller lanes at the edges. These spaces, which remind one of a historical city center, seem familiar, but in this context they deviate slightly from the expected pattern, creating unexpected views. The glimpses from the windows are directed: while the young children look out at their playground, the older pupils look out onto a neutral landscape from their classroom windows. From the corridors, they look at each other; there the interaction and the distraction that connection creates are desired. Who got to the top of the jungle gym first? Are the others already outside? What did you make? Show us what you have practiced. Next year I will also be with the big kids over there! Even the gym has a window; not to the outside, because it is located underground, but from the hallway onto the action on the fields.

Die Farbe Grün

Das Tal ist so üppig begrünt, dass die Verwendung der Farbe für Gebautes fast kühn anmutet. Zu kühn, denn im Wettbewerb war die gesamte Schule so grün, dass der Kontrast zu der zart beigen Bebauung ringsum den Bauherren zu krass erschien. Nun also weniger Grün, dafür wohl dosiert und wohl platziert. Zum Beispiel wenn die Sonne auf die Gebäude scheint, dann nämlich fährt der textile Sonnenschutz herunter und verdeckt die großen Gläser der Gebäudehülle mit tannengrünem Textil. Und auch auf den Spielplätzen ist das Grün dominant. Nicht die Natur selbst, denn die Plateaus, auf denen die Spielgeräte stehen, sind als Dächer oder Sockel Teil der gebauten Topografie. Der grüne Fallschutz imitiert einen Spielteppich mit langen Fransen, an einer Kante umgeschlagen wölbt er sich auf, zeigt eine heller grüne Unterseite. Hier und dort stehen drei kleine gummigrüne Berge. Die Außenanlage erinnert an einen Comic, denn ja, diese Schule ist für Kinder gebaut.

The Color Green

The valley is so lushly green that the use of color for buildings seems almost daring. Too daring, because in the competition, the entire school was so green that the contrast with the delicate beige of the surrounding buildings seemed too blatant for the client. So now there is less green, but what remains is in good proportion and well placed. For example, when the sun shines on the buildings, the sunscreen descends and hides the large windows of the building envelope behind fir-green textile. Green is also dominant in the playgrounds. Not nature itself, because the plateaus on which the play equipment stands are part of the built topography of roofs or plinths. The green fall protection mimics a play carpet with long fringes; turned up on one side, it arches up, showing a bright green underside. Here and there are three small green rubber mountains. The outdoor area is reminiscent of a comic, because yes, this school is built for children.

Neuer Kanzlerplatz
Bonn

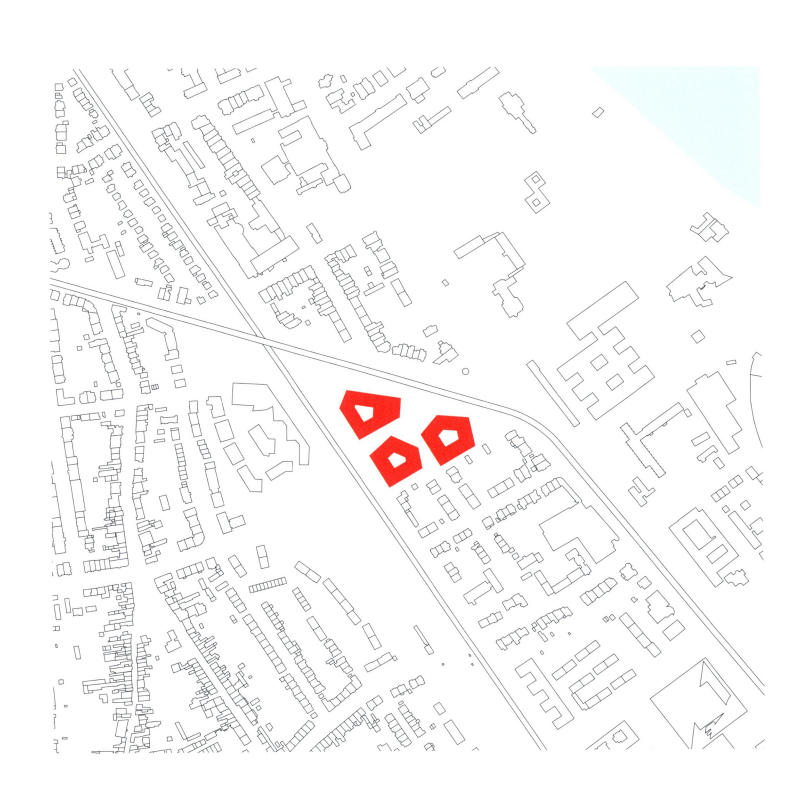

Im Jahr 2019 stehen die Zeichen am Bundeskanzlerplatz auf Neuanfang. 12 Meter tief ist die gewaltige Baugrube, in der die Arbeiten an den Fundamenten die Dimensionen des Büroensembles Neuer Kanzlerplatz bereits grob skizzieren. Nachdem der Bonn-Berlin-Beschluss 1991 dem ehemaligen Regierungsviertel die Existenzgrundlage entzogen hatte, konnte es sich wider Erwarten mit dem UN-Campus, einem internationalen Kongresszentrum, der Museumsmeile und nicht zuletzt als Standort von drei DAX-Konzernen und zahlreichen weiteren Institutionen neu profilieren. Doch bislang fehlte diesem „neuen Bonn" ein klangvoller Auftakt, eine Willkommensgeste mit durchaus erwünschter Fernwirkung. Schon einmal, 1969, hatte man nach einer Lösung dieser Aufgabe gesucht und am Bundeskanzlerplatz das Bonn-Center errichtet. Es ist kein einfaches Grundstück, die dreieckige Form, die sich durch die Überfahrt eines Autobahnzubringers und eine Bahntrasse ergibt, ist dabei noch eine geringere Herausforderung als die Barrierewirkung dieser beiden stark frequentierten Achsen. Und doch hätte als Ort kaum etwas Besseres gewählt werden können als diese Spitze.

Mit einer schlüssigen dreiteiligen Gebäudekonstellation um einen 100 Meter hohen Büroturm überzeugten JSWD in dem 2015 ausgelobten zweistufigen Qualifizierungsverfahren. Dieses Ensemble erscheint stark genug, um Bezüge zu seinem vielfältigen und verkehrsumtosten Umfeld herzustellen, ohne die Fokussierung auf sein Zentrum zu verlieren. Die Grundrisse der drei sechs- bis siebengeschossigen Baukörper sind in der Form unregelmäßiger Fünfecke geplant, ihre Kanten folgen akkurat den Grundstücksgrenzen, während die Binnenräume sich zum Zentrum hin verjüngen. Das Innere dieses Quartiers ist offen gestaltet und einsehbar; mit Ausnahme der Vorfahrt ist es den Fußgängern vorbehalten. Mit einem großzügigen Grünraum führt das neue Büroquartier die Freiflächen der südlich angrenzenden Wohnbebauung fort, das Grün zieht sich über Pflanzinseln und Solitärbäume in das einladend gestaltete Quartiersinnere.

Die in den einander zugewandten Gebäudeköpfen liegenden Foyers werden schwellenlos über den zentralen Platz erschlossen. Dieser öffentliche Raum scheint in die Foyers hineinzufließen, da die Untersichten und Rückwände der Fassadentypologie entsprechend gestaltet werden.

Die Fassaden der drei fünfeckigen Baukörper sind als außen liegendes Tragwerk aus hellem Stahlbeton konzipiert. Bei gleicher Anmutung liegt technisch bedingt das Tragwerk des Hochhauses auf der Innenseite der Fassade, während die filigrane Struktur aus Glasfaserbeton außen vorgehängt wird. Abhängig vom Standpunkt des Betrachters scheint sich die Netzstruktur der Gebäudehüllen zusammenzuziehen oder aufzuweiten. Jeder Baukörper ist einzeln wahrnehmbar, das Quartier erscheint jedoch als harmonische Einheit.

Das Hochhaus entwickelt sich aus dem großen Ganzen 28 Geschosse in die Höhe, ohne die Hülle zu durchstoßen, und setzt damit das gewünschte Zeichen für den Neubeginn. Rund 4500 Menschen werden ab 2022 am Neuen Kanzlerplatz arbeiten, aber ein Vielfaches davon wird er als Landmarke täglich grüßen.

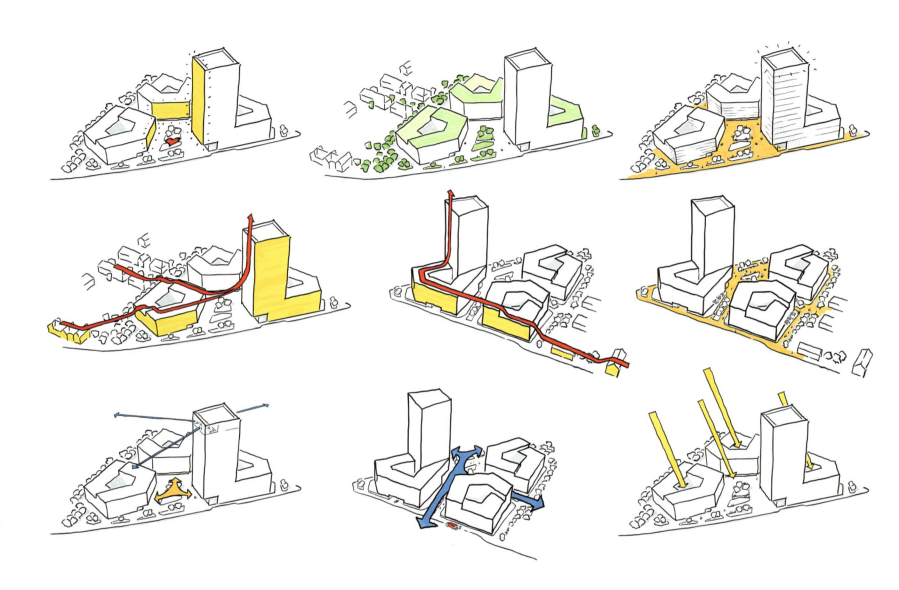

New Chancellor Square
Bonn

All the signs point to a new start at Bundeskanzlerplatz in 2019. The massive excavation is 12 meters deep; one can already make out the dimensions of the new office buildings at New Chancellor Square based on the work taking place on their foundations. After the 1991 Berlin-Bonn decision robbed the government quarter of its *raison d'être*, it was able to distinguish itself anew against all expectations through the UN campus, an international congress center, the Museum Mile, and, last but not least, as the headquarters location for three DAX companies and numerous other institutions. But somehow this "new Bonn" was missing a resounding kick-off, a welcoming gesture with the desired effect far afield. In 1969, a solution to this task had already been sought and was realized through the construction of the Bonn-Center at Bundeskanzlerplatz. The triangle that is formed by a highway feeder road and a set of train tracks is not an easy site. The shape of the site is, however, less challenging than the barrier effect that these two highly frequented infrastructure axes have on it. And yet the location could not have been better chosen.

The two-step qualification procedure, which was announced in 2015, was won by JSWD, who designed a coherent, three-part constellation of buildings around a 100-meter office tower. This ensemble seems strong enough to develop relationships to its diverse and busy environment without losing the focus on its center. The floor plans of the three six-to-seven-story buildings are planned as irregular pentagons; their edges follow the boundaries of the plot accurately, while the interstitial spaces point towards the central square, narrowing as they approach it. The interior of the new quarter has an open design and is visible from outside; it is reserved for pedestrians with the exception of a driveway. The office quarter's generous green space serves as a continuation of the open spaces in the neighboring residential area; plant islands and solitary trees stretch into the invitingly designed interior of the quarter.

The foyers of the buildings face one another and can be reached threshold-free via the central square. As a result of design choices on the undersides and back walls of the facades, this public space seems to flow into the foyers. The facades of the three pentagonal buildings are characterized by an external support structure of light-colored reinforced concrete. The same impression is achieved through the supporting structure of the high-rise, which had to be located on the inside of the facade for technical reasons; a delicate structure of fiberglass concrete is affixed to the outside. Depending on the observer's location, the netting structure of the building envelopes appear to expand or contract. Each building can be perceived on its own; the quarter, however, also appears as a harmonious unit.

The high-rise extends from all of this to a total of 28 stories without piercing the envelope, so setting the stage for a new beginning. From 2022 onward, around 4,500 people will work at the New Chancellor Square, but many, many more will greet it daily as a landmark.

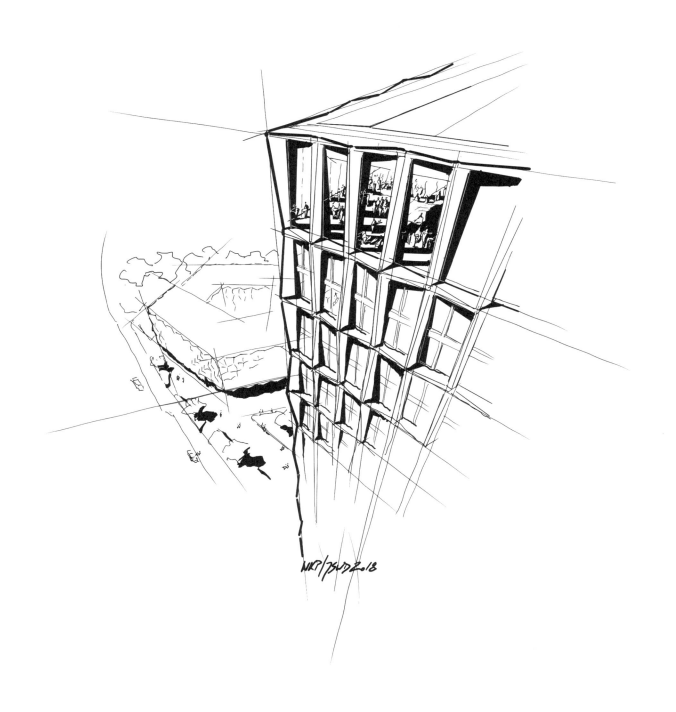

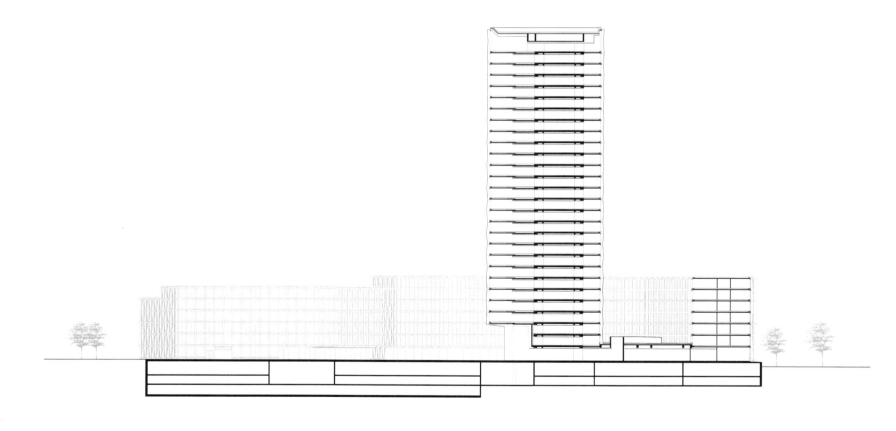

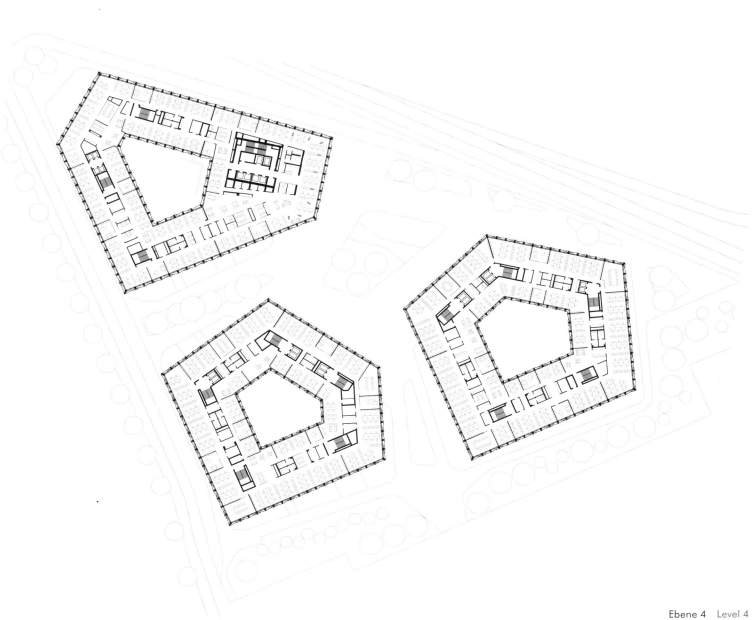

Ebene 4 Level 4

Die geografische Mitte
The Geographic Middle

Dass ausgerechnet ein leuchtender Mercedes-Stern zu einem Wahrzeichen der kleinen Bundeshauptstadt am Rhein wurde, war bestimmt nicht geplant. So, wie vieles hier nicht oder nur unter dem Siegel der Verschwiegenheit oder dem Vorbehalt des Provisoriums geplant wurde.

It was certainly not the plan that a lighted Mercedes logo, of all things, would become a symbol of the little capital on the Rhine. Like so much here, it too was planned behind closed doors or only ever meant to be temporary.

Ansichtskarte aus den frühen 1970er Jahren mit dem noch jungen Bonn-Center
Postcard from the early 1970s with the recently constructed Bonn Center

Genau 20 Jahre nach ihrem Dienstantritt als Regierungssitz war die Stadt Bonn durch eine umfangreiche Eingemeindung so angewachsen, dass sich ihr geografischer Mittelpunkt vom historischen Zentrum auf eine Kreuzung an der Grenze zwischen Innenstadt und Regierungsviertel verschob, die damals erst kurze Zeit den Namen Bundeskanzlerplatz trug.
Der geografische Mittelpunkt ist eine Formalie, die im tatsächlichen Leben einer Stadt mal weniger, mal mehr Bedeutung hat. In Bonn war

Exactly 20 years after it assumed the role of the seat of government, the city of Bonn had grown so much as a result of extensive incorporation that its geographic middle had shifted from the historic center to an intersection at the border between the inner city and the government quarter, which had just been renamed Bundeskanzlerplatz.
The geographic middle is a formality that varies in importance over the course of a city's existence. In Bonn it became important in 1969 when the Bonn-Center, designed by Berlin architect Friedrich Wilhelm Garasch

Arne Hilbert (Geschäftsführer, Art-Invest RE)

„Im Bonner Bundesviertel, in direkter Nachbarschaft zur Museumsmeile besteht für uns die einmalige Möglichkeit, ein Grundstück mit besonderer Strahlkraft zu entwickeln. Auf dem geschichtsträchtigen Areal des ehemaligen Bonn-Centers entsteht ein modernes Büroquartier mit städtebaulicher Relevanz. So schaffen wir mit einer spektakulären Architektur den gebührenden Rahmen für einen attraktiven Stadtplatz. Das Highlight unseres Prestige-Projektes bildet das 101,50 Meter hohe Hochhaus, welches als weithin sichtbare Landmarke das Quartier im Stadtgefüge verankert. Wir sind uns unserer hohen Verantwortung für Bonn bewusst und freuen uns, mit dem Neuen Kanzlerplatz einen echten Impulsgeber schaffen zu dürfen."

Arne Hilbert (managing director, Art-Invest RE)

"In Bonn's federal district, in the immediate vicinity of the museum mile, we have the unique opportunity to develop a property with special appeal. A modern office district with a high level of relevance for the urban fabric of the city is being built on the historically important site of the former Bonn Center. Through this spectacular architecture, we are creating the right surroundings for an attractive city square. The 101.5-meter-high skyscraper is the highlight of our prestige project; as a landmark that can be seen from afar, it anchors the neighborhood in the urban fabric. We are aware of our great responsibility for Bonn and are happy to be able to create a real impetus for the future through the new Kanzlerplatz."

Sprengung des Bonn-Centers am 19. März 2017   Demolition of the Bonn Center, March 19, 2017

Konrad-Adenauer-Büste auf dem Bundeskanzlerplatz, Hubertus von Pilgrim, 1981
Bust of Konrad-Adenauer at Bundeskanzlerplatz, Hubertus von Pilgrim, 1981

Kanzlerbungalow und -limousine, Bonn, 1965
The chancellor's bungalow and limousine, Bonn, 1965

sie 1969 insofern bedeutend, als ebendort das von dem Berliner Architekten Friedrich Wilhelm Garasch entworfene Bonn-Center eröffnet wurde, bestehend aus einem 18-geschossigen Hochhaus, einem fünfgeschossigen Seitenflügel und einer eingeschossigen Ladenzeile. Außer den von Botschaften und Bundestagsfraktionen genutzten Büros und Konferenzräumen wurden hier ein hochklassiges Hotel, ein Restaurant, ein Friseur, ein Supermarkt, Bankfilialen und eine Art Kulturkeller mitgeplant. Die privaten Bauherren boten nun erstmals in dem als Dauerprovisorium sich etablierenden Bundesviertel neben Arbeitsplätzen auch eine Art von Alltagsinfrastruktur.

Das Bonn-Center, in der Literatur auch als Analogie zum Berliner Europa-Center bezeichnet, wurde zu einer modernen Variante des Bonner Stadtzentrums. Dies alles geschah nicht ohne den Hintergedanken, dass sich der mit äußerster Nüchternheit geplante Gebäudekomplex auch nach einem möglichen Ende der Ära als Regierungssitz weiterhin lukrativ nutzen lassen sollte. Der gut 8 Meter hohe Mercedes-Stern auf dem Dach des Bonn-Centers war zunächst nichts weiter als ein Markenzeichen: Leuchtreklame, jedoch äußerst prominent platziert, da Bonn als Bundeshauptstadt ansonsten wenig Zeichenhaftes bot. Allzu einfach war es, in dem in fast jedem *Tagesschau*-Bericht leuchtenden Stern zugleich

and made up of an 18-story high-rise, a five-story wing and a single-story shopping area, was opened. In addition to the offices and conference rooms, which were used by embassies and parliamentary groups, a high-end hotel, a restaurant, a hairdresser, a supermarket, bank branches and a basement for cultural uses were planned. The private developers offered the government quarter, which had established a sort of long-term provisional status, new jobs and day-to-day infrastructure for the first time. The Bonn-Center, described in the literature as analogous to Berlin's Europa-Center, became a modern version of Bonn's city center. This all happened to some extent with the ulterior motive that the office complex, which was planned with the utmost forethought, should also be able to be used profitably even after the era of Bonn as the seat of government had passed. The 8-meter high Mercedes logo on the roof of the Bonn-Center was no more than a brand at first: illuminated advertising, albeit in a prominent place. Bonn as the seat of the federal government did not offer many other symbols. It was all too easy to recognize the logo, glowing in nearly every *Tagesschau* report, as a symbol of the economic potency of the Bonn Republic—which was true in some sense: after all, from Adenauer to Kohl, no other brand was ever considered for the chancellor's limousine. The geographic middle of the city began to lose importance as the

ein Symbol für die Wirtschaftskraft der Bonner Republik zu erkennen – was auf gewisse Weise zutraf, denn von Adenauer bis Kohl kam als Kanzlerlimousine keine andere Automarke infrage.

Weniger Bedeutung hatte die geografische Mitte der Stadt, als das Bonn-Center mit dem Auszug des Hotels 1988 erst langsam, mit dem fortschreitenden Umzug der Bundesregierung dann immer deutlicher zu schwächeln begann. Der zunehmende Verkehr machte den Standort zu einer Insel, Verfall und Tristesse stellten seine Funktion infrage. Auch wenn sich der Stern auf dem Dach weiterdrehte – was sich darunter abspielte, machte dem eigentlichen Zentrum der Stadt keine Konkurrenz mehr. Doch in der Bundesstadt, wie Bonn sich ohne parlamentarische Funktionen nennen darf, dauert es, bis Entscheidungen gefällt und Hoffnungen begraben werden. Längst war der mitten im ehemaligen Bundesviertel in die Höhe geschossene Post Tower zum Wahrzeichen der neuen Bonner Geschichte geworden, als das Kölner Unternehmen Art-Invest Real Estate das Bonn-Center 2014 aus einem Insolvenzverfahren übernahm. Die aufsehenerregende Sprengung des Komplexes am 19. März 2017 machte schließlich Platz für Neues und bot den Bonnern die Gelegenheit, Abschied zu nehmen von einer längst vergangenen Vergangenheit.

Bonn-Center began to decline; slowly at first, with the closing of the hotel, and then more and more quickly with the progressing move of the federal government. Increasing traffic made the site into an island; deterioration and dreariness called its functionality into question. Even though the Mercedes logo on the roof still turned, the building below it was no longer able to compete with the actual city center. However, in the Federal City, as post-parliamentary Bonn is permitted to call itself, there is always a lag before decisions are reached and hopes are put to rest. When the Cologne company Art Invest Real Estate purchased the Bonn-Center at a foreclosure auction in 2014, the Post Tower in the middle of the former government quarter had already long been the symbol of the new chapter of Bonn's history. The spectacular demolition of the complex on March 19, 2017 finally cleared the way for something new and offered Bonn's residents the opportunity to take leave of a long-since ended chapter.

Projektteam JSWD auf der Sohle der 12 Meter tiefen Baugrube
The JSWD project team at the bottom of the 12-meter-deep construction pit

Konversionen

Conversions

LEVERKUSEN-OPLADEN   LEVERKUSEN OPLADEN

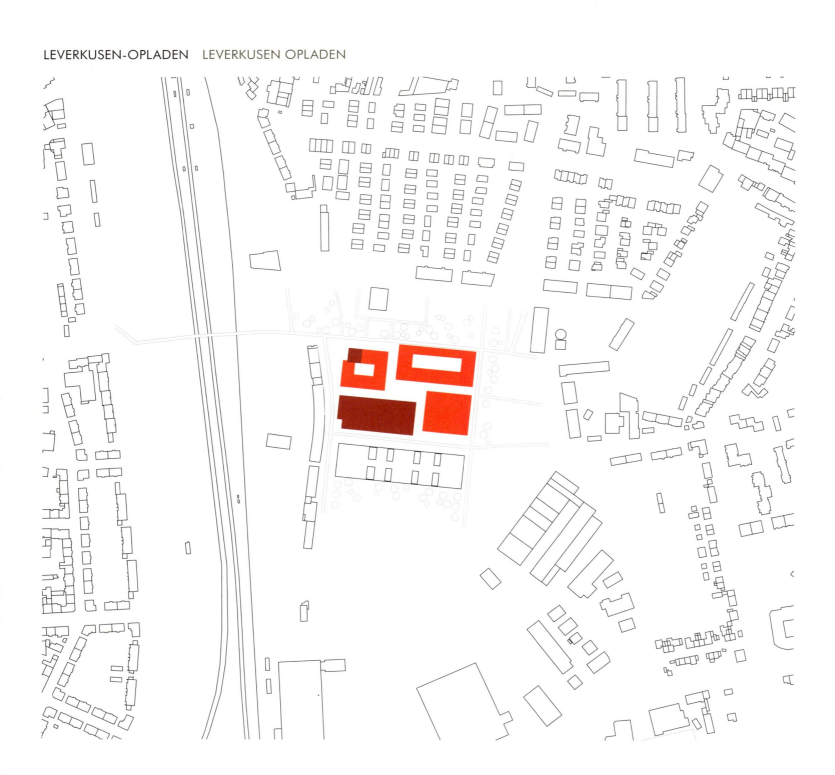

KÖLN-BAYENTHAL   COLOGNE BAYENTHAL

Campus Werk Opladen
Leverkusen

Im Stadtteil Opladen praktiziert die Stadt Leverkusen auf einer Gesamtfläche von gut 70 Hektar nachhaltige Baulandpolitik. Auf dem Gelände des 2003 geschlossenen Bahn-Ausbesserungswerks entwickelt sie die Neue Bahnstadt Opladen, ein durchmischtes Stadtviertel, das neben einem Uni-Campus Wohnraum und Arbeitsplätze bieten wird, aber auch Möglichkeiten zum Einkaufen und zur Freizeitgestaltung. 100 Jahre lang war Opladen Eisenbahnerstadt; einen großen Impuls zum Strukturwandel wird der hier neu angesiedelte Campus der Fakultät für Angewandte Naturwissenschaften der TH Köln geben. Charakteristisch für Opladen und entsprechend für die Neue Bahnstadt ist die Lage an der Zugstrecke Köln–Wuppertal. Zwar profitiert das Areal von der guten Verkehrsanbindung, es muss sich aber mit seiner Entwicklung dieser Gegebenheit anpassen. Zwei neue Brücken stellen eine Verbindung zwischen der West- und der Ostseite her. Die Westseite schließt an das historische Zentrum an, die hier liegenden 12 Hektar Bahnbrache sollen bis 2020 entwickelt werden. Die Ostseite mit dem ehemaligen Bahnausbesserungswerk ist mit der Erschließung des Areals, dem Bau von Wohnsiedlungen mit Spiel- und Grünflächen sowie dem großen Neubau der TH Köln schon einige Schritte weiter. Während der Planung stellte sich die Frage, wie mit dem Bestand an historischen Industriegebäuden umzugehen ist, denn insbesondere bei den großen Hallen ist eine wirtschaftliche Nachnutzung nur schwer vorstellbar, weshalb sie zunächst eilig abgerissen wurden; erst später, nach eingehender Untersuchung, befand man andere Gebäudeteile für erhaltenswert. Charakteristische Einzelbauten wie Kesselhaus, Magazin und Wasserturm werden auch in Zukunft an die Geschichte des Ortes erinnern, während die Neubauten mit schlüssig eingewebten Zitaten seine neue Identität stärken.
Im Zentrum des Areals östlich der Bahntrasse entsteht nach Plänen von JSWD die Cube Factory 577. Die dort vorgefundene fünfschiffige Hallenlandschaft wurde 2019 zu einem großen Teil abgebrochen. In den kommenden Jahren soll sich an dieser Stelle mit drei Neubauten und einer Bestandshalle ein lebendiges und offenes Quartier entwickeln, sorgsam eingewebt in die Struktur der Neuen Bahnstadt. Dem historischen Raster folgend, verteilten JSWD die zukunftsorientierten Nutzungen auf vier voneinander unabhängig entwickelbare Baufelder, die sich windmühlenförmig um einen zentralen Platz legen. Das Bürohaus am Anger schließt den historischen Würfelbau ein. Im Wohnhaus am grünen Kreuz sind die Wohnungen zum Park Grüne Mitte und in den ruhigen Gartenhof orientiert, die Apartments für die Studierenden liegen in der Quartiersmitte. Das Park- und Boardinghouse wächst, dank Systembauweise dem Stellplatzbedarf entsprechend, sukzessive bis auf 500 Stellplätze an. Das direkt angeschlossene Boardinghouse orientiert sich mit allen Wohneinheiten auf den im Osten anschließenden Park Grünes Kreuz. Flexibilität erlaubt auch das Gewerbehaus am Boulevard, es wird in den ehemaligen Bahnhallen 4 und 5 entstehen. Die langen Hallen können dem Bedarf entsprechend in unterschiedlich große Segmente für Sport, Einzelhandel und Gastronomie aufgeteilt werden. Auch wenn die neuen, an diesem Ort stark nachgefragten Nutzungen zum Teil neue Gebäude forderten, legen die

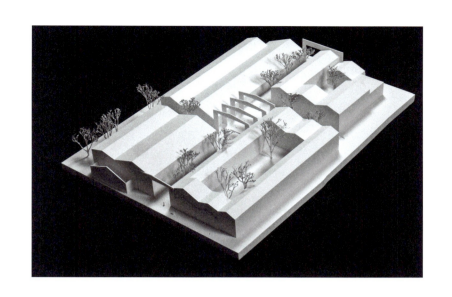

Architekten großen Wert darauf, den Industriecharakter der Bahnstadt mit den Ziegelfassaden, den Kubaturen und Strukturen der Neubauten zeitgemäß fortzuschreiben.

Campus Plant Opladen
Leverkusen

In the district of Opladen, the city of Leverkusen is practicing sustainable building land management on a total area of more than 70 hectares. On the grounds of a railway repair site, which was closed in 2003, the city is developing Opladen's New Bahnstadt, a mixed-use district that will offer residential space and workplaces and a university campus, but also opportunities for shopping and leisure activities. For 100 years, Opladen was a railroad town; TH Cologne's new campus for their Faculty of Applied Sciences will give a major boost to structural change. The location along the train route Cologne-Wuppertal is characteristic of Opladen and accordingly for the New Bahnstadt as well. The area benefits from good transport links, however, its new development needs to take this situation into account. Two new bridges connect the west and east sides. The west side is adjacent to the historic center; the 12 acres of fallow land located here will be developed by 2020. The east side, with the former railway repair shop, is already a few steps ahead; the a development of the area, including the construction of housing with playgrounds and green areas as well as the TH Cologne's large new building, has already begun. During the planning process, the question arose as to how to deal with the historic industrial buildings. An economically efficient reuse was particularly difficult to imagine, especially in the case of the large halls, which is why they were quickly demolished. Later, after a thorough investigation, other buildings were deemed worthy of preservation. Characteristic individual buildings such as the boiler house, deposit, and water tower will continue to recall the history of the place in the future, while the new constructions will strengthen its new identity by coherently integrating references to the historic structure.
The Cube Factory 577 is being built in the center of the area east of the railway line following plans by JSWD. The five-aisled hall complex located there was largely demolished in 2019. Over the next few years, three new buildings and an existing hall will be used to develop a lively and open neighborhood carefully woven into the structure of the New Bahnstadt. Following the historical layout, JSWD distributed the future-oriented uses to four independently developable construction sites which are arranged around a central square like the blades of a windmill. The office building on the Anger incorporates the historic cube building. In the residential building at the green crossing, the apartments are oriented toward the Green Center Park and the quiet garden courtyard; the student accommodations are located in the district center. Thanks to the modular design, the parking structure is gradually growing to accommodate up to 500 parking spaces. In the boarding house, which is directly connected to the parking structure, all of the residential units are oriented toward the adjacent Green Crossing Park to the east. The commercial building on the boulevard also permits flexibility; it will be constructed in former railway halls 4 and 5. The

long halls can be divided into segments of different sizes for sports, retail, and dining spaces. Although the new uses, which are in great demand in this location, sometimes required new buildings, the architects placed great importance on continuing the industrial character of the Bahnstadt in a contemporary way through the brick facades, cubature, and structures of the new buildings.

FLOW Tower
Köln

Bis in die 1980 Jahre war das Gustav-Heinemann-Ufer in Köln-Bayenthal ein lebendiger Bürostandort. Große Konzerne besetzten die begehrten Logenplätze mit repräsentativen Solitären und großen Gesten. Doch die Uferbereiche südlich des Rheinauhafens verloren mit der Zeit ihre Attraktivität als Gewerbestandort zugunsten der kaum 1 Kilometer Luftlinie entfernt gelegenen Innenstadt. Die teils eigenwilligen architektonischen Hinterlassenschaften standen oft jahrzehntelang leer, bis sich jemand an eine Nachnutzung heranwagte. So erging es auch dem elfgeschossigen Haus der Deutschen Industrie am Bayenthaler Rheinufer. Nach dem Auszug des Bundesverbandes der deutschen Industrie 1999 war das Hochhaus – mit den geschwungenen Flanken und kupferfarben verspiegelten Scheiben ganz offensichtlich ein Kind der frühen 1970er Jahre – als Bürostandort trotz seiner hervorragenden Lage nicht mehr vermarktbar. 13 Jahre stand es leer, bis eine Reihe von Studien, die JSWD im Auftrag des damaligen Eigentümers durchgeführt hatte, zu der Erkenntnis führte, dass nur eine Umnutzung als Wohnhaus mit einer vorgelagerten Mantelbebauung der ungewöhnlichen Landmarke neue Perspektiven eröffnen würde. Denn während der Büromarkt weitgehend gesättigt war, herrschte in Köln ein immenser Bedarf an Wohnraum. Zudem versprach eine entsprechende Nachverdichtung, die direkt an die populären Wohnquartiere in Bayenthal anschließt, für diese den lange vermissten direkten Anschluss an das Rheinufer herzustellen.
Doch erst ein Verkauf der Immobilie führte schließlich zur Umsetzung. Während für die Mantelbebauung FLOW Living, bestehend aus fünf Wohngebäuden und einem Büroriegel, an der Uferstraße ein städtebaulicher Wettbewerb ausgeschrieben wurde (Preisträger: ASTOC), wurde JSWD auf Basis der Vorstudien mit der Konversion des Verwaltungsbaus in ein Wohngebäude mit dem Titel FLOW Tower beauftragt. Zur Auflage dieser Direktvergabe machte die Stadt allerdings, dass das Projekt eng vom Gestaltungsbeirat begleitet würde. Das Hochhaus wurde für den Umbau bis auf sein stählernes Skelett entkernt, die charakteristische Dynamik der spiegelgleich geschwungenen konkaven Flanken blieb dabei erhalten. Von der eigenwilligen Ästhetik der 1970er Jahre erzählen auch die aufwendig gestockten Sichtbetonoberflächen der Stahlbetonkerne, die an der südlichen Stirnseite des Gebäudes sowie partiell in den Fluren weiterhin sichtbar blieben. Erschlossen wird das Hochhaus, das nun das Zentrum eines Wohnquartiers bildet, stadt- und rheinseitig, damit es als Filter und nicht länger als Barriere zwischen Veedel und Ufer wahrgenommen wird. Die zeittypisch kupferfarben bedampfte Fassade konnte JSWD aus bauphysikalischen und funktionalen Gründen zwar nicht erhalten, die Architekten

zitieren aber ihre starke Horizontale mit weißen, teils gelochten Brüstungsbändern, die sich an den Längsseiten geschossweise versetzt zu Balkonen aufweiten. Da die auskragenden Balkonplatten zudem einem Brandüberschlag entgegenwirken, konnten dort bodentiefe Fenstertüren eingesetzt werden, sodass die Anmutung und das Erleben des Gebäudes nun der neuen Nutzung, dem Wohnen, entsprechen. Um die Erschließungskerne, die keilförmig zwischen den Scheiben liegen, gruppieren sich insgesamt 132 Wohnungen. In den Regelgeschossen sind es Zwei- bis Fünfzimmerwohnungen, deren variable Grundrisse von der organischen Kontur geprägt sind.

Außergewöhnliche Lösungen fanden sich für Krone und Sockel des ehemaligen Verwaltungsbaus. In einem aufgesetzten Staffelgeschoss wurden vier Penthouses mit Dachterrassen geplant. Das umlaufend auskragende Dach nimmt die Form der darunterliegenden Geschosse auf. Ein dritter Wohntypus konnte dank doppelter Geschosshöhe und Geländeversprung in das ehemals raumhoch verglaste Erdgeschoss eingebaut werden. Anstelle der Lobby wurden dort 13 dreigeschossige Stadthäuser mit eigenem Garten eingesetzt.

Während das eigenwillig spiegelnde Haus der Deutschen Industrie, gestärkt auch durch seine solitäre Exposition, nie den Anschluss an die Stadt gesucht hatte, spielt der FLOW Tower als Wohnlandmarke im neuen Gewand nun eine Vermittlerrolle und steht zudem weithin sichtbar auch für das Potenzial ungewöhnlicher Konversionen.

FLOW Tower
Cologne

Until the 1980s, the Gustav-Heinemann-Ufer in Cologne-Bayenthal was a lively office location. Large corporations occupied the coveted box seats with representative stand-alone buildings and big spatial gestures. However, over time the river bank areas south of the Rheinauhafen lost their attractiveness as a business location; businesses settled instead the inner city, which is barely 1 kilometer away as the crow flies. The somewhat idiosyncratic architectural legacy often stood empty for decades until someone ventured to reuse it. This was the case for the eleven-story House of German Industry on the banks of the Rhine in Bayenthal. After the Federal Association of German Industry moved out in 1999, the skyscraper—an obvious heritage of the early 1970s with its curved flanks and copper-colored mirrored windows—was no longer marketable as

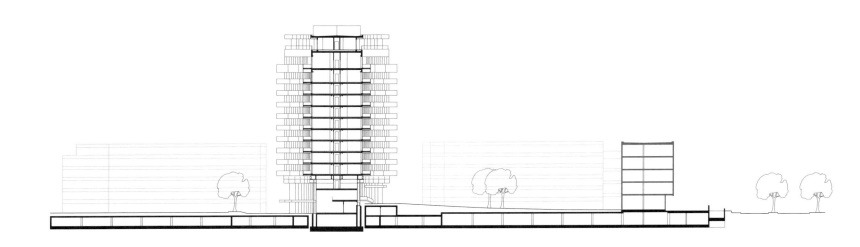
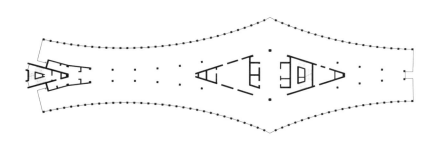
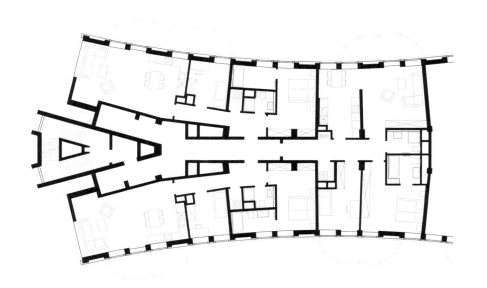

an office building despite its excellent location. It stood empty for 13 years until a series of studies carried out by JSWD on behalf of the then-owner led to the conclusion that only a conversion into a residential building with flanking construction would open up new perspectives for the unusual landmark. In fact, while the office market was largely saturated, there was an immense need for housing in Cologne. In addition, a corresponding densification which connects directly to the popular residential areas in Bayenthal promised to create a long-missed direct connection to the banks of the Rhine for these areas.

In the end, the sale of the property finally led to the implementation. The flanking construction, FLOW Living, consisting of five residential buildings and an office building along Uferstraße, won an urban development competition (won by ASTOC) and JSWD was commissioned to convert the administrative building into a residential building entitled FLOW Tower on the basis of the preliminary studies. As a stipulation of the direct award, the city, however, required that the project be closely monitored by a design advisory board.

The skyscraper was gutted down to its steel skeleton for the remodeling; the characteristic shape of the mirror-like curved concave flanks was preserved. The elaborate, stacked concrete surfaces of the reinforced concrete cores, which remained visible on the southern end of the building and partially in the hallways, are also testament of the idiosyncratic aesthetics of the 1970s. The skyscraper, which now forms the center of a residential district, is being connected on the city and Rhine sides, so that it will now be perceived as a filter and no longer a barrier between the neighborhood and the river bank. Although JSWD was not able to preserve the copper-colored facade typical of the era for structural and functional reasons, the architects cited their strong horizontal lines with white, partly perforated parapet strips, which extend on the long sides to form staggered balconies. As the cantilevered balcony slabs also prevent fire from moving from one story to another, floor-to-ceiling French windows could be used there, so that the look and feel of the building now corresponds to its new residential use. A total of 132 apartments is grouped around the access cores, which are located in wedge-shaped spaces between the panes. On the standard floors, there are two- to five-room apartments whose variable floor plans are characterized by organic contours.

Exceptional solutions were found for the top and bottom floors of the former administrative building. Four penthouses with roof terraces have been planned for an additional, set back top floor. The surrounding projecting roof takes on the shape of the floors below. The ground floor could be successfully converted into a third type of residential space thanks to its double story height and terraces. Instead of the lobby, 13 three-story townhouses, each with their own garden, now occupy this space.

While the idiosyncratically mirrored House of German Industry, strengthened by its stand-alone exposure, never sought a connection to the city, the FLOW Tower now plays an intermediary role in its new guise as a residential brand and is also a widely visible example of the potential of unusual conversions.

Die Auseinandersetzung mit Veränderung
Dealing with Change

Konversionen haben JSWD schon durchgeführt, lange bevor die Themen nachhaltige Baulandpolitik und Umnutzung von Bestandsbauten politisch und gesellschaftlich so viel Beachtung fanden wie heute. Die Fragen danach, welche Erfahrungen das Büro dabei gemacht hat und welche Chancen und Risiken darin stecken, beantwortet Jürgen Steffens (Partner, JSWD).

JSWD carried out conversions long before the issues of sustainable building land policy and the conversion of existing buildings had received as much political and social attention as they enjoy today. Jürgen Steffens (Partner, JSWD) answers questions about what experiences the office has gathered and what opportunities and risks conversions hold.

Blick über den Deutzer Bahnhof zu den Constantin Höfen   View over the Deutzer train station to the Constantin Höfen

In Zukunft werden Architekten und Stadtplaner sich insbesondere in den Ballungsräumen intensiv mit dem Recycling von Flächen und Gebäuden auseinandersetzen müssen. Wie macht man als Architekt aus dieser Pflicht eine Kür?
Jürgen Steffens: Städte befinden sich in einem ständigen Erneuerungsprozess. Dieser fordert von allen Beteiligten, den Kommunen, den Entwicklern, den Bürgern und Planern, ein hohes Maß an Dialogfähigkeit und Anpassungsbereitschaft. Für viele bedeutet Veränderung an sich nichts Positives, und das macht diesen Prozess zu einer enormen Herausforderung. Ich würde die Auseinandersetzung damit aber nicht als Pflicht betrachten, sondern als eine ureigene Aufgabe der Architektur und Stadtplanung. Köln wurde von der römischen Stadt bis heute immer wieder überplant, erweitert, erneuert. Diese räumlichen und gesellschaftlichen Entwicklungen stellen uns immer wieder vor neue Herausforderungen, die wir gerne annehmen. So beteiligen wir uns an den in der Stadtgesellschaft geführten Diskussionen gerne als Moderatoren und Informationsträger.

Die Stadtbereichsplanung ist doch sogar die Grundfeste von JSWD …
JS: Alle vier Partner haben an der RWTH studiert, dort hat uns Volkwin Marg als Inhaber des Lehrstuhls für Stadtbereichsplanung sehr geprägt. Sein Ziel war und ist die Weiterentwicklung der Stadt als eine Vision des permanenten gesellschaftlichen Wandels. Bei der Lösungsfindung spielte aber immer die Spurensuche nach den beständigen Werten des jeweiligen Ortes eine große Rolle. Und so hat es unser Büro auch immer gemacht – bis heute. Über die Stadtbereichsplanung sind wir auch zu Hochbauaufgaben gekommen. Ein Beispiel: Im Jahr 2000 haben wir den Wettbewerb für das ICE-Terminal Köln-Deutz/Messe gewonnen, in dem wir auch eine städtebauliche Entwicklung im direkten Umfeld des Bahnhofes vorgeschlagen haben. Infolgedessen konnten wir auf einem angrenzenden, brach liegenden Grundstück die Constantin Höfe bauen. Sie waren eines unserer ersten großen Hochbauprojekte, mit denen wir weitere Bauvorhaben akquirieren konnten.

Ihr erstes Konversionsprojekt war die Halle 11, die sehr prominent im Rheinauhafen liegt. Wie sehen Sie sie heute?
JS: Die Architektur, die wir für den Umbau der Halle 11 gewählt haben, ist zeitlos. Sie hat ein klares und für den Betrachter verständliches Konzept, mit dem neue und alte Formen miteinander verwoben werden. Das wirkt heute wie damals sehr selbstverständlich und unaufgeregt. Unsere Eingriffe in die alte Substanz haben dem Gebäude nicht geschadet. Aller-

Bahnhofshalle mit freigelegter Kuppelkonstruktion
Station building with exposed dome construction

In the future, architects and urban planners will have to deal intensively with the recycling of areas and buildings, especially in urban areas. How can architects adapt this task to allow more freedom?
Jürgen Steffens: Cities are in a constant process of renewal. This demands a high degree of dialogue capability and willingness to adapt from all concerned: municipalities, developers, citizens, and planners. Many don't regard change as positive in and of itself, and that makes this process a huge challenge. However, I would not regard the negotiation with change as a duty, but as a task inherent to architecture and urban planning. Cologne has been re-planned, expanded, and renewed over and over again, from the original Roman city until today. These spatial and social developments constantly present us with new challenges, which we gladly accept. For example, we are happy to assume the role of moderators and sources of information in the discussions conducted in the urban society.

Urban planning is even the foundation of JSWD…
JS: All four partners studied at RWTH, where Volkwin Marg, the head of the Department of Urban Planning, made a strong impression on us. His goal was and is the further development of the city as a vision of permanent social change. When finding a solution, however, the search for clues to the consistent values of each location always played a major role. And that's how our office has always been—until today. Urban planning led us to building design and construction. For example: in 2000, we won the competition for the ICE terminal Köln-Deutz/Exhibition Center, in which we also proposed development in the immediate vicinity of the station. Consequently, we were able to build the Constantin Höfe on an adjacent vacant plot. That was one of our first large construction projects, which later allowed us to acquire further construction projects.

Your first conversion project was Hall 11, which enjoys a very prominent location in the Rheinauhafen. How do you see it today?
JS: The architecture that we chose for the renovation of Hall 11 is timeless. It has a clear and understandable concept which interweaves new and old forms. Now as then, it feels very natural and rational. Our interventions in the old substance did not harm the building. However, today I would certainly design the staircase access to the roof terraces and the technical structures on the top floor differently.

Although each conversion is always treated individually: what are the criteria that determine whether you can transport the qualities of the past into the future?

dings würde ich die Treppenaufgänge auf die Dachterrassen und den Technikaufbau auf dem letzten Geschoss heute sicher anders machen.

Obwohl jede Konversion individuell behandelt wird: Nach welchen Kriterien entscheiden Sie, ob Sie die Qualitäten des Vergangenen in die Zukunft transportieren können?
JS: Das Wohnen in Hochhäusern wurde lange Zeit nur mit den Brennpunkten in Chorweiler oder Kölnberg assoziiert, nun wird es in oder nahe der Innenstadt und in gut funktionierenden Quartieren zunehmend populär – und teurer. Da plädieren wir natürlich für den Erhalt dieser Objekte. Ein weiterer wirtschaftlicher Grund für den Erhalt eines Hochhauses ist, dass im Fall eines Abbruchs des Gebäudes in der Regel eine Verdichtung an selber Stelle in gleichem Maße nicht genehmigungsfähig ist. Aber sprechen wir über die Architektur: Jedes Haus hat seinen Charme, und den von einer Nutzung in die andere zu transferieren, ist ein sehr spannender Prozess. Unsere beiden kürzlich realisierten Projekte in Köln und Frankfurt brachten ganz unterschiedliche Voraussetzungen mit. Beim FLOW Tower war es gewünscht, aus dem Bürohaus deutlich ablesbar ein Wohngebäude zu machen. Dagegen setzte das Marketing für Wohnungen in der Walter-Kolb-Straße genau auf das Alleinstellungsmerkmal der Konversion. Die hohen Decken und die gewaltigen Stützen dieses Bürohochhauses aus den 1980er Jahren verleihen den Wohnungen einen besonderen Charme.

Häuser mit Geschichte lassen sich also besser vermarkten?
JS: Ja, eindeutig. Wir folgen da gewissermaßen einer gesellschaftlichen Strömung. Die Menschen schauen lieber zurück als nach vorne. So wird Dingen, Häusern oder Quartieren, die eine Geschichte haben, mit der man sich individuell verbinden kann, mehr Wert zugesprochen als dem Neuen. Das Neue alleine gilt heute nicht mehr als identitätsstiftend.

JS: Living in high-rise buildings was long associated with problem areas like Chorweiler or Kölnberg. Today, it is becoming ever more popular— and expensive—in and near the city center and in well-designed neighborhoods. Of course we plead for the preservation of these buildings. Another economic reason for the preservation of skyscrapers is that, when they are demolished, the construction of the same density in the same area is usually not possible. But let's talk about architecture: every building has its own charm, and transferring it from one use to another is a very exciting process. The two projects that we have recently realized in Cologne and Frankfurt had very different requirements. At the FLOW Tower, the client wanted to turn a former office building into a clearly legible residential building. In contrast, the marketing campaign for the apartments in Walter-Kolb-Strasse focused on the unique selling point of the conversion. The high ceilings and massive support columns of the 1980s' office tower give the apartments a special charm.

Historischer Speicher Halle 11, Bernhard Below, 1898
Historical storage hall 11, Bernhard Below, 1898

So would you say that buildings with history can be marketed better?
JS: Yes, definitely. In a sense, we are following a social movement. People prefer to look back than forward. Thus, objects, homes, or districts that have a history with which one can individually connect are given more value than the new. Newness alone is no longer considered a foundation for identity.

Building in Germany is complicated: is it possible to realize all the nice-to-haves? Can all the requirements and standards be met? Is it even worth it? Or do we need more flexibility to make conversions less complex and expensive in the future?
JS: We always try to limit the financial uncertainties of implementation with calculations that also show the risks. But conversion projects cannot be exactly calculated in advance. Old buildings usually have at least one surprise in store. The conversion of a building is based on the legal standards at the time the conversion is conducted. If a building is 30 years

Revitalisierung der Halle 11 im Rheinauhafen, 2009   Renovation of Hall 11 in Rheinauhafen, 2009

Bauen in Deutschland ist kompliziert: Sind alle Wünsche realisierbar? Sind alle Auflagen und Standards erfüllbar? Rechnet es sich überhaupt? Oder brauchen wir mehr Flexibilität, damit Konversionen in Zukunft weniger aufwendig und kostspielig möglich sind?

JS: Wir versuchen immer, die finanziellen Unwägbarkeiten der Umsetzung mit Kalkulationen, die auch die Risiken aufzeigen, in Grenzen zu halten. Doch Konversionsprojekte können nicht vorab auf den Cent genau kalkuliert werden. Mit alten Gebäuden erlebt man Überraschungen. Bei einer Umnutzung eines Gebäudes werden die rechtlichen Maßstäbe zum Zeitpunkt der Fertigstellung der Umnutzung zu Grunde gelegt. Wenn ein Gebäude 30 Jahre oder älter ist, ergeben sich zum Teil große Zwänge, den aktuellen Auflagen gerecht zu werden. Hier wäre ein maßvoller Blick auf die Umsetzung von Vorschriften im Sinne einer Abwägung – was ist sinnvoll, was ist nicht sinnvoll – wünschenswert. Ein ganz anderer Aspekt ist, dass das Angebot auf dem Wohnungsmarkt in Deutschland extrem determiniert ist, hier findet kaum etwas Neues statt. Wenn wir das Geschehen durch unsere Architektenbrille betrachten, sehen wir, dass viel mehr möglich wäre. Aber für einen Investor, der sein Produkt allein daran orientiert, was er auf dem Markt bereits einmal erfolgreich platziert hat, erscheint das Neue immer als Risiko. So entsteht auch im Käuferverhalten eine gewisse Eintönigkeit. Wenn die Entwickler nur die Breite des Marktes als Richtschnur nehmen, kommen immer die gleichen Wohnungstypen heraus. Mehr Mut aufseiten der Investoren würde sich garantiert positiv auf die Vielfalt der Möglichkeiten auswirkten. Dass es Auflagen gibt, die Baustandards festlegen, ist bis zu einem gewissen Maß zu akzeptieren. Wenn sie reiner Selbstzweck sind, wird es schwierig.

Revitalisiertes Bürohochhaus in Frankfurt-Sachsenhausen, 2018
Renovated high-rise office building in Frankfurt-Sachsenhausen, 2018

Denken Sie beim Entwurf eines Gebäudes heute auch an die Möglichkeit, dass sich die Nutzung in 20 Jahren einem ganz anderen Bedarf anpassen lassen muss? Wohnen im The Icon Vienna oder Büros in der Ecole Centrale Clausen …

JS: Selbstverständlich denken wir auch über eine Nachnutzung unserer Gebäude nach. Derzeit gibt es in den Ballungsräumen einen hohen Bedarf an Schulbauten, zum einen, weil der Zuzug enorm ist, zum anderen, weil in der Schulentwicklungsplanung Fehler gemacht wurden. Doch wenn die Peaks dieses Bedarfs wieder abgebaut werden, stellt sich unweigerlich die Frage, wie in ferner Zukunft überzählige Schulbauten zu nutzen sind. Kann man da vielleicht ein Altenheim draus machen? Wir versuchen dem ein wenig vorzugreifen, indem wir schon bei der Planung von Neubauten Antworten auf die Fragen von morgen suchen.

old or older, there are sometimes major constraints to meeting current requirements. I would plead for a moderate assessment of the implementation of regulations—considering what makes sense, what doesn't—in the spirit of compromise. An entirely different aspect is that the supply on the housing market in Germany is extremely predetermined; not much new happens here. When we look at what is happening from an architectural perspective, we see that much more is possible. But for an investor who orients their product solely on what they have already successfully placed on the market, trying something new always appears to be a risk. This creates a certain monotony in the buyer's behavior as well. If the developers only take the existing variation in the market as a guideline, then they will always produce the same types of apartments. More courage on the part of investors would certainly have a positive effect on the variety of outcomes. That there are requirements that set building standards is to some extent acceptable. If they are pure end in itself, it makes things difficult.

When designing a building today, do you also think about the possibility that its use can be adapted to a completely different need in 20 years' time? Maybe living in The Icon Vienna or offices in the Ecole Centrale Clausen…

JS: Of course, we also think about a reuse of our buildings. Currently there is a high demand for school buildings in metropolitan areas, both because of high immigration and because mistakes have been made in the past in school development

Bürohochhaus vor der Umnutzung
Office tower high-rise before conversion

planning. But when the current extremes have passed, the question will inevitably arise of how to use surplus school buildings in the distant future. Is it possible to build a retirement home there? We try to anticipate this by looking for answers to the needs of tomorrow when planning new buildings.

Thyssenkrupp Quartier
Essen

Die Konzerne Thyssen und Krupp schlossen sich 1999 zu einem Unternehmen zusammen, das heute weltweit über 161000 Mitarbeiter beschäftigt. Damit verschmolzen auch zwei der bedeutendsten deutschen Industriellendynastien mit je eigener Historie und Kultur zu einer neuen Organisation. Nachdem beschlossen worden war, das neue Hauptquartier von Düsseldorf auf das ehemalige Werksgelände der Krupp AG in Essen zu verlegen, sollte auch ein neues Bild, eine neue Corporate Architecture, definiert werden. 2006 fand ein internationaler offener Realisierungswettbewerb statt, den JSWD zusammen mit Chaix & Morel et Associés gewannen. Das Preisgericht lobte an dem Entwurf, dass die städtebaulich vertraute Struktur des Campus eine eigenständige Adresse bilde, indem sie einen städtischen Erlebnisraum schaffe. Die bebauten und die unbebauten Flächen seien so gestaffelt, dass die Gebäudestandorte mit den Freiräumen und dem zentralen Flanierboulevard bestens verflochten würden.

Der Thyssenkrupp-Campus entstand 2010–2014 auf einer über 20 Hektar großen Fläche der ehemaligen Krupp'schen Gussstahlfabrik, westlich der Essener Innenstadt. In zwei Bauabschnitten wurden bislang acht der dreizehn im Masterplan angelegten Neubauten errichtet. Die städtebaulich klare Anordnung der Einzelgebäude schafft Orientierung und spiegelt zugleich interne Zusammenhänge des Unternehmens wider. Als gliederndes Landschaftselement dient die großflächige Wasserachse. Sie wird von diagonal verlaufenden Stegen gekreuzt, die die Gebäude verbinden, ein Kontrapunkt zur ansonsten rechtwinkligen Struktur des Quartiers. In der Flucht dieses zentralen Boulevards steht das Gebäude Q1, in dem die Unternehmenszentrale sitzt. Mit seiner Höhe von 54 Metern überragt es zwar alle anderen Gebäude auf dem Campus, herausgehoben wird es aber vielmehr durch seine Komposition aus zwei aufeinander stehenden Winkelbauten. Sie formen einen beeindruckenden, von schlanken Brücken durchzogenen Luftraum oberhalb des Foyers und fassen ihn ein wie ein Fensterrahmen, genauer gesagt: wie ein überdimensionales Doppelfenster. Dessen „Scheiben" sind jeweils 26 x 28 Meter groß und wirken dennoch filigran, weil das Glas von vergleichsweise dünnen Stahlseilen gehalten wird. Das Motiv des Fensters macht das immerhin elfgeschossige Q1 zu einem *point de vue*. Der Blick durch das markante Gebäude, entweder in den Himmel oder auf die Landschaft, erzeugt ein Bild von Offenheit, das für das gesamte Thyssenkrupp Quartier steht. So wie die Belegschaft ist auch die Öffentlichkeit eingeladen, diesen Campus jederzeit zu benutzen; alle Außenanlagen sind frei zugänglich.

Westlich des Boulevards reihen sich die fünf Verwaltungsgebäude der unterschiedlichen Geschäftsbereiche auf. In ihnen wiederholt sich, leicht variiert, das Thema zweier zusammengefügter L-förmiger Volumen, die eine kommunikative Mitte umschließen – mal einen Innenhof, mal ein Foyer. Durch die geschickte Höhenstaffelung wirken auch diese Bausteine trotz ihrer Größe offen und zugänglich, und sie bilden räumlich die (Unter-)Adressen innerhalb des Unternehmensgefüges ab. Ihre zumeist geschosshohen Glasfassaden erlauben Ein- und Ausblicke und behalten damit den Kontakt zum Campusleben.

An der Ostseite des Boulevards steht das lang gestreckte dreigeschossige Q2, das Gebäude mit dem größten Publikumsverkehr. Das hat zum einen mit dem Mitarbeiterrestaurant und der öffentlichen Cafeteria im Erdgeschoss zu tun, zu der vor allem zur Mittagszeit die Beschäftigten aus allen Richtungen

herbeiströmen. Zum anderen empfängt der Konzern im Q2 seine Gäste, hier befinden sich ein Sitzungs- und Veranstaltungssaal für bis zu 1000 Personen, der Aufsichtsratssitzungssaal und weitere Konferenz- und Besprechungsräume nebst Serviceflächen. Wer über die große Treppe in das erste Obergeschoss hinaufsteigt, kann dort eine Analogie zur städtebaulichen Struktur des Campus erkennen. Alle Räume sind wiederum entlang einer großzügigen Achse des doppelgeschossigen Foyers aufgereiht, das als kommunikative Begegnungszone dient. Sie schafft Orientierung und Klarheit. Eine Besonderheit am südlichen Ende des Q2 ist der Raum der Stille. Durch eine gewöhnliche Tür gelangt man zunächst in einen langen Gang, der zu einem doppelgeschossigen Raum mit ganz eigener Atmosphäre führt. Von der Decke ist ein objekthafter Kubus abgehängt, dessen Innenseite aufwendig mit Tausenden kleinen

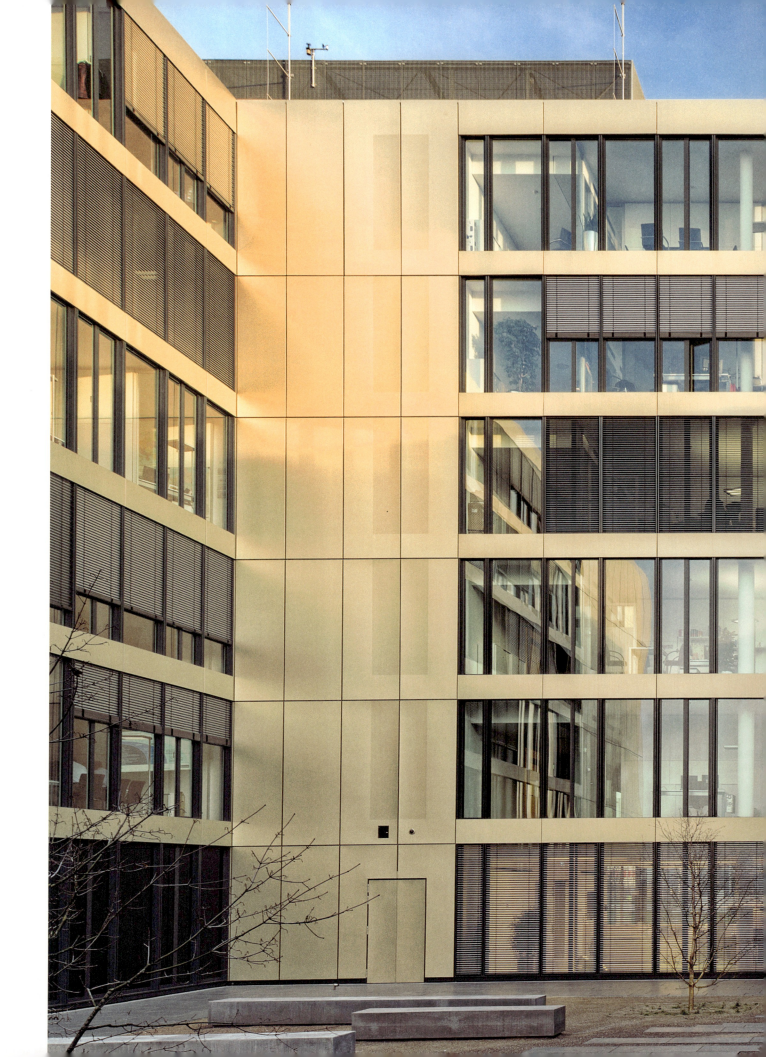

Titanblechzungen verkleidet ist, die das einfallende Oberlicht bläulich reflektieren. Unter diesem Kubus finden Mitarbeiter und Gäste einen Raum zur inneren Einkehr und Entspannung, der überdies die interkulturelle, überkonfessionelle Kommunikation fördern soll, die sich im Grenzbereich zwischen Privatsphäre und Arbeitswelt abspielt. Der Raum der Stille illustriert im Kleinen das gewisse Mehr, ein löbliches Übermaß, das die Architekten und der Bauherr mit diesem Campus geschaffen haben.

Thyssenkrupp Quarter
Essen

In 1999, the companies Thyssen and Krupp merged into one firm, which today employs more than 161,000 staff worldwide. This merger also combined two of the most important German industrial dynasties, each with their own history and culture, into a new organization. After it had been decided to move the new headquarters to the former Krupp AG factory site in Essen, the decision was also reached to create a new image and a new corporate architecture. In 2006, an open international realization competition was held which was won by JSWD, together with Chaix & Morel et Associés. The jury praised the design for using the familiar campus structure to create a unique address and an urban experience space. The built and unbuilt areas are staggered in order to optimally integrate the buildings, open spaces and the central boulevard into the overall spatial concept.

The Thyssenkrupp Campus was constructed between 2010 and 2014 on a more than 20-hectare area west of the Essen inner city which had been the location of the former Krupp steel foundry. As of today, eight of the thirteen new buildings set out in the masterplan have been realized in two construction phases. The clear organization of the individual buildings relative to each other aids in the orientation and simultaneously reflects internal connections within the company. The landscape is structured around an large axial water element. The water element is crossed by diagonal footbridges that connect the buildings, a direct counterpoint to the otherwise rectilinear structure of the quarter. Building Q1, in which the corporate headquarters is located, forms the focal point of this central boulevard. At a height of 54 meters, it towers above all of the other buildings on the campus; however, it is its design, a composition of two L-shaped buildings perched one atop the other, which makes it stand out. They form an impressive airspace above the foyer which is criss-crossed by slender bridges. They surround the space like a window frame, or, more specifically: like an oversized double window. Its "windowpanes" are 26 meters be 28 meters each but still feel delicate, since the glass is held in place by comparatively thin steel cables. The window motif makes the eleven-story Q1 into a point de vue. The view through the striking building, either into the heavens or of the landscape, creates a sense of openness which infuses the entire Thyssenkrupp Quarter. Both employees and the public are invited to use the campus: the grounds and its facilities are freely accessible.

The five administrative buildings of the various business units are arranged in a row on the western side of the boulevard. In these buildings, the theme of two intersecting L-shaped building sections has been repeated, albeit in a slightly different way for each building; the Ls enclose a communicative middle-point in each building—sometimes a courtyard, sometimes a foyer. Through cleverly staggered heights, these building components feel open and inviting despite their size; spatially, they represent the various divisions of the company. Their mostly floor-to-ceiling glass facades permit views from both inside and out and therefore maintain contact with life on the campus.

The elongated Q2 building, which receives the largest number of public visitors, is located on the eastern side of the boulevard. The number of visitors can be explained by the employee restaurant and public cafeteria on the ground floor, to which employees from everywhere in the city flock during lunchtime. In addition, Q2 is where the company receives its visitors; a conference and event hall for up to 1,000 people, the board meeting room, further conference and meeting rooms, and their respective service areas are located here. Anyone who climbs the large staircase to the first floor will recognize an analogy to the organizational structure of the campus. All of the rooms are arranged along the long axis of the two-story foyer, which serves as a generously proportioned communicative meeting zone. This element aids in orientation and clarity. A special feature at the southern end of the Q2 building is the quiet room. Passing through a normal door, one comes at first to a long hallway which leads to a two-story-high room with a unique atmosphere. A cuboid object is suspended from the ceiling; its interior has been elaborately clad with thousands of thin titanium strips which lend the light a bluish cast. Beneath the object, employees and guests can find a space for inner reflection and relaxation; furthermore, this space is intended to promote intercultural, interdenominational communication at the intersection of private life and work. The quiet room is just one small example of the little extra something, the laudable abundance, which the architects and the client have created with this campus.

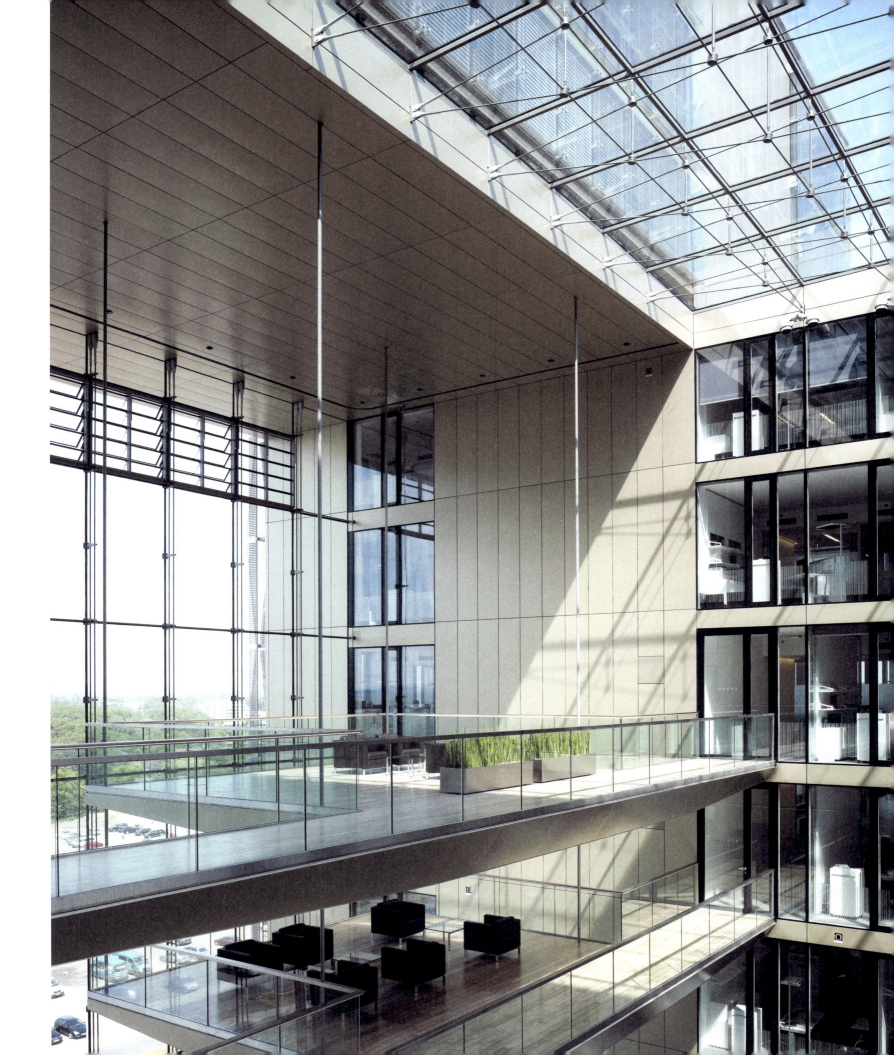

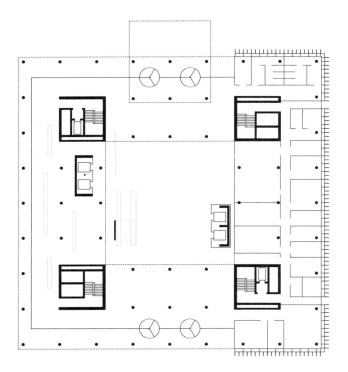

Ebene 0 Level 0

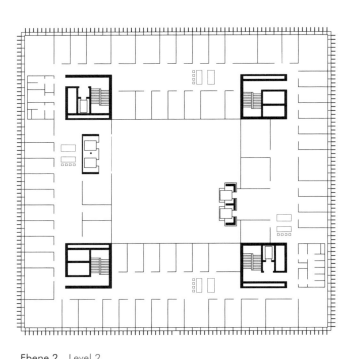

Ebene 2 Level 2

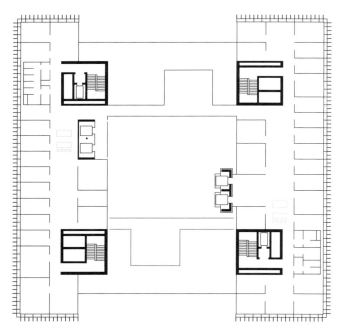

Ebene 7 Level 7

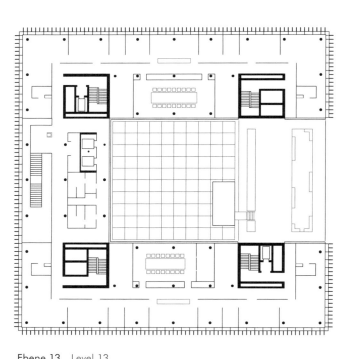

Ebene 13 Level 13

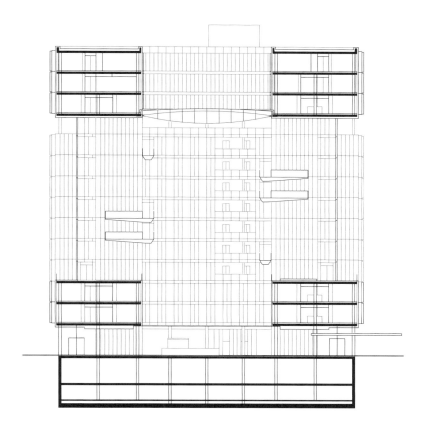
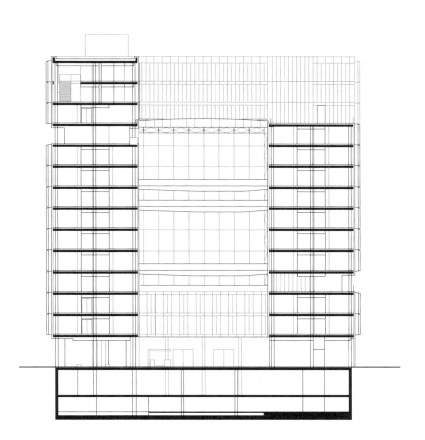

199

Fassade und Identität
Facade and Identity

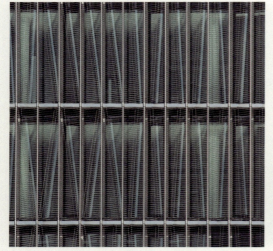
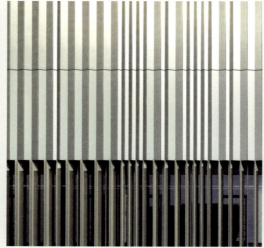

Fassadenfamilie (v. l.): Q1, Q2, Q5, Kita (u.)   Facade family (from left): Q1, Q2, Q5, day care center (below)

Ob Aufspaltung, Fusion oder Ausgliederung – der Thyssenkrupp-Konzern steht einmal mehr vor größeren Umstrukturierungen. Die Campus-Architektur der Essener Zentrale ist auf solche Veränderungen vorbereitet.

Whether division, fusion or demergers—the Thyssenkrupp company is once again faced with larger-scale restructuring. The campus architecture of the headquarters in Essen is ready for these kinds of changes.

Die Essener Gussstahlfabrik Fried. Krupp, ab 1811
The Essen cast steel factory Fried. Krupp, from 1811

Baustelle mit Kruppschem Stammhaus, 2010
Construction site with the original Krupp company building (*Stammhaus*), 2010

Die Gussstahlfabrik Fried. Krupp wurde im Zweiten Weltkrieg weitgehend zerstört und nach Kriegsende bis auf wenige Bauten demontiert. An die industrielle Vergangenheit des einst gewaltigen Areals im Essener Westviertel erinnern nur noch wenigen Relikte. Wer die Straßenbahn an der Haltestelle namens Thyssenkrupp verlässt, erblickt sofort das monumentale Tiegelgussdenkmal an der Altendorfer Straße. Das Denkmal, 1935 vom Berliner Bildhauer Arthur Hoffmann entworfen, konnte wegen kriegsbedingter Materialknappheit erst 1955 eingeweiht werden. Ein 22 Meter langes Bronzerelief illustriert, wie Arbeiter in mehreren Schritten Gussstahl herstellen – eine Schlüsseltechnologie des Industriezeitalters, die der Unternehmensgründer Friedrich Krupp an diesem Ort ab 1823 entwickelte. Auch das ehemalige Aufseherhaus, später als Krupp'sches Stammhaus bezeichnet, ist ein anschauliches Zeugnis der Unternehmensgeschichte. Es wurde 1961 zum 150-jährigen Firmenjubiläum originalgetreu rekonstruiert, wenige Meter von seinem ursprünglichen Standort entfernt. Das kleine Fachwerkhaus mit Schiefergiebel und Ziegelausfachung sollte zeigen: Auch die Schwerindustrie hat einmal klein angefangen. In der Nachkriegszeit war dies ein Versuch, an die vermeintlich unschuldige Gründerzeit zu erinnern, ein Versuch der Selbstvergewisserung nach einer Zeit, in der Krupp als „Waffenschmiede des Reiches" galt.

Der fast zwei Jahrhunderte andauernde Erfolg der Krupp AG wäre ohne die ständige Bereitschaft zum Wandel niemals möglich gewesen; dasselbe gilt für die Düsseldorfer Thyssen AG. Die Fusion der beiden Konzerne hat mit dem Thyssenkrupp-Campus eine neue Zeitschicht auf dem historischen Gelände in Essen entstehen lassen. 2019 sieht der Mischkonzern der Aufspaltung in zwei Sparten entgegen: *Materials* und *Industrials*. Regelmäßig ist in der Wirtschaftspresse über den Verkauf der profitablen Aufzugsparte zu lesen, und es wird auch über eine mögliche Fusion von Thyssenkrupp mit dem indischen Konzern Tata Steel spekuliert. Die Campusstruktur wurde genau wegen solcher Umstrukturierungen und Reorganisationen ausgewählt, denn ihre Bausteine können flexibel belegt, separat betrieben und bei Bedarf durch neue ergänzt werden. Umso wichtiger war es den Architekten, dass allen internen Veränderungen zum Trotz die Familienzugehörigkeit der Gebäude ablesbar bleibt. So wie enge

The Friedrich Krupp steel foundry was extensively destroyed during the Second World War; after the end of the war, just a few buildings were spared from demolition. Today, only a handful of relics remind one of the industrial past of the once enormous site in the western section of Essen. Anyone alighting at the Thyssenkrupp tram stop cannot miss the massive monument to crucible steel casting (*Tiegelgussdenkmal*) in Altendorfer Straße. The monument, which was designed in 1935 by Berlin sculptor Arthur Hoffmann, could only be dedicated in 1955 as a result of war-related material shortages. A 22-meter-long bronze relief illustrates how workers produce cast steel in several steps—a key technology of the industrial era which was developed by company founder Friedrich Krupp at this location in 1823. The former overseer's cottage, later described as the Krupp original company building (*Stammhaus*), is a demonstrative reference to the company's history. For the 150th company anniversary, it was faithfully reconstructed in 1961 just meters from its original location. The small half-timbered house with slate gable ends and brick infills is intended to show that even heavy industry began small. In the post-war period, this was an attempt to hark back to the supposedly innocent era of industrial expansion, an attempt at self-assurance after a period in which Krupp had become the "armorer of the Reich."

The success of Krupp AG, which has been maintained for nearly two hundred years, would not have been possible without the willingness to change; the same is true of the Düsseldorfer company Thyssen AG. The merger of the two companies and the resultant construction of the Thyssenkrupp Campus have inscribed a new time layer onto the historical site in Essen. In 2019, the conglomerate was divided into two: *Materials* and *Industrials*. The financial press frequently features articles about the sale of the profitable elevator division, as well as speculation about a possible merger between Thyssenkrupp and the Indian company Tata Steel. The campus structure was selected precisely for its ability to accommodate these types of restructurings and reorganizations, since its building blocks can be flexibly occupied, run separately, or, if needed, supplemented by new construction. For this reason, it was all the more important to the architects that the "family affiliation" between the buildings remained legible independent of any and all internal changes. Like

Kinetischer Sonneschutz des Gebäudes Q1   Kinetic sun protection on building Q1

Verwandte einander durch die Ähnlichkeit ihrer Gesichter erkennen, so sind auch die Fassaden einander ähnlich, ohne repetitiv oder vervielfältigt zu wirken.
„Schale und Kern" lautete ein gestalterisches Leitprinzip für die Zentrale und die Verwaltungsgebäude. Während die hof- und foyerseitigen Fassaden glatte Oberflächen haben, sind die Außenseiten mehrschichtig konzipiert und wirken dadurch wie das Relief einer Schale. Dabei stellt Edelstahl als quasi hauseigenes Material nachvollziehbar einen übergeordneten Zusammenhang her. Die flächigen „Kernseiten" der Gebäude sind mit speziell beschichteten Stahlblechpaneelen verkleidet, während die Campusfassaden durch den außen liegenden Sonnenschutz geprägt sind. Raumhohe Glasflächen – eine Chiffre der klassischen Moderne – bilden den eigentlichen Raumabschluss. Der davor montierte Sonnenschutz, der die Räume vor Überhitzung schützt, verkörpert den gewissenhaften Umgang mit den natürlichen Ressourcen, den die Gegenwart fordert.

close relatives who recognize each other by the similarity of their faces, the facades are also similar without seeming repetitive or copied.
"Peel and kernel" is the name of the overarching design principle for the main headquarters and the administrative buildings. While the interior facades facing foyers and courtyards have smooth surfaces, the outward-facing facades have multiple levels and therefore feel like a relief of a fruit peel. The steel used for these external facades is a logical choice based on the company's history and creates an overarching relation between the buildings. The extensive "kernel sides" of the buildings are clad with specially coated steel panels, while the campus facades are all characterized by their internal sun protection. Floor-to-ceiling glass panels—typical for classical modernism—form the actual spatial boundary. The sun protection, which is mounted in front of the glass and protects the rooms from overheating, embodies the conscientious approach to natural resource use demanded by today. The sun protection facades, in their variously

Darstellung der glatten Kerne im Modell   Model showing the smooth cores

In ihren unterschiedlich konstruierten Formen erzählen die Sonnenschutzfassaden des Campus von Innovation, sie stellen Akkuratesse und Präzision in den Vordergrund und illustrieren den hohen technologischen Anspruch des Unternehmens wie auch der Architekten.

Die Varianten hierarchisieren zudem die Gebäude auf dem Campus. Die raffinierteste und komplexeste Fassade befindet sich am Hauptquartier (Q1). Hierfür wurde eine neuartige Kombination aus Vertikal- und Horizontallamellen erfunden, die zugleich freien Ausblick und Schutz vor Sonnenstrahlung bietet. Dazu wurde das altbewährte Prinzip des Fensterladens zu einer neuen Gestalt weiterentwickelt. Über 400000 horizontale Edelstahllamellen sind mit ca. 3150 drehbaren Stielen verschraubt, die sich von 1280 Linearmotoren zentral gesteuert je nach Sonnenstand verdrehen. So verändert sich je nach Wetterlage das gesamte Fassadenbild wie ein filigranes kinetisches Kunstwerk. Beim Forum (Q2) sind es gekantete Lochbleche in unterschiedlicher Breite, die sich den Lichtverhältnissen entsprechend aufdrehen. Durch die 25-prozentige Lochung des dünnen Stahlblechs ergibt sich aber auch im geschlossenen Zustand eine gute Durchsicht. Der Bau wirkt von außen wie mit einem leichten Vorhang verhüllt. Die Verwaltungsgebäude (Q5 und Q7) hingegen werden von einem Raster aus feststehenden vertikalen Edelstahlprofilen gegliedert, hinter dem sich klassische Raffstorelamellen motorisiert auf und ab bewegen.

Edelstahl rostet nicht. Bei regelmäßiger Reinigung wirkt das Material immer wie neu. Es suggeriert Zeitlosigkeit und steht für das Jetzt. Angesichts der anstehenden Veränderungen bei Thyssenkrupp hat sich der Wirt des Mitarbeiterrestaurants etwas Kurioses einfallen lassen: Vor den Eingang des Q2, am Ufer des Wasserbeckens, ließ er sich aus fünf Containern, wie man sie von Baustellen kennt, eine kleine Kneipe zusammenschustern, in der man sich nach Feierabend auf ein Bier verabreden oder informelle Treffen abhalten kann. Auf diese Trapezblechbude ist – durchaus mit einem Augenzwinkern – ein Fachwerk aus Ziegelsteinen aufgemalt. Offenbar bedarf es derzeit eines rustikalen Ortes, an dem die Belegschaft an alte Zeiten denken und der Zukunft entgegensehen kann.

constructed forms, tell a story of innovation. They place accuracy and precision in the foreground and illustrate the high technological demands of both the company and the architects.

The variations also create a hierarchy of buildings on the campus. The most refined and complex facade graces the main building (Q1). For this building, an innovative combination of vertical and horizontal lamellae was invented, which simultaneously allows a free view while affording protection from the sun. The tried-and-trusted principle of the window shutter was evolved into a new design. More than 400,000 horizontal stainless steel lamellae are fastened with approximately 3,150 rotatable shafts, which are centrally turned by 1,280 linear motors according to the position of the sun. Depending on the weather, the entire facade changes like a delicate kinetic sculpture. In the forum (Q2), angled perforated plates of varying widths shift following the changing light conditions. Through the 25 percent perforation of the thin steel sheets, it is still possible to look through even when the plates are closed. From the outside, the building seems to be obscured by a light curtain. The administrative buildings (Q5 and Q7), on the other hand, have been articulated through a grid of static, vertical stainless steel profiles, behind which classic, motorized exterior blinds are mounted.

Stainless steel does not rust. When cleaned regularly, the material seems perpetually new. It suggests timelessness and stands for the now. In light of the coming changes at Thyssenkrupp, the proprietor of the employee restaurant thought up something curious: directly in front of the entrance to Q2, he had five shipping containers cobbled together into a small bar in which people can have a beer after work or hold informal meetings. The steel panel sides are painted—with a good portion of well-meaning humor—like a half-timbered house with brick infills. It seems that there is a need for a rustic space in which the employees can both think back to the old days and look forward to the future.

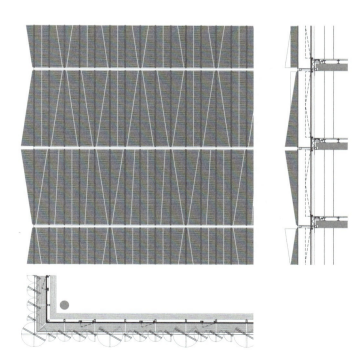

205

Haus und Hof

House and Yard

KORSCHENBROICH   KORSCHENBROICH

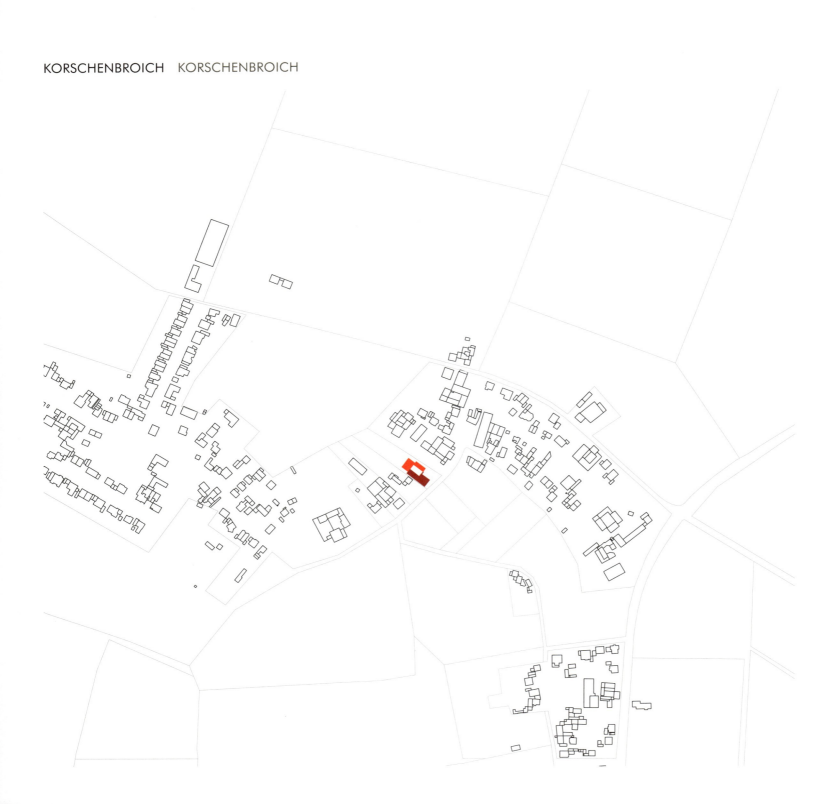

KÖLN-WEISS COLOGNE WEISS

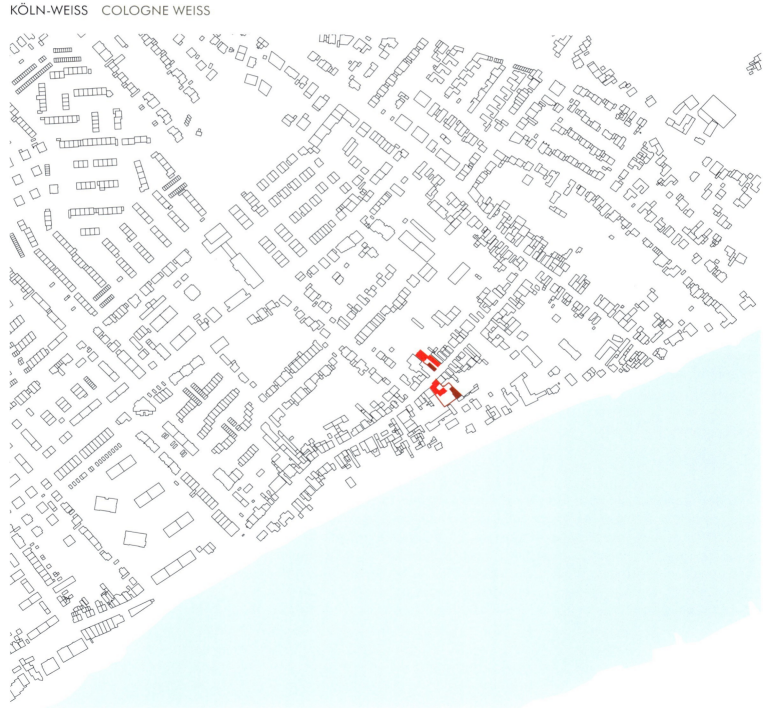

Hofanlage Zgoll
Korschenbroich

Als Standort für ihren neuen Firmensitz erwarb die Zgoll Konferenzraum GmbH einen ehemaligen Bauernhof in einem der idyllisch-ländlich geprägten Ausläufer des niederrheinischen Städtchens Korschenbroich. Hier geht der Blick zwar weit über die Felder, doch die kleinteilige gewachsene Struktur verlangt einen sensiblen Umgang mit Material und Maßstab, wenn Altes überdacht oder Neues hinzugefügt wird. Der Bauherr wünschte sich einen identitätsstiftenden Ort, an dem die großzügigen Ausstellungs- und Schulungsräume für Konferenztechnik mit den eigenen Büros und Werkstätten als Einheit ablesbar sein sollten.
Der Blecherhof bestand ursprünglich aus vier Baukörpern mit unterschiedlichen Nutzungen. Wohngebäude, Scheune und Lager gruppierten sich um einen Innenhof, dessen Proportion und Öffnung nach Südosten sich in der 2019 fertiggestellten Sanierung und Erweiterung wiederfinden.
Für die Hofanlage besteht kein Denkmalschutz. Zwei kleinere Bestandsgebäude, die sich nur schwer den geplanten Nutzungen hätten anpassen lassen, konnten durch Neubauten ersetzt werden. Erhalten wurden die ehemalige Scheune sowie das daran angebaute, leicht zurückversetzte Stallgebäude. Mit zwei zweigeschossigen Baukörpern, die die einfache Satteldachkubatur des Bestands aufgreifen, wurde der Hof an drei Seiten neu gefasst. Die Zufahrt für die Mitarbeiter, gleichzeitig Anlieferung, führt entlang der beiden Neubauten auf die Rückseite des Ensembles.
Die ehemalige Scheune wird nun als Showroom genutzt. Der Kundeneingang liegt an deren Stirnseite, zur Straße hin orientiert. Der Einbau einer schwarzen Stahlkonstruktion, die wie ein Haus im Haus wirkt, zoniert den Großraum und bildet eine kommunikative Galerieebene aus. Das regionaltypische Ziegelmauerwerk der Fassaden von Scheune und Stall wurden saniert, die Dächer wurden mit einer schwarzen Doppel-Stehfalzdeckung neu gedeckt. Straßen- und hofseitig wurden Fensteröffnungen und Türen vergrößert, um die Publikumsbereiche einladend zu öffnen. Inspiriert von diesem Materialkanon erhielten die Neubauten eine horizontal ausgerichtete vorgehangene und geschuppte Tonziegeldeckung. Diese über Dach und Fassaden geführte Haut lässt die Häuser skulptural anmuten, was der gesamten Hofanlage als Ensemble ein zeitgemäß-stilvolles wie lokal-historisch verankertes Erscheinungsbild verleiht.

Farmstead Zgoll
Korschenbroich

The Zgoll Conference Room GmbH acquired a former farm in one of the idyllic rural foothills of the town of Korschenbroich in the Lower Rhine region as the location for its new company headquarters. Here the view extends far over the fields; the new interpretation of old structures or the addition of new ones requires a sensitive handling of material and scale which respects the small-scale organic structure of the existing built space. The client wanted a place which would consolidate their identity, where spacious exhibition and training rooms

for conference technology would be combined with their offices and workshops and be readable as a coherent whole.

The Blecherhof originally consisted of four structures with different uses. Residential buildings, a barn and a warehouse were grouped around an inner courtyard, whose proportion and orientation to the south-east are still evident in the renovation and expansion which was completed in 2019.

The farmstead does not have listed status. Two smaller existing buildings that would have been difficult to adapt to the planned uses were therefore replaced by new buildings. The former barn and the slightly recessed stable building attached to it were preserved. The courtyard was redesigned on three sides through the construction of two two-story buildings which adopted the simple gable roof of the existing structures. The employee access road, which is also the delivery entrance, is located along the two new buildings at the rear of the ensemble.

The former barn is now used as a showroom. The customer entrance is located on the front side of this building, facing the street. The installation of a black steel structure which looks like a house within a house divides the large area into zones and forms a communicating gallery level. The regionally typical brick masonry of the barn and stable facades was renovated; the roofs were covered with a new layer of black double standing seam roofing. On the street and courtyard sides, the window openings and doors were enlarged in order to open the public areas in an inviting manner. Inspired by this canon of materials, the new buildings were enclosed in a horizontally aligned, scaled red brick curtain wall facade. This exterior skin, which extends over both the facades and the roof, gives the buildings a sculptural appearance, and lends the entire courtyard as an ensemble a contemporary, stylish and locally historically anchored appearance.

Wohnen im Dorf
Living in the Village

Dorfstraße in Weiß, 1928
Village street in Weiß, 1928

Der Stadtteil Weiß liegt südlich der Kölner Innenstadt und hat durch den ihn im Osten umfließenden Rheinbogen eine besonders innige Beziehung zu dem mächtigen Strom entwickelt. So ist in Weiß, dessen Name sich aus dem mittelhochdeutschen Wort für Wiese ableitet, die Geschichte des ehemaligen Fischerdorfs heute noch deutlich ablesbar. Insbesondere die erhaltene Kleinteiligkeit der dörflichen Struktur entlang der Weißer Hauptstraße, die über die Jahre nur behutsam ergänzt und fortgeschrieben wurde, erzählt von der Geschichte des früheren Fischerdorfes. Mit zwei Neubauten, die sich schräg gegenüber inmitten des historischen Ortskerns befinden, entwickelten JSWD in einem für das Büro ungewöhnlich kleinen Maßstab zeitgemäße Spielarten des lokalen Typus von Haus und Hof.

The district of Weiß is located south of Cologne's city center. The district has developed a particularly close relationship with the Rhine as a result of the loop of the river that flows around it to the east. In Weiß, whose name is derived from the Middle High German word for meadow, the history of the former fishing village which was located here can still be clearly read today. The preserved small-scale nature of the village structure along Weiß' main street, which has been carefully added to and updated over the years, tells the story of the former fishing village particularly well. Through two new buildings diagonally opposite one another in the middle of the historic town center, JSWD developed contemporary versions of the local type of house and yard on an unusually small scale for the office.

Gartenseite des neuen Hofhauses   Garden side of the new courtyard building

Haus F

Direkt an der Dorfstraße gelegen, fanden JSWD eine Situation vor, die bislang gut ohne den rechten Winkel zurechtgekommen war. Das Cluster aus Häusern und Höfen zeichnete eine Chronologie des Wachsens und Bleibens, in der es nie eine große Lösung gegeben hatte. In diesem Sinne schreiben JSWD die Struktur fort und schufen straßenseitig eine schmale Lücke, die sie gleich wieder schlossen. Dabei passten sie sich den ungeschriebenen Regeln des dörflichen Wachstums an, ließen Giebelständiges auf Traufständiges folgen, zogen den Versatz der Flucht in die Tiefe vor und machten aus einer großen Idee ein Ensemble, das die feine Körnung der Nachbarschaft reflektiert.

Die Bauherren hatten sich ein großzügiges Haus für die Familie gewünscht. Privat sollte der Neubau sein, obwohl er eine Front zur Straße hat und das Grundstück mit dem kleinen Hotel im Altbau teilt. Die ehemalige Schreinerei war zwischenzeitlich eine Apotheke und ist mittlerweile ebenfalls im Besitz der Bewohner.

Zur Dorfstraße hin macht der Neubau sich klein, imitiert das Dörfliche mit seinem spitzen Giebel und tritt gut zwei Schritte hinter den Altbau zurück. Doch der Blick bleibt am Neuen hängen, denn es treibt ein seltsames Spiel mit Vertrautem und Besonderen: Vertraut ist die Farbe der Fassade, das satte Dunkelrot, das aus der Palette der Backsteine entnommen wurde, doch es sind schmale, eloxierte Metallpaneele – vollkommen ortsfremd und dennoch willkommen. Mehr braucht diese Fassade nicht, die Funktionales – die Haustür, das Garagentor, die Fenster – nur andeutet, nicht zeigt.

Was an der Straßenfront so schmal beginnt, gewinnt durch die L-Form des Grundrisses, die den räumlichen Gegebenheiten folgt, in der Tiefe an Weite und Höhe. Im rechten Winkel schließt sich Neues an Altes an und lässt einen kleinen Hof entstehen. Als Freiplatz für das Café genutzt, bringt er der Familie Licht und Abstand.

House F

JSWD found a spatial situation located directly along the village's main street which had done without right angles quite well up until now. The cluster of houses and courtyards outlined a chronology of incremental growth, in which there had never been a major overhaul. JSWD continued this incremental accretion of the structure, creating a narrow gap on the street side, which they immediately closed again. In doing so, they adapted to the unwritten rules of village growth, allowed gable end to follow long end, straightened the mismatch in the alignment and turned a big idea into an ensemble which reflected the fine grain of the neighborhood. The clients wanted a spacious house for their family. The new building should be private, despite the fact that its front faces the street and it shares the property with the small hotel in the adjoining historic building. The

Giebelständiger Einschub zur Straße
Gable-end insertion toward the street

Historisches Fischerhaus mit zeitgenössischem Pendant   Historic fisherman's house and its contemporary counterpart

Kochen, Essen und Wohnen im Erdgeschoss sind eins, auf Türen wurde verzichtet, nur eine Stufe, ein Richtungswechsel, eine einläufige Treppe und das über dem kurzen Schenkel des Grundrisses bis ins spitze Dach offene Atrium kennzeichnen die Bereiche, ohne sie zu begrenzen. Die Offenheit nimmt in der Tiefe des Hauses zu, der Blick fällt geradeaus in den Gartenhof, wo filigrane Stützen vor der großflächig verglasten Fassade kaum ins Gewicht fallen.

Haus J
Wenige Schritte die Dorfstraße hinauf widmete sich JSWD rund fünf Jahre später auf der gegenüberliegenden Seite einer ähnlichen Bauaufgabe wie im Falle von Haus F. Auf einem ebenfalls direkt an der Straße gelegenen Grundstück fanden sie ein historisches Fischerhaus mit zahlreichen Anbauten und Erweiterungen vor. Auch hier haben dir früheren Nutzer nicht nur gewohnt, sondern auch gearbeitet. Von der Fischerei über die Schreinerei, von einer Autowerkstatt bis zur Heißmangel hinterließen die verschiedenen Tätigkeiten bauliche Zeugnisse. Die Architekten entschieden sich, das Grundstück aufzuräumen und – konform mit der Erhaltungssatzung des Ortes – nur das Fischerhäuschen zu erhalten. Nicht zuletzt wegen seiner geringen Deckenhöhe dient es nun zwar nur noch als Fahrradgarage und Ausweichfläche, doch stellt es eine direkte und authentische Verknüpfung zwischen der gewachsenen Struktur des

former carpenter's workshop, which was converted to a pharmacy at one point, is now also owned by the residents.

The new building turns its small end towards the village street, imitating the village with its pointed gable and receding behind the adjoining historic building a good two steps. But the eye remains fixed on the new, because it plays with both familiar and special elements: the color of the facade, the rich dark red that was taken from the nearby bricks, is familiar, but it is made up of narrow, anodized metal panels – completely foreign and unfamiliar, yet still welcoming. This facade does not need anything else; the functional aspects – front door, garage door, windows – are mere suggestions.

What begins so narrowly on the street front gains in depth and width due to the L-shape of the floor plan, which follows the spatial conditions of the lot. The new building meets the existing ones at a right angle, creating a small courtyard. Used as an open space for the café, it offers the family both light and privacy.

The kitchen, dining and living rooms have been unified on the ground floor. There are no doors; a single step, a change of direction, a single-flight staircase and an atrium which extends through the short side of the floor plan to the pointed roof characterize the areas of the building without walling them off. The openness increases with the depth of the house; the view from inside falls straight into the garden courtyard, where delicate

historischen Ortskerns und dem neu geschaffenen Familiensitz her. Die Neubauten – das „Langhaus" für die Kinder und das „Scheunenhaus" – sind zweigeschossig mit Satteldach und wurden dem Bestand entsprechend giebelständig an der Straßenfront ausgerichtet. Der durch die Positionierung des „Langhauses" entstehende schmale Hof weitet sich in der Tiefe und wird an seinem „Kopfende" von dem eingeschossigen „Scheunenhaus" gefasst. Mit einem großen offenen Raum zum Wohnen, Essen und Kochen sowie dem Schlafbereich der Eltern nimmt Letzteres die gesamte Grundstücksbreite ein. Breite Fensterfronten öffnen sich sowohl auf den Hof wie auch zum rückwärtig anschließenden Garten, sodass der Baukörper eine einladende Transparenz erhält. Erschlossen werden die beiden Neubauten über einen gemeinsamen Eingang im Hof, der so an ihrer Schnittstelle platziert ist, dass die bauliche Zweigliederung im Inneren zugunsten der derzeitigen Nutzung als Einfamilienhaus quasi aufgehoben wird. Während der Sanierung fiel die Entscheidung, das Fischerhäuschen von seinem ehemals weißen Putz zu befreien, um den darunter liegenden Backstein freizulegen. Durch seine Kubatur und Farbigkeit inspiriert, wirken die Neubauten mit ihrem lichtgrauen mineralischen Putz, generiert aus dem hellsten Ton des Ziegels, skulptural, fast abstrakt – und dennoch maximal neutral. In diesem Duktus sind auch die Ziegeldeckung ohne Dachüberstand und der in die betonierte Hoffläche übergehende Sockel gehalten, die die Form auf ein Minimum reduzieren. Doch die handwerkliche Detaillierung der horizontalen Besenstruktur des Putzes oder die in allen drei Bauteilen ohne Leibung eingesetzten Lärchenholzfenster erzeugen eine wohltuende Haptik. Und nicht zuletzt schafft auch die Positionierung der Häuser als kleines Hofensemble eine familiäre Atmosphäre, in der Nähe immer gegeben, aber nicht zwingend ist.

supports in front of the large glazed facade are barely noticeable.

House J

About five years later, JSWD realized a construction project similar to Building F on the opposite side of the street a little further along. On a plot of land that also directly fronted the street, they found a historic fisherman's house with numerous additions and extensions. Here, too, previous users had not only lived, but also worked. From a fishery to a carpenter's workshop, from a car repair shop to hot mangle, each of the various activities left its own traces on the built structures. The architects decided to tidy up the property and – in accordance with the village's conservation statutes – only to preserve the fisherman's house. Because of its low ceiling height, it now only serves as a bicycle garage and additional storage space; however it creates a direct and authentic link between the organic structure of the historic town center and the newly created family home. The new buildings – the "long house" for the children and the "barn house" – have pitched roofs and have been aligned with their gables to the street front in order to blend with the surrounding historic buildings. The narrow courtyard created by the positioning of the two-storied "long house" widens the further back it goes and is enclosed at its "head end" by the one-story "barn house." The latter takes up the entire width of the property and encloses a large open space for living, eating and cooking, as well as the parents' sleeping area. Wide windows open onto both the courtyard and the rear garden, giving the building an inviting transparency. The two new buildings are accessed via a common entrance in the courtyard, which is positioned at their interface in such a way that the physical division between the two building sections is virtually eliminated inside, to the benefit of the current use as a single-family home.

During the renovation, the decision was made to remove the existing white plaster from the facade of the fisherman's house in order to expose the brick underneath. The new buildings, which are clad in light gray mineral plaster generated from the brightest tone of the brick, have been inspired by this historical building's cubature and colorfulness; they appear sculptural, almost abstract – and yet maximally neutral. This style continues in the roof tiles without roof overhang and the plinth which merges with the concrete surface of the courtyard, both of which reduce the shape to a minimum. But the skillful detailing of the horizontal "broom structure" on the plaster facade and the larch-framed windows, which have been used in all three building section components without reveal, create a pleasant feel. And last but not least, the positioning of the buildings as a small courtyard ensemble creates a familiar atmosphere in which closeness is always present but never forced.

Bundesumweltministerium
BMU Berlin

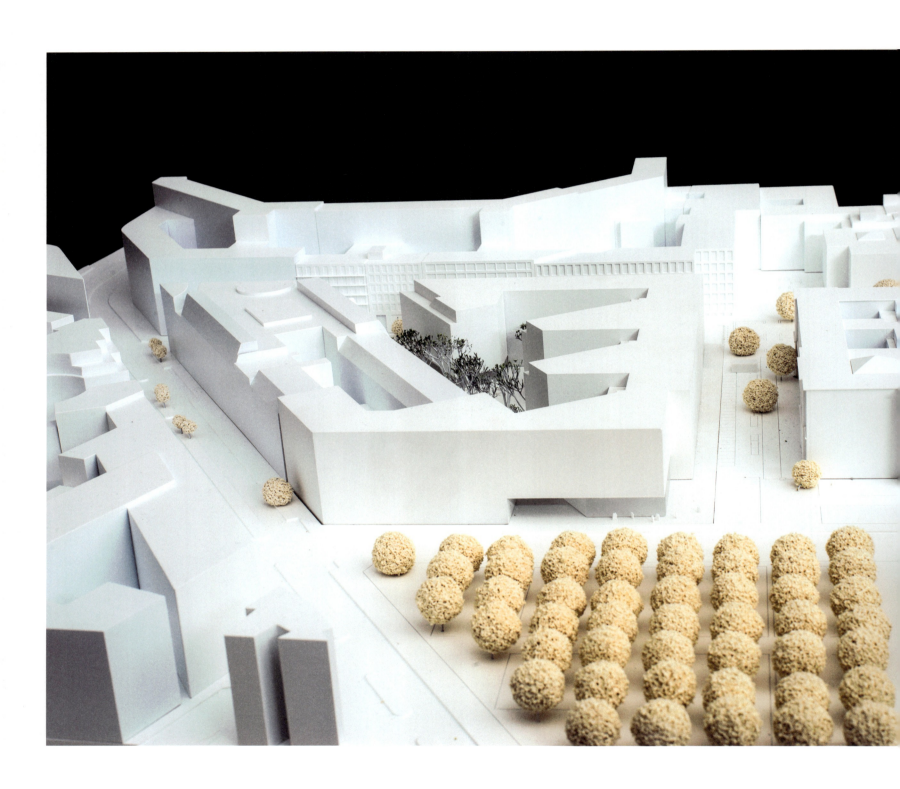
222

Erweiterung Dienstgebäude des Bundesministeriums für Umwelt, Naturschutz und nukleare Sicherheit, Berlin-Mitte

Es ist eine Selbstverständlichkeit, dass der Sitz des Bundesministeriums für Umwelt, Naturschutz und nukleare Sicherheit (BMU) ein Leuchtturmprojekt für nachhaltiges Bauen sein muss. Doch gepaart mit der Forderung nach maximaler Ausnutzung und hoher Verdichtung des mitten in Berlin gelegenen Grundstücks ergibt sich eine fast widersprüchliche Aufgabe, die zu lösen 25 Teams aus Architekten und Landschaftsarchitekten eingeladen waren. JSWD und RMP Stephan Lenzen Landschaftsarchitekten (Bonn) überzeugten mit dem Entwurf einer urbanen und zeitgemäßen Arbeitswelt, die sich organisch mit einem Landschaftsgarten verknüpft, und wurden mit einem von zwei ersten Preisen ausgezeichnet.

Das denkmalgeschütze Bestandsgebäude des BMU sitzt an der schrägen Westflanke des Grundstücks, an seinem südlichen Kopf schließt die Vattenfall Energiezentrale an. Mit ihrem Neubau zeichnen JSWD die Kanten sauber nach und schließen den bis dahin an drei Seiten offenen Block. Die neue Großfigur des Ministeriums entspricht der Körnung der Umgebung, die von eindrucksvollen historischen Solitärbauten wie dem direkt benachbarten Abgeordnetenhaus Berlin, dem Gropiusbau oder dem Bundesrat geprägt ist. Verschiedene Epochen nutzten unterschiedliche Ansätze, um die großen Volumina zu gliedern und zu erschließen. JSWD kontrastieren hier die formale Strenge des Äußeren mit einer organischen Öffnung des Baukörpers im Inneren. Dadurch entsteht ein großzügiger, mit dem Gebäude verzahnter Blockinnenraum, der parkähnlich gestaltet und mit Bäumen bepflanzt wird. Die grüne Mitte des Blocks, so die Jury, werde damit zum eigentlichen identitätsstiftenden Ort für das gesamte Gebäudeensemble und strahle dies auch in den Stadtraum aus.

JSWD entwickelten für die Fassade eine umlaufende Struktur aus Recyclingbeton-Fertigteilen, wodurch auch die charakteristische Hülle den Anspruch an ein energieeffizientes Lowtech-Haus kommuniziert. Die tiefen Laibungen schützen die Büros vor zu starker Sonneneinstrahlung und sommerlicher Überhitzung, während die sich nach unten verjüngenden Elemente den Blick vom Arbeitsplatz nach draußen freigeben.

Die knapp 30000 Quadratmeter Nutzfläche des siebengeschossigen Erweiterungsbaus des BMU sind in vier Schichten organisiert: In den beiden Untergeschossen befinden sich Parkplätze und die Lieferzone; im Erdgeschoss verbinden sich die Sondernutzungen mit dem Gartenraum; die Arbeitswelt verteilt sich auf sechs Bürogeschosse und darüber liegt die Dachlandschaft mit Sonnendeck. Der homogen gestaltete Block erhält durch einen zweigeschossigen Rücksprung an der Niederkirchnerstraße eine eindeutige Zäsur, die auf der dem Abgeordnetenhaus zugewandten Seite einen Vorplatz entstehen lässt, der den hier gelegenen Haupteingang wirkungsvoll in Szene setzt. Durch die großzügige Magistrale erhält der Gebäudekomplex eine klare Ordnung. An drei Punkten dieser zentralen Achse bilden offene Treppen und Erschließungskerne repräsentative Zugänge zu den Büroetagen. Die großen, flexibel teilbaren Konferenz- und Schulungsräume sowie die Kantine sind mit Ausrichtung auf den Landschaftsgarten an der Magistrale aufgefädelt, was den Mitarbeitern und Besuchern des Hauses die Orientierung erleichtert. Die Büroetagen sind je nach Lage als Zwei- oder Dreibund ausgebildet, wobei die Struktur so flexibel ist, dass sie sich als Zellen- oder Kombibüros sowie als Cluster organisieren lassen. Die über zwei Geschosse gestaltete Dachlandschaft ist in Teilen intensiv begrünt und mit Sitzstufen und Terrassen einladend gestaltet, während der extensiv begrünte Bereich Platz für Fotovoltaikmodule bietet.

Federal Ministry of the Environment (BMU), Berlin

Building Extension of the Federal Ministry for the Environment, Nature Conservation and Nuclear Safety, Berlin-Mitte

It goes without saying that the extension of the headquarters of the Federal Ministry for the Environment, Nature Conservation and Nuclear Safety (BMU) had to be a beacon project for sustainable construction. However, the demand for maximum utilization, combined with the high-density location in the center of Berlin, resulted in an almost contradictory task, which 25 invited teams of architects and landscape architects had to solve. The jury awarded one of two first prizes to JSWD Architekten from Cologne and RMP Stephan Lenzen Landschaftsarchitekten from Bonn. The winning design creates an urban and contemporary working environment that is organically linked to a landscape garden.
The existing site consists of the historical BMU building located on the sloping west side of the property and the Vattenfall Energy Center adjacent to the south. JSWD's new building extension neatly traces the edges and closes the block from east to west, which was previously open on three sides. The new large-scale structure respectfully responds to the scale and density of the surroundings, which is characterized by impressive historical buildings from various epochs, such as the directly neighboring Berlin House of Representatives, the Gropius building or the Federal Council building. In their design, JSWD juxtaposes the formal rigor of the exterior building structure with an organic, soft green opening onto its interior. This creates a spacious, park-like courtyard with numerous trees that interlaces with the new building extension. According to the jury, the green center becomes the actual identity for the entire building block and radiates into the surrounding urban space.
For the facade, JSWD developed an encompassing structure made of prefabricated elements produced from recycled concrete. Through this design, the distinctive facade visually communicates the aspiration to be an energy-efficient, low-tech building. The deep soffits protect the offices from excessive sunlight and overheating in summer, while the downward tapering elements allow visual connection from the offices to the outside.
The nearly 30000 square meters of usable space in the BMU's seven-story extension are organized into four programmatic layers, which are seamlessly interwoven with the new landscaped space and Berlin-Mitte. Two underground levels accommodate parking spaces and the delivery zone. Special-purpose spaces at street level expand towards and connect with the inner garden. Here, a two-story recess along Niederkirchnerstrasse forms a clear break in the homogeneously designed block, which creates a forecourt on the side facing

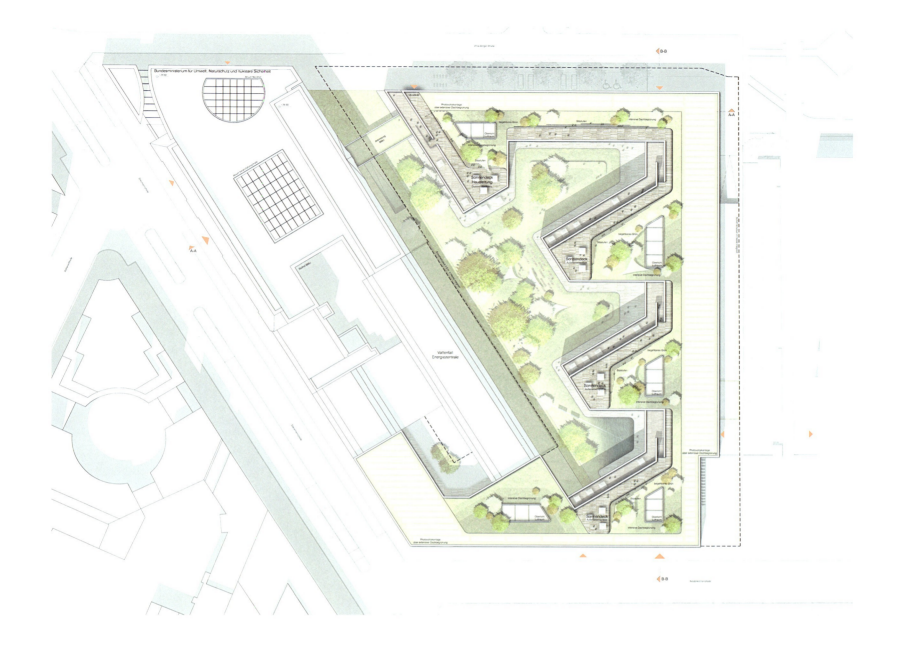

the House of Representatives, effectively framing the main entrance. Above, office spaces are spread over six floors organized by a generous 'avenue' that runs through the building providing order. At three points on this central axis, open stairs and access points form prestigious entrances to the office floors. The large, flexibly divisible conference rooms, training rooms and the canteen are located along this avenue with a view towards the landscaped inner courtyard, offering clear orientation for employees and visitors alike. Depending on the location, the office floors are designed as two or three-tier units; however, the flexible structure also allows the layout of single or combined clusters.
The landscaped roof extends over two levels, which are partially greened and designed with inviting seating steps and terraces. The extensively greened area offers space for photovoltaic panels.

Nachhaltige Quartiersentwicklung
Sustainable Urbanism

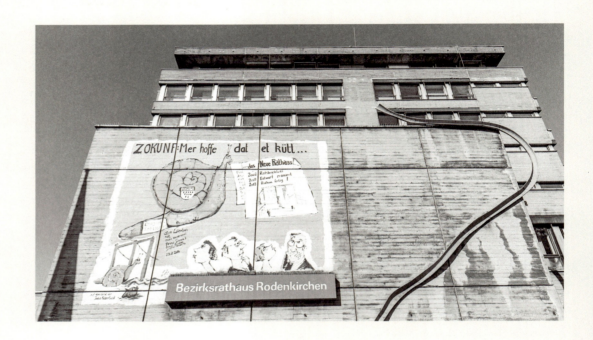

Ein Gespräch mit Christian Mammel und Mario Pirwitz (beide Associate Partner, JSWD) über Zeitgeist, Wandlungsfähig- und Langlebigkeit von Architektur und Städtebau in Zeiten des Klimawandels.

A conversation with Christian Mammel and Mario Pirwitz (both Associate Partners, JSWD) about the spirit of the times and the adaptability and longevity of architecture and urban development in the era of climate change.

Herr Mammel und Herr Pirwitz, Sie stehen als Associate Partner gewissermaßen für die nachwachsende Generation bei JSWD. Wie nehmen Sie die gegenwärtigen Klimaschutzproteste der noch weitaus jüngeren „Generation Greta" wahr?
Christian Mammel: Mir gefällt daran, dass das Thema in der Mitte der Gesellschaft angekommen ist, auch wenn es vielleicht ein wenig einseitig betrieben wird. Ich sehe zugleich aber auch die Gefahr eines „grünen Populismus". Alle wollen jetzt nachhaltig sein, wissen aber oft nicht recht, was das bedeutet. Das betrifft auch Bauherren. Selbstverständlich sind unsere Gebäude alle energieeffizient. Wir beziehen den Begriff der Nachhaltigkeit aber auch auf die Gestaltung. Was über viele Jahrzehnte hinweg als „schön" gilt und funktioniert, wird akzeptiert und bleibt erhalten.

Mr. Mammel and Mr. Pirwitz, as associate partners you represent the younger generation at JSWD. How do you perceive the current climate protests of the much younger "Generation Greta?"
Christian Mammel: What I like is that the topic has reached the center of society, even if it's perhaps a little one-sided. At the same time, I also see the danger of "green populism." Everyone wants to be sustainable now, but they often don't really know what that means. This also applies to building owners. Naturally, all of our buildings are energy-efficient. We relate the concept of sustainability to sustainable design. Buildings that are considered "beautiful" and functional for many decades remain well-accepted and are thus spared the wrecking ball.
Mario Pirwitz: Viewed on an urban planning scale, we observe

Mario Pirwitz: In einem städtebaulichen Maßstab betrachtet, beobachten wir, dass beispielsweise Stadträume der 1960er und 1970er Jahre immer weniger Akzeptanz genießen. Das liegt nicht nur daran, dass die damalige Qualität des Baumaterials aus heutiger Sicht oft minderwertig ist, sondern vor allem an dem unsensiblen Umgang im Bezug auf dauerhafte städtebauliche Grundsätze.

Meinen Sie das Rathaus Rodenkirchen, das bald durch einen Neubau von JSWD ersetzt wird?
CM: Das Rathaus Rodenkirchen wird vor allem deswegen abgerissen, weil sich seit über 40 Jahren niemand darum gekümmert hat, obwohl das Gebäude denkmalwürdig gewesen wäre. Heute ist die Substanz zerschlissen. Aber auch der Stadtraum um das Rathaus ist problematisch: Es gibt viele undefinierte Restflächen, dunkle Ecken, in denen sich niemand wohl fühlt und die mit dazu geführt haben, dass das Gebäude keine Akzeptanz mehr erfahren hat.

Was wurde falsch gemacht?
CM: Vielleicht müsste die Frage eher lauten: Woran liegt es, dass andere städtebauliche Konzepte beliebter sind? Sehr viele Menschen fühlen sich in klassischen Stadträumen wohl, die Gründerzeitviertel mit Blockrandbebauung und durchgehender Traufhöhe haben vor über 100 Jahren funktioniert und werden vermutlich in 50 Jahren noch genauso gefragt sein. Das mag konservativ klingen, ist aber erstmal nur eine Feststellung. Seit den 1950er Jahren haben Architekten und Stadtplaner sich nicht gescheut, diese bewährten Strukturen zu negieren und maßstabsprengende Solitäre zu bauen, auch um die autogerechte Stadt zu verwirklichen. Diese Brüche sehen wir heute als Fehler an.

Können Sie nachvollziehen, warum Ihre Kollegen von damals diese Brüche wagten?
MP: Es gab eine Aufbruchstimmung, eine neue Zeit stand bevor. Die Technikbegeisterung war groß, der reibungslose Verkehrsfluss stand im Fokus, dadurch haben sich die Dimensionen und der Maßstab

that the urban spaces of the 1960s and 1970s enjoy less and less acceptance, for example. This is not only due to the fact that the quality of the building material at that time was often inferior from today's point of view but above all to the insensitive disregard of long-standing urban planning principles.

Are you referring to the Rodenkirchen town hall, which will soon be replaced by a new JSWD building?
CM: The Rodenkirchen town hall will be demolished due to over 40 years of neglect, even though the building was worthy of preservation. The building's substance is simply worn out. In addition, the urban space surrounding the town hall is problematic. For example, there are many undefined residual areas and unpleasant dark corners, which is why the building is no longer accepted.

What did the designers do wrong?
CM: Perhaps the question should be: Why is it that other urban planning concepts are more accepted? A lot of people feel comfortable in classic urban spaces. Industrial-era neighborhoods with perimeter development and continuous eaves worked well more than 100 years ago and will probably still be in demand 50 years from now. That may sound conservative, but it's my observation. Since the 1950s, architects and urban planners have not shied away from negating these tried and tested structures and building base structures of a completely different scale; these designs were also part of their effort to realize the car-friendly city. Today we regard these disruptions as mistakes.

Can you understand why your colleagues from that time period dared to take these steps?
MP: There was an optimistic spirit, a new era was imminent. The enthusiasm for technology was great. The focus was on the smooth flow of traffic, which changed the dimensions and scale of the city. Today there is a countermovement across Europe that wants to regain the pedestrian spaces that were once lost to motorists.

Der sperrige Solitär des Bonn-Centers aus den 1960er Jahren inmitten einer grünen, aber unstrukturierten Restfläche. The bulky solitaire of the Bonn Center from the 1960s amidst a green but unstructured surrounding area.

Der maßstäblich eingegliederte Neue Kanzlerplatz verknüpft die angrenzenden Stadtquartiere. The New Chancellor Square integrated to scale links the bordering city districts.

der Stadt verändert. Heute gibt es europaweit eine Gegenbewegung, die die einst an die Autofahrer verlorenen Räume für die Fußgänger zurückgewinnen will.

CM: Für uns geht es im Entwurf immer um den Kontext, das ist vielleicht der größte Unterschied zu den Kollegen, die vor über 50 Jahren als Architekten arbeiteten. Damals mag derjenige die meiste Aufmerksamkeit bekommen haben, dessen Entwurf sich am stärksten vom Bestand unterschied. Wir sehen das heute anders. Ein gutes Beispiel ist das Gebäude, in dem sich unser eigenes Büro befindet: Es fügt dem Ort eigentlich nur eine klare Kante hinzu und plötzlich verwandelt sich der ehemals zerfaserte Restraum zu einem Platz, auf dem jeden Tag das Leben spielt. Das halten wir für deutlich nachhaltiger, als eine große architektonische Geste zu bauen, die vielleicht dem Zeitgeist entspricht, aber in absehbarer Zeit nicht mehr verstanden wird.

MP: Ein gutes Beispiel für unseren Ansatz ist der Bundeskanzlerplatz in Bonn. Dort stand vorher eine Hochhausscheibe aus den 1960er Jahren, die viele unbrauchbare Restflächen erzeugt hat. Unser Entwurf für den Neuen Kanzlerplatz übernimmt zwar die Idee einer Landmarke mit einem 100 Meter hohen Punkthochhaus, kombiniert sie aber mit drei flacheren Blockbauten, mit denen eine Verdichtung der Stadt entsteht, die mit Gassen und Plätzen urbane Aufenthaltsqualitäten schafft …

CM: … und sich vor allem mit den umliegenden Bereichen vernetzt. Auf den ersten Blick sieht man da vielleicht nur unregelmäßige fünfeckige Blöcke, erst auf den zweiten Blick ist zu erkennen, dass die Formen der Baukörper sich in erster Linie aus den vorhandenen Wegen und Blickbeziehungen der Nachbarschaft entwickeln. Wir halten es für sehr nachhaltig, wenn sich ein großes neues Volumen wie der Neue Kanzlerplatz in die Stadt integriert und von den Menschen angenommen wird.

Ein Abriss ist aber doch nie nachhaltig, da die Energie, die für den Bau verwendet wurde, verloren geht. Wie entscheiden Sie, ob es sinnvoller ist neu oder weiterzubauen?

CM: Da spielen viele Kriterien eine Rolle. Es gibt Gebäude, die sich keiner neuen Nutzungen zuführen lassen, zum Beispiel Bürogebäude, bei denen tragende Trennwände eine Aufteilung im Sinne heutiger Arbeitswelten blockieren oder deren immense Gebäudetiefe ausschließlich Großraumbüros zulassen. Diese unflexiblen Strukturen verlieren irgendwann ihre Berechtigung.

MP: Beim Schwarz Projekt Campus war es uns wichtig, dass jeder der 5000 Arbeitsplätze die gleiche Qualität hat, in den Baukörpern also keine Rückseiten oder benachteiligten Ecken entstehen. Das erlaubt es dem Bauherrn, die Flächen jederzeit im Bestand neu aufteilen zu können.

Könnten denn diese Büros eines Tages auch in Wohnungen umgewandelt werden?

Die Neue Mitte Porz übernimmt existierende kleinteilige Strukturen.
Porz' New Center adopts existing detailed structures.

CM: For us, design is always about context, which is perhaps the biggest difference between us and the colleagues who worked as architects over 50 years ago. At that time, the designs that contrasted with their contextual surroundings received the most attention. Today it's a different story. The building in which our own office is located is a good example: it added a clear edge to the square, and suddenly the formerly frayed residual space was transformed into a place that is now filled with everyday activities. We consider this to be significantly more sustainable than building a large architectural gesture that may correspond to the spirit of the times but will likely no longer be appropriate in the future.

MP: A good example of our approach is the Bundeskanzlerplatz in Bonn. There existed a high-rise building from the 1960s, which created many unusable remaining areas. Our design for the new square adopts the idea of a landmark with a 100-meter high-rise building, but combines it with three flat block buildings that create urban density, with streets and squares…

CM: … and above all, it is interconnected with the surrounding areas. At first glance, you may only see irregular pentagonal blocks, but a second look reveals that the building shapes were primarily developed from the existing paths and visual relationships of the existing neighborhood. We consider it very sustainable if a large new volume like the Bundeskanzlerplatz is integrated into the city and is well accepted by the residents.

However, a demolition is never sustainable because the energy that was used for the construction is lost. How do you decide whether it makes more sense to construct a new building or adapt the existing one?

CM: Many criteria play a role in that decision. There are buildings

Das Stadtzentrum von Porz vor der Revitalisierung mit der nicht weiter nutzbaren Kaufhausruine. The town center of Porz before the revitalization, with the department store ruin that can no longer be used.

CM: Der Entwurf ist nicht darauf angelegt, aber ausgeschlossen ist das nicht.

Beim FLOW Tower in Köln ist es gelungen ...

CM: Das Gebäude war eine Ikone der 1970er Jahre, aber durch jahrelange Vernachlässigung nicht mehr als Bürostandort vermarktbar. Als um den Solitär herum nach und nach ein hochwertiges Wohnquartier entstand, das auch den Straßenlärm abschirmte, wurde der Umbau des FLOW Tower zu Wohnungen überhaupt erst zu einer Option. Durch die städtebauliche Ergänzung hatte das Gebäude wieder eine Zukunft.

MP: Da hat es funktioniert. Beim Projekt Neue Mitte Porz wurde zunächst untersucht, ob sich das alte Hertie-Kaufhaus für neue Nutzungen eignen könnte. Allerdings wären dabei so viele andere städtebauliche Nachteile entstanden, dass Abriss und Neubau deutlich sinnvoller erschienen – und dadurch auch ein neues Stück Stadt entstehen kann.

CM: Der Hertie-Bau in Porz konnte aufgrund seiner enormen Raumtiefe nur als Kaufhaus funktionieren. Die zukünftige kleinteiligere Stadtstruktur wird es den Bewohnern erleichtern, ihre jahrzehntelang blockierte Mitte wieder als Stadtzentrum zu sehen.

Bei der Erweiterung des Bundesministeriums für Umwelt in Berlin spielte das Thema Lowtech eine Rolle. Was ist darunter zu verstehen?

CM: Lowtech bedeutet, dass ein Gebäude weitgehend ohne die übliche technische Gebäudeausrüstung auskommt, dass es aber auch so organisiert ist, dass alle

Heutiger FLOW Tower: Hochwertiger Wohnraum anstelle von nicht mehr zeitgemäßen Bürogrundrissen
The present-day FLOW Tower: high-quality living space instead of the outdated office ground plan

Das ehemalige BDI-Hochhaus in Köln mit seiner markanten Grundform stand lange leer. The former BDI high-rise in Cologne with its striking basic form stood empty for a long time.

that cannot be repurposed, for example office buildings in which load-bearing partition walls block spatial revisions and modernization in accordance with today's standards or whose immense building depth only allows open-plan offices. These inflexible structures eventually lose their justification.

MP: With the Schwarz Project Campus, it was important to us that each of the 5,000 workplaces has the same quality so that no unfavorable corners were created in the buildings. This allows the client to be able to redistribute the space in the existing building at any time.

Could these offices one day be converted into apartments?

CM: The design was not based on this possibility, but it is not ruled out.

This was successfully achieved with the FLOW Tower in Cologne...

CM: The building was an icon of the 1970s, but due to years of neglect it was no longer marketable as a commercial office building. The conversion of the FLOW Tower into apartments only made sense after a high-end residential area had been developed around its base, which also shields it from street noise. Thanks to this urban expansion, the building had a future again.

MP: Well, it worked there, but it doesn't work everywhere. In the New Center project in Porz, we first examined whether the old Hertie department store could be suitable for reuse. However, there would have been so many other urban disadvantages that demolition and new construction seemed much more sensible and allowed for the creation of a new neighborhood.

CM: Due to its enormous depth, the Hertie building in Porz could only function as a department store. The future small-grain urban structure will make it easier for residents to once again see this area, which has been blocked for decades, as the city center.

The subject of low-tech played a role in the extension of the Federal Ministry for the Environment in Berlin. How should we understand this term?

Räume Tageslicht erhalten, es möglichst wenig innen liegende Räume hat usw. In Berlin wollen wir versuchen, ohne beweglichen Sonnenschutz auszukommen, weil der besonders störungs- und reparaturanfällig ist. Diese Dinge sind bereits im Entwurf angelegt.

MP: Die Haustechnik veraltet heute unheimlich schnell und muss dann mit hohem Aufwand nachgerüstet oder ersetzt werden. dadurch weniger Energie verbrauchen, nicht weil es auf besonders energieeffizienter Technik beruht, sondern weil es diese Technik erst gar nicht benötigt. So ein Haus wird heute, morgen und übermorgen funktionieren.

MP: Oft wird heutzutage der Faktor Mensch vergessen, der durch sein Verhalten, etwa indem er hin und wieder mal ein Fenster öffnet, ein hochkompliziertes

CM: Low-tech means that a building can largely do without the usual technical building services, but it also has to do with spatial organization: all rooms have daylight, create as few windowless interior rooms as possible, etc. In Berlin we wanted to try to get by without a movable sun protection system, because it is particularly susceptible to faults and repairs. We set out these goals in the design.

conference areas through the inner courtyard. As a result, the building will consume less energy, not as a result of particularly energy-efficient technology, but because it does not need this technology in the first place. A building like that will work today, tomorrow and the day after tomorrow.

MP: People are often forgotten by the system. But of course, through their behavior, for example by

Blick in die grüne Mitte des zukünftigen Schwarz Projekt Campus (Stand Wettbewerb)
View into the green center of the future Schwarz Project Campus (competition phase)

CM: Die Planung eines Lowtech-Gebäudes erfordert allerdings viel Hightech, denn über Simulationen überprüfen wir bereits am digitalen Modell, welche Auswirkungen unsere baukonstruktiven Entwurfsentscheidungen auf das Raumklima haben werden. Beim BMU haben wir bewusst einen einfachen Ansatz gewählt: Alle Büros liegen an der Fassade, es wird viel natürliches Licht über eingezogene Innenhöfe in die Konferenzbereiche gelangen. Das Gebäude wird Haustechniksystem schnell ad absurdum führen kann.

Haben Sie Vorbilder für Lowtech-Konzepte?

CM: Die Planer stehen da noch relativ am Anfang. Mit dem Büro von Werner Sobek haben wir bereits bei einigen Projekten zusammengearbeitet, und da kam schon mehrfach die Frage auf: Kann man das alles nicht ein bisschen einfacher machen? So einfach ist es dann natürlich nicht, schon

MP: Today's building technology is becoming obsolete quickly and then has to be retrofitted or replaced with great effort.

CM: However, the planning of a low-tech building requires a lot of high-tech, because we use simulations to check in digital models which effects our design decisions will have on the indoor climate. At the BMU, we deliberately chose a simple approach: all of the offices are located along the facade, and lots of natural light will enter the opening a window every now and then, they can quickly reduce a highly complicated building services system to absurdity.

Do you have role models for low-tech concepts?

CM: The planners are still at the beginning of this relatively new process. We have already worked with Werner Sobek's office on a number of projects, and the question has arisen several times: can we simplify this? It is not that easy, of

Gesamtperspektive des Schwarz Projekt Campus in Bad Friedrichshall (Stand Wettbewerb)
Overall perspective of the Schwarz Project Campus in Bad Friedrichshall (competition phase)

gar nicht in der Kommunikation mit den Bauherren, denn die müssen lernen, dass der Verzicht auf Technik zu ihrem Vorteil sein kann, sofern sie die gesamte Lebensdauer ihres Gebäudes in Betracht ziehen.

MP: Eine wichtige Frage ist auch, welches Baumaterial das nachhaltigste ist. Holz rückt derzeit zu Recht wieder in den Fokus. Wenn wir allerdings alle unsere Gebäude aus Holz bauen wollten, wäre es schnell komplett verbraucht. Naturstein hat nachweislich die beste Energiebilanz, er hält ewig, muss nur einmal aus dem Steinbruch geschnitten, bearbeitet und zur Baustelle gebracht werden. Aber wer baut sich heute ein Haus aus Naturstein? Nachhaltig ist seit jeher, das Material zu verwenden, welches lokal vorhanden ist. Recyclingbeton, bei dem zerkleinerter Abbruchbeton statt Sand und Kies als Zuschlagstoff verwendet wird, ist in einer Stadt wie Berlin in großen Mengen verfügbar. Unser Erweiterungsbau für das BMU könnte daher der weltweit größte mit Recyclingbeton errichtete Neubau werden.

CM: Auch ohne Holz und Grün an den Fassaden kann ein Gebäude nachhaltig sein. Einfachheit, Klarheit, Flexibilität und Schönheit haben für uns dabei mindestens genauso viel mit dem Begriff Nachhaltigkeit zu tun wie Energieeffizienz.

course, especially when it comes to communicating with the building clients, because they have to learn that doing without technology can be an advantage if they take the entire life cycle of their building into account.

MP: Another important question is which building material is the most sustainable. Wood is rightly coming back into focus. However, if we wanted to build all of our buildings out of wood, it would quickly be completely used up. Natural stone has proven to have the best energy balance, it lasts forever, only has to be cut from the quarry, processed and taken to the construction site. But who constructs a building of natural stone these days? It has always been sustainable to use locally available materials. Recycled concrete, which uses crushed concrete as an aggregate instead of sand and gravel, is available in large quantities in a city like Berlin. Our extension for the BMU could therefore become the largest new building in the world built with recycled concrete.

CM: A building can be sustainable even without wood and greenery on its facade. For us, simplicity, clarity, flexibility and beauty have at least as much to do with the notion of sustainability as energy efficiency.

Ausgewählte Bauten und Projekte 2000–2020
Selected Buildings and Projects 2000–2020

Schwarz Projekt Campus, Bad Friedrichshall ■1
für for Schwarz Immobilien Service GmbH & Co. KG
1. Preis Wettbewerb 1st award competition 2017
Fertigstellung 1. Bauabschnitt ca. completion 1st construction phase approx. 2025

Masterplan Koelnmesse 3.0, Köln Cologne ■2
für for Koelnmesse AG
1. Preis Wettbewerb 1st award competition 2016
Fertigstellung 1. Bauabschnitt ca. completion 1st construction phase approx. 2023

Ecole Brouch Primary school, Esch, Luxemburg Luxembourg
für die Stadt for the City of Esch
1. Preis Wettbewerb 1st award competition 2013
Fertigstellung 1. Bauabschnitt ca. completion 1st construction phase approx. 2021

Hybrid.M, München-Moosach Munich Moosach ■3
für die for Stadtwerke München
1. Preis Wettbewerb 1st award competition 2014
mit with LAND
Fertigstellung ca. completion approx. 2022

Neuer Kanzlerplatz, Bonn ■4
für die for Art-Invest RE
1. Preis Wettbewerb 1st award competition 2015
Fertigstellung ca. completion approx. 2022

Waldviertel, Wohnquartier Residential Area in Rodenkrichen, Köln Cologne
für die for Bauwens GmbH & Co. KG + Convalor PP GmbH
1. Preis Wettbewerb 1st award competition 2013
Fertigstellung ca. completion approx. 2022

Cube Factory 577, Leverkusen
für die for CUBE Real Estate GmbH
1. Preis Wettbewerb 1st award competition 2017
Fertigstellung ca. completion approx. 2022

Moxy Hotel, Flughafen Köln/Bonn ■5
für die for Art-Invest RE
1. Preis Wettbewerb 1st award competition 2018
Fertigstellung ca. completion approx. 2022

Rathaus und Janshof, Brühl ■6
für die Stadt for the City of Brühl
1. Preis Wettbewerb 1st award competition 2017
mit with RMP Landschaftsarchitekten
Fertigstellung ca. completion approx. 2021

Neue Mitte Porz, Köln Cologne
Direktauftrag von direct commission from moderne stadt mbh, Köln
Machbarkeitsstudie feasibility study 2015
Fertigstellung Haus 1 ca. completion building 1 approx. 2021

Ergänzungsbau Theaterhaus Stuttgart ■7
für die Landeshauptstadt for the state capitol of Stuttgart
3. Preis Wettbewerb 3rd award competition 2020

Masterplan Bezirk Ouhai, Wenzhou, China ■8
für die Stadt for the city of Wenzhou
Wettbewerb competition 2020
mit with Artform

Büro- und Geschäftshaus Luisenstraße, Düsseldorf
für for Becken Development GmbH
1. Preis Wettbewerb 1st award competition 2018
Projektstart project start 2020

9

11

13

15

10

12

14

16

Betriebshöfe der Stadt Work yard of the City of **Wolfsburg** und der and the **Wolfsburger Abfallwirtschaft + Straßenreinigung** ■9
Zuschlag award 2014
Fertigstellung 1. Bauabschnitt completion 1st construction phase 2020

Bürogebäude der AOK mit Gesundheitszentrum, Pforzheim ■10
für die for AOK Baden-Württemberg
1. Preis Wettbewerb 1st award competition 2018
Projektstart ca. project start approx. 2020

Erweiterung Landratsamt Alb-Donau-Kreis, Ulm
für den for Alb-Donau-Kreis
1. Preis Wettbewerb 1st award competition 2015
Fertigstellung completion approx. 2020

Bezirksrathaus Rodenkirchen, Köln Cologne
für die Gebäudewirtschaft der Stadt Köln for the building management oft he City of Cologne
1. Preis Wettbewerb 1st award competition 2018
Projektstart ca. project start approx. 2020

Masterplan Fort Zbarz, Warschau, Polen Warsaw, Poland ■11
für for Atenor S. A.
Wettbewerb competition 2019
mit with Grupa 5 Architekci

Erweiterung des Bundesumweltministeriums Expansion Ministry **BMU, Berlin** ■12
für die for Bundesanstalt für Immobilienaufgaben BImA
1. Preis Wettbewerb 1st award competition 2019
mit with RMP Landschaftsarchitekten

UKSH – Universitätsklinikum University Medical Center **Schleswig-Holstein, Campus Kiel** ■13
für for BAM Deutschland AG + Vamed Health Project GmbH
Zuschlag award ÖPP-Verfahren 2014
mit with HDR, tsj, ash
Fertigstellung completion 2019

UKSH – Universitätsklinikum University Medical Center **Schleswig-Holstein, Campus Lübeck**
für for BAM Deutschland AG + Vamed Health Project GmbH
Zuschlag award ÖPP-Verfahren 2014
mit with HDR, tsj, ash
Fertigstellung completion 2019

The Icon Vienna, Wien, Österreich Vienna, Austria ■14
für die for SIGNA Development, Wien
Eigentümer owner Allianz RE
1. Preis Wettbewerb 1st award competition 2013
mit with BEHF architects
Fertigstellung completion 2019
beantragt applied for LEED Platin + BREEAM Excellent

Parkhaus + Wohnen in Echternach, Luxemburg Luxembourg ■15
für die for MC Luxembourg
Direktauftrag direct commission 2019, Entwurf concept

Wohn- und Geschäftcenter in Atlanta, USA ■16
für die for Jamestown LP, Atlanta
1. Preis Wettbewerb 1st award competition 2019
mit with Handel Architects

BürgerRatHaus, Essen
für die Stadt for the City of Essen
Ankauf Wettbewerb acquisition competition 2019
mit with GINA Barcelona Architects

17

19

23

18

20

22
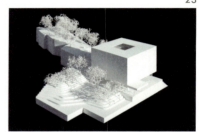
24

Showroom Zgoll, Korschenbroich
für die for zgoll: GmbH
Direktauftrag direct commission 2016
Fertigstellung completion 2019

Neues Kesselhaus, Gelsenkirchen ■17
für die for Vivawest Wohnen GmbH
1. Preis Wettbewerb 1st award competition 2014
Fertigstellung completion 2018

Hauptverwaltung der GAG Headquarter, Köln Cologne ■18
für die for GAG Immobilien AG
1. Preis Wettbewerb 1st award competition 2015
Fertigstellung completion 2018

Wohn- und Geschäftshaus Kolb 13, Frankfurt a. M.
für die for MEAG MUNICH ERGO AM GmbH
Direktauftrag direct commission 2013
Fertigstellung completion 2018
KfW 70

Bahnhofsareal HBF + Busbahnhof Main Railway Station + Bus Terminal Wuppertal ■19
für die Stadt for the City of Wuppertal
1. Preis Wettbewerb 1st award competition 2004
Fertigstellung completion 2018

Ecole Centrale Clausen, Luxemburg Luxembourg
für die Stadt Luxemburg for the City of Luxembourg
1. Preis Wettbewerb 1st award competition 2008
Fertigstellung completion 2017

Büro- und Geschäftshaus Europe Plaza, Stuttgart
für die for Fay Projects GmbH
1. Preis Wettbewerb 1st award competition 2008
Fertigstellung completion 2017
DGNB Platin

FLOW Tower, Köln Cologne
für die for GARBE Immobilien-Projekte GmbH + ABG Gruppe
Direktauftrag direct commission 2012
Fertigstellung completion 2017

Haus der Europäischen Geschichte House of European History, Brüssel, Belgien Brussels, Belgium ■20
für das for the EU-Parlament und die and the EU-Kommission
1. Preis Wettbewerb 1st award competition 2010
mit with Chaix & Morel et Ass. + TPF Engineering
Fertigstellung completion 2017

Straßenmeisterei und Rettungswache, Magstadt ■21
für den Landkreis for the district of Böblingen
1. Preis Wettbewerb 1st award competition 2017

Deutsches Tapetenmuseum, Kassel ■22
für das Land Hessen for the federal state of Hesse
2. Preis Wettbewerb 2nd award competition 2017

House of Elements, Essen ■23
für die for HOCHTIEF PE GmbH/TEAMRHEINRUHR PE GmbH
Direktauftrag direct commission 2014
Mieter tenant Brenntag Group
Fertigstellung completion 2017
LEED Gold

Büros + Wohnen Offices + Living in Navile Tre, Bologna, Italien Italy
für for Valdadige Costruzioni, Verona
1. Preis Wettbewerb 1st award competition 2008
mit with cfk architetti
Fertigstellung Bürohaus completion of office building 2016

Helios Klinik, Schleswig
für die for HELIOS Kliniken Gruppe
Zuschlag award 2011
mit with HDR
Fertigstellung completion 2016

Medienzentrum des SWR Media Center SWR, Baden-Baden ■24
für den for SWR Südwestfunk
2. Preis Wettbewerb 2nd award competition 2016

25

27

29

31

26

28

30

32

Kurt-Masur-Schule Primary School, **Leipzig** ■25
für die Stadt for the City of Leipzig
1. Preis Wettbewerb 1st award competition 2008
Fertigstellung completion 2015
PHHP-Standard

Haus F, Köln-Weiß Cologne Weiß
Bauherr privat private client
Direktauftrag direct commission
Fertigstellung completion 2015

Center for Windpower Drives, CWD, Aachen ■26
für den for BLB NRW
Zuschlag award 2011
Fertigstellung completion 2015

Sitz der Luxemburgischen Finanzaufsicht, CSSF Headquarter, **Luxemburg** Luxembourg ■27
für die for Commission de Surveillance du Secteur Financier
Zuschlag award 2011
mit with architecture & aménagement S.A.
Fertigstellung completion 2015

Siemens Campus, Erlangen
für die for Siemens RE
3. Preis Wettbewerb 3rd award competition 2014

Thyssenkrupp Quartier Thyssenkrupp Quarter **Essen** ■28
für die for ECE Projektmanagement G.m.b.H
1. Preis Wettbewerb 1st award competition 2007
mit with Chaix & Morel et Ass.
Eigentümer owner Thyssenkrupp AG
Fertigstellung completion 2010–2014
DGNB Gold (Q1)

Wohnquartier Residential Area **Reiterstaffel, Köln** Cologne
für die for Corpus Sireo Real Estate
2. Preis Wettbewerb 2nd award competition 2010
Fertigstellung 5 MF-Wohnhäuser completion 5 MF apartement buldings 2014

Fraunhofer-Institute Fraunhofer Instituts **ILT + IPT, Aachen**
für die for Fraunhofer-Gesellschaft e.V.
Zuschlag award 2009
Fertigstellung completion 2014

Zentrale der Enervie AG Enervie Headquarter, **Hagen**
für die for Enervie Südwestfalen Energie + Wasser AG ■29
1. Preis Wettbewerb 1st award competition 2011
Fertigstellung completion 2014
LEED Gold

Meet + Eat, Herzogen-Aurach
für die for Adidas AG ■30
Ankauf Wettbewerb acquisition competition 2014

Seniorenwohnhaus, Düren ■31
Direktauftrag von der direct commission from Seniorenhaus GmbH der Cellitinnen zur Hl. Maria
Fertigstellung completion 2013

AOK Regionaldirektion mit Kundencenter, Essen ■32
für die for HOCHTIEF PE GmbH + Bauwens GmbH & Co. KG
1. Preis Wettbewerb 1st award competition 2010
Fertigstellung completion 2013
DGNB Gold

Telekom Flagship-Store, Köln Cologne
Direktauftrag von der direct commission from Telekom AG
Fertigstellung completion 2013

Nano-Institut, LMU München Munich
für das for Staatliches Bauamt München
2. Preis Wettbewerb 2nd award competition 2013

Kita Day Care Center **Miniapolis, Thyssenkrupp Quartier** Thyssenkrupp Quarter **Essen**
Direktauftrag von der direct commission from Thyssenkrupp RE
Betreiber operator DRK Nordrhein Soziale Dienste gGmbH
Fertigstellung completion 2012

 33
 35
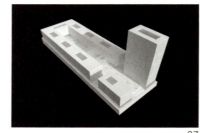 37
 39

 34
 36
 38
 40

Musikzentrum Music Center, Bochum ■33
für die Stadt for the City of Bochum
2. Preis Wettbewerb 2nd award competition 2012

GreenCity Zürich, Schweiz Zurich, Switzerland ■34
für die for Losinger Marazzi AG, Bern
1. Preis Baufeld 1st award construction field B6
Wettbewerb competition 2012

Siemens Headquarter, München Munich
für die for Siemens RE
Wettbewerb competition 2011

Messehalle Süd, Berlin
für die for Messe Berlin GmbH
3. Preis Wettbewerb 3rd award competition 2011
mit with Chaix & Morel et Ass.

Thyssenkrupp-Haus, Berlin ■35
für die for Thyssenkrupp AG
2. Preis Wettbewerb 2nd award competition 2011
mit with Chaix & Morel et Ass.

Telekom Flagship-Store, Frankfurt a. M.
Direktauftrag von der direct commission from Telekom AG
mit with Interbrand
Fertigstellung completion 2011

ICE-Terminal Köln Messe/Deutz, Köln Cologne
für die for DB Station & Service AG + DB Netz AG
1. Preis Wettbewerb 1st award competition 2000
Sanierung Altbau bis restrcuturing of old buildiung until 2010

Fraunhofer-Institut Fraunhofer Institute TZA, Darmstadt ■36
für die for Fraunhofer-Gesellschaft e.V.
Zuschlag award 2007
Fertigstellung completion 2010

Bâtiment Office Center Jean Monnet 2, Luxemburg Luxembourg ■37
für die for the EU-Kommission über das Land through the country of Luxemburg
1. Preis Wettbewerb 1st award competition 2010
mit with Chaix & Morel et Ass. + architecture & aménagement S.A.

Halle 11 im Rheinauhafen, Köln Cologne
für die for Pareto GmbH + Provinzial RE
1. Preis Wettbewerb 1st award competition 2003
Fertigstellung completion 2009

Bahnhof Railway Station Cessange, Luxemburg Luxembourg ■38
für das for Ministère des Transports Luxembourg
3. Preis Wettbewerb 3rd award competition 2009

Fraunhofer-Institut Fraunhofer Institute IZS, Stuttgart ■39
für die for Fraunhofer-Gesellschaft e.V.
1. Preis Wettbewerb 1st award competition 2009

MED Campus Graz, Österreich Austria
für die for Medizinische Universität Graz
Wettbewerb competition 2009
mit with Chaix & Morel Ass.

Wohn- und Geschäftshaus Maternusplatz mit Kopfbebauung, Köln Cologne
Direktauftrag von der direct commission from Maternusplatz GmbH 2001
Fertigstellung completion 2009

Hotel am Quai de Seine, Paris, Frankreich France ■40
für for Cofitem-Cofimur, Paris
1. Preis Wettbewerb 1st award competition 2004
mit with Chaix & Morel Ass.
Fertigstellung completion 2008

 41
 43
 45
 47
 42
 44
 46
 48

Bahnhofsareal HBF Main Railway Station Area **Luxemburg** Luxembourg ■41
für die Stadt for the city of Luxemburg
1. Preis Wettbewerb 1st award competition 2005
Machbarkeitsstudie feasibility study 2008

Bühnen Köln, Oper + Schauspielhaus Opera and Playhouse, City of Cologne ■42
für die Stadt Köln
1. Preis Wettbewerb 1st award competition 2008
mit with Chaix & Morel Ass.
gestoppt stopped 2010

Bahnhofsareal HBF Main Railway Station Area **Bonn**
für die Stadt for the City of Bonn
1. Preisgruppe Wettbewerb 1st award group competition 2008

Grundschule Primary School **OGTS Mainzer Straße, Köln** Cologne ■43
für die Gebäudewirtschaft der Stadt Köln for the estate management of the City of Cologne
Zuschlag award 2005
Fertigstellung completion 2007

Constantin Höfe, Köln-Deutz Cologne Deutz ■44
für die for HOCHTIEF Projektentwicklung GmbH
Direktauftrag direct commission 2004
Fertigstellung completion 2006

Zentrale Zone Flughafen München Central Zone Airport Munich
für die for Flughafen München GmbH
1. Preisgruppe Wettbewerb 1st award group competition 2006

Internationales Kongresszentrum Bundeshaus Bonn, IKBB
für die Stadt for the City of Bonn
Ankauf Wettbewerb aquisition competition 2005

Fraunhofer-Institut Fraunhofer Institute **IZI, Leipzig**
für die for Fraunhofer-Gesellschaft e.V.
Ankauf Wettbewerb aquisition competition 2005

Kunsthochschule für Medien Art College, **KMH, Köln** Cologne ■45
Direktauftrag vom direct commission from BLB NRW 2002
Fertigstellung completion 2005

5 Schwebebahnhöfe Suspension Railway Stations, **Wuppertal** ■46
für die for WSW, Stadt City of Wuppertal
1. Preis Wettbewerb 1st award competition 1994
Fertigstellung completion 1999–2004

Art'otel im Rheinauhafen, Köln Cologne ■47
für for Gädeke & Landsberg
1. Preis Wettbewerb 1st award competition 2004
mit with Chaix & Morel Ass.

Campus Westend, Frankfurt a. M.
für die for Goethe-Universität Frankfurt a. M.
3. Preis Wettbewerb 3rd award competition 2004

Innenstadt Recklinghausen
für die Stadt for the City of Recklinghausen
1. Preis Wettbewerb 1st award competition 2004

Siemens Campus Isar-Süd, München Munich ■48
für die for Siemens AG
1. Preis Wettbewerb 1st award competition 2002
mit with BSV Büro für Stadt- und Verkehrsplanung
Masterplanung master planning 2003

Helene-Lohmann-Realschule Secondary School, **Witten**
für die Stadt for the City of Witten
1. Preis Wettbewerb 1st award competition 1999
Fertigstellung completion 2003

Gründungspartner
Founding Partners

JÜRGEN STEFFENS

Geboren 1960 in Trier | 1982–1989 Architekturstudium an der RWTH Aachen | 1989–1992 Mitarbeit im Büro von Behnisch + Partner, Stuttgart | 1992–1995 Assistent an der RWTH Aachen | 1992 Gründung des Büros Jaspert & Steffens Architekten in Köln mit Konstantin Jaspert | Seit 2000 Partner im Büro JSWD | 2001–2004 Lehrtätigkeit an verschiedenen deutschen Hochschulen | 2005 Professor i. V. an der TU Darmstadt | Seit 2003 im Vorstand des Vereins koelnarchitektur e. V., seit 2006 Vorstandsvorsitzender | Seit 2009 Gesellschafter der JSWD Architekten GmbH + Co. KG | Seit 2015 Gastprofessur an der School of Architecture and Design, Beijing Jiaotong University, China

Born 1960 in Trier (Treves), Germany | 1982–1989 studied architecture at RWTH Aachen | 1989–1992 worked at Behnisch + Partner, Stuttgart | 1992–1995 assistant at RWTH Aachen | 1992 cofounded Jaspert & Steffens Architekten in Cologne with Konstantin Jaspert | Since 2000 partner at JSWD | 2001–2005 teaching at various German universities | 2005 substitute professor at TU Darmstadt | Since 2003 member of the board of koelnarchitektur e. V. association | Since 2006 chairman of the board | Since 2009 shareholder at JSWD Architekten GmbH + Co. KG | Since 2015 visiting professorship at the "School of Architecture and Design", Beijing Jiaotong University, China

FREDERIK JASPERT

Geboren 1965 in Köln | 1986–1987 Studium Musik- und Theaterwissenschaften an der Universität Köln | 1987–1994 Architekturstudium an der RWTH Aachen | 1989 Mitarbeit im Büro Behnisch + Partner, Stuttgart | 1994 Diplom, Friedrich-Wilhelm-Preis der RWTH Aachen I 1995–1999 Mitarbeit im Büro von Gerkan, Marg und Partner (gmp), Hamburg/Aachen | 1996–2001 Assistent bei Prof. Volkwin Marg an der RWTH Aachen | 1998 Gründung des Büros WJD Architekten in Köln mit Olaf Drehsen | Seit 2000 Partner im Büro JSWD | Seit 2009 Gesellschafter der JSWD Architekten GmbH + Co. KG | 2010–2011 Gastprofessur an der RWTH Aachen

Born 1965 in Cologne, Germany | 1986–1987 studied music and drama at the University of Cologne | 1987–1994 studied architecture at RWTH Aachen | 1989 worked at Behnisch + Partner, Stuttgart |1994 Diploma, Friedrich Wilhelm Award of RWTH Aachen | 1995–1999 worked at Gerkan, Marg und Partner (gmp), Hamburg/Aachen | 1996–2001 assistant to Prof. Volkwin Marg at RWTH Aachen | 1998 founded WJD Architekten in Cologne with Olaf Drehsen | Since 2000 partner at JSWD | Since 2009 shareholder at JSWD Architekten GmbH + Co. KG | 2010–2011 visiting professorship at RWTH Aachen

OLAF DREHSEN

Geboren 1967 in Düren | 1987–1994 Architekturstudium an der RWTH Aachen | 1990–1993 Mitarbeit im Büro Behnisch + Partner, Stuttgart | 1994–1995 Mitarbeit im Büro Kowalski, Düsseldorf | 1995 Gründung eines eigenen Architekturbüros in Aachen | 1995–1998 Mitarbeit im Büro von Gerkan, Marg und Partner (gmp), Hamburg/Aachen | 1998 Gründung des Büros WJD Architekten in Köln mit Frederik Jaspert | Seit 2000 geschäftsführender Partner im Büro JSWD | Seit 2009 geschäftsführender Gesellschafter der JSWD Architekten GmbH & Co. KG I Seit 2019 Dozent an der UFS University of South Florida, SACD School of Architecture and Community Design, USA I Ab August 2020 Professor an der SACD

Born 1967 in Düren, Germany | 1987–1994 studied architecture at RWTH Aachen | 1990–1993 worked at Behnisch + Partner, Stuttgart | 1994–1995 worked at Kowalski in Düsseldorf | 1995 founded own architecture firm in Aachen | 1995–1998 worked at the office of Gerkan, Marg und Partner (gmp), Hamburg/Aachen | 1998 co-founded WJD Architekten in Cologne with Frederik Jaspert | Since 2000 managing partner at JSWD | Since 2009 sole managing partner of JSWD Architekten GmbH & Co. KG I Since 2019 Associate Professor at the UFS University of South Florida, SACD School of Architecture and Community Design, USA I From August 2020 Professor at SACD

KONSTANTIN JASPERT

Geboren 1961 in Trier | 1982–1989 Architekturstudium an der RWTH Aachen | 1989 Diplom, Friedrich-Wilhelm-Preis der RWTH Aachen | 1989–1992 Mitarbeit im Büro Schuster Architekten, Düsseldorf | 1991–1996 Assistent bei Prof. Volkwin Marg an der RWTH Aachen | 1992 Gründung des Büros Jaspert & Steffens Architekten in Köln mit Jürgen Steffens | 1999 Berufung in den BDA Köln | Seit 2000 Partner im Büro JSWD | 2001 Lehrauftrag an der Fachhochschule Koblenz | 2001–2004 Mitglied im Vorstand des BDA Köln | Seit 2009 Gesellschafter der JSWD Architekten GmbH + Co. KG

Born 1961 in Trier (Treves), Germany | 1982–1989 studied architecture at RWTH Aachen | 1989 Diploma, Friedrich Wilhelm Award of RWTH Aachen | 1989–1992 worked at Schuster Architekten, Düsseldorf | 1991–1996 assistant to Prof. Volkwin Marg at RWTH Aachen | 1992 cofounded Jaspert & Steffens Architekten in Cologne with Jürgen Steffens | 1999 appointment to the Cologne branch of the Association of German Architects (BDA) | Since 2000 partner at JSWD, Cologne| 2001 lecturer at the Koblenz University of Applied Sciences | 2001–2004 member of the board of the Cologne branch of the Association of German Architects (BDA) | Since 2009 shareholder at JSWD Architekten GmbH + Co. KG

Associate Partner
Associate Partners

MARIO PIRWITZ

Geboren 1978 in Aachen I 1999–2006 Architekturstudium an der RWTH Aachen I 2006 Diplom mit Auszeichnung I Verleihung der „Springorum Denkmünze" der RWTH Aachen für herausragende wissenschaftliche Leistungen I Bis 2005 Mitarbeit in verschiedenen Architekturbüros, u. a. tp bennett, London I Ab 2006 Mitarbeit im Büro Orbit Architects, London I 2007–2011 Projektleiter und Team Director im Büro Orbit Architects, London I 2011–2013 Projektleiter im Büro JSWD I Ab 2013 Projektpartner im Büro JSWD I Seit 2016 Gastkritiker und -redner an der Bartlett School of Architecture, London, und an der TH Köln I Seit 2017 Associate Partner im Büro JSWD

Born 1978 in Aix-la-Chapelle, Germany | 1999–2006 studied architecture at RWTH Aachen I 2006 diploma with honours I Awarded the "Springorum Medal" for outstanding academic achievements at RWTH Aachen I Until 2005 worked in various architecture offices, including tp bennett, London I 2007 research associate to the Chair of Supporting Structures, RWTH Aachen, Prof. Martin Trautz I 2011–2013 project manager at JSWD I Since 2013 project partnership at JSWD I Since 2016 guest critic and speaker at the Bartlett School of Architecture, London and at the TH Cologne I Since 2017 Associate Partner at JSWD

TOBIAS UNTERBERG

Geboren 1976 in Oberhausen I 1997–2000 Architekturstudium an der TU Dortmund I 2000–2004 Architekturstudium an der RWTH Aachen I 2004–2013 Projektleiter im Büro von Gerkan Marg und Partner (gmp), Aachen I 2008 Red Dot Design Award I 2013 Projektleiter im Büro JSWD I Ab 2014 Projektpartner im Büro JSWD I Seit 2017 Associate Partner im Büro JSWD

Born 1976 in Oberhausen, Germany I 1997–2000 studied architecture at TU Dortmund Germany I 2000–2004 studied architecture at RWTH Aachen I 2004–2013 project manager at the office of Gerkan Marg und Partner (gmp), Aachen I 2008 Red Dot Design Award I 2013 project manager at JSWD I Since 2013 project partnership at JSWD I Since 2017 Associate Partner at JSWD

CHRISTIAN MAMMEL

Geboren 1977 in Köln I 1997–2003 Architekturstudium an der RWTH Aachen I 2003 Diplom mit Auszeichnung I Verleihung der „Springorum Denkmünze" der RWTH Aachen für herausragende wissenschaftliche Leistungen I Bis 2004 Mitarbeit in verschiedenen Architekturbüros, u. a. Stücheli Architekten, Zürich I Seit 2004 Mitarbeit im Büro JSWD, Köln I 2007 Wissenschaftlicher Mitarbeiter am Lehrstuhl für Tragkonstruktionen, RWTH Aachen, Prof. Martin Trautz I Seit 2009 im Vorstand von koelnarchitektur e.V. I Ab 2009 Associate Partner im Büro JSWD

Born 1977 in Cologne, Germany I 1997–2003 studied in architecture at RWTH Aachen I 2003 diploma with honours I Awarded the "Springorum Medal" for outstanding academic achievements at RWTH Aachen I Until 2004 worked in various architecture offices, including Stücheli Architekten, Zurich I Since 2004 has worked at JSWD I 2007 research associate at the Chair of Supporting Structures, RWTH Aachen, Prof. Martin Trautz I Since 2009 member of the board of the koelnarchitektur e.V. association I Since 2009 Associate Partner at JSWD

PATRICK JAENKE

Geboren 1975 in Köln I 1995–2001 Architekturstudium an der RWTH Aachen I 1997–1998 Mitarbeit im Büro Hentrich Petschnigg und Partner (HPP), Köln I 2000–2001 Mitarbeit im Büro JSWD I 2001–2003 Mitarbeit im Büro von Gerkan Marg und Partner (gmp), Aachen I 2003–2009 Mitarbeit im Büro JSWD I Ab 2009 Associate Partner im Büro JSWD

Born 1975 in Cologne, Germany I 1995–2001 studied architecture at RWTH Aachen I 1997–1998 worked at the office of Hentrich-Petschnigg und Partner (HPP), Cologne I 2000–2001 worked at the office of JSWD I 2001–2003 employed at the office of Gerkan Marg und Partner (gmp), Aachen I 2003–2009 worked at JSWD I Since 2009 Associate Partner at JSWD

Mitarbeiter
Employees

2000–2020

Abraham Klagsbrun I Adam Wuttke I Agata Maiwald I Agnes Sobotta I Alessandro Zanola I Alexander Derstroff I Alexander Kreft I Alexandra Limar I Alexander Mielsch I Alexander Scholtysek I Alexandra Voss I Alia Mortada I Alicia Pedrosa Moreno I Alicja Bergmann I Alisa Rinderspacher I Ameline Dumouchel I Anastasiia Korovina I András Bódi I André Siering I Andrea Marxen I Andreas Lepert I Andreas Meyer I Andreas Rump I Andrés Conesa Rosique I Anette Rickert I Anika Knöll I Anna Becker I Anna Rozwadowska I Anna Rzymelka I Anna Schulz I Annabelle von Reutern I Anne Korfmacher I Annelen Schmidt I Annika Obst I Ann-Kristin Crusius I Anthea Dirks I Antonio Molina I Aresch Dastouri I Armin Memic I Armin Tillmann I Arno Pollmanns I Arzu Bastug I Asmaa Hithnawi I Barbara Jeanrond I Bartosz Czempiel I Bastian Scholz I Bernd Schultz I Bilal Sinir I Bin Yang I Burak Kilic I Carlota Estaun Martinez I Carolin Amann I Carsten Saggau I Celia Bosc I Chen Jiang I Chiara Fetha I Christian Klein I Christian Mammel I Christian Rothe I Christiane Lafeldt I Christina Codjambopoulo-Lindemann I Christoph Helbig I Christoph Köstel I Christoph Wildhack I Claire Dupré I Claudia D'Aloisio I Cora Kwiatkowski I Corinna Granich I Dagmar von Stranz I Daria Emsermann I Daria Smirnova I Dario Luzzi I Dierk Königs I Désirée Schmitz I Dirk Martin Claßen I Dominic Wanisch I Dominik Rosauer I Dongwei Liu I Efstratios Sianidis I Ekin Dilek I Elena Chernyak I Elena Kantorovitch I Elena Orlova I Elena Sarigelinoglu I Elisabeth Mohrs I Ellen Wölk I Elmar Schmidt-Bleker I Emilia Schulz I Emily Manzer I Eugen But I Eva Rüth I Fabio Galicia I Fangyuan Zhang I Fedaa Alsoki I Florian Gast I Florian Husemeyer I Francisco Fajardo I Franziska Humperdinck I Frank Hillesheim I Frank Peter Jäger I Frederike Wernicke I Friederike Legler I Gerd Frerichs I Gergana Ivanova-Stanoeva I Gerrit Sauer I Guido Litjens I Han Feng I Hannah Warrach I Heike Frohnapfel I Helmut Schröder I Henning Schwieters I Henriette Kosel I Hilke Fett I Holger Kirsch I Hyesu Kim I Ikenna Tony Obinna I Ilse Kampers I Inka Kunz I Irini Galarza I Irmhild Wollatz I Isabella Lorenz I Isabelle Diamant I Iva Baze I Jan Haloschan I Jan Jermer I Jan Mikolayczak I Jakob Hense I Jennifer Maldener I Jens Robert Angres I Joachim Haupt I Joanna Rutkowska I Jochen Wink I Joep Kuijs I Johanna Schmidt I Johanna Veith I Julia Benning I Julian Gross I Julian Wachsmann I Julica Grzybowski I Jürgen Frehr I Kai Grosche I Kai Hauck I Kamal Kafi I Kareem Elnems I Karim Amer I Karsten Hansen I Katharina Cembik I Katharina Horsthemke I Katharina Merten I Katja Vidic I Kejun Luo I Kerstin Tulke I

Kim Karen Steffens I Klemens Becker I Larissa Kranich I Lars Goose I Laura Dorfmüller I Laura Harzheim I Laura Marche I Laura Offermann I Marleen Stauth I Lejla Huskic I Linh Le I Lisa Bornholdt I Lisa Ehses I Luisa Jung I Luz Gutiérrez Gómez I Maen Shams Edden Alsaghir I Maic Auschrat I Maria Kühlem I Maria Pitsiladi I Maria Renner I Marie Reinartz I Mario Pirwitz I Marleen Stauth I Maroua Ben Othman I Martin Böhmer I Martin Heddinga I Martin Mellis I Martin Oehme I Matteo Giovanelli-Dürfeld I Matthes Langhinrichs I Matthias Bockstruck I Mazen Alshash I Mehtap Saltan I Mei Zhen Wan I Michael Backes I Michael Hahn I Michael Landin I Michael Pflüger I Mikulasch Adam I Minjeong Kang I Min Guo I Mirca Österreich I Miriam Berndt I Mirco Birkhold I Mohamed Adel Abdelmonem I Mohammed Al-Jabber I Moritz Weiss I Nadine Lubeley I Nadine Keller I Naghmeh Malek I Nastaran Eidani Asl I Nathalie Carton Lou I Nicola Sauerland I Nicolas Capo Rhode I Nicolas Velz I Nils Kubischek I Nina Breuer I Olga Metzger I Omar Alayli I Omar Malass I Pascal Martis I Patrick Jaenke I Patrick Jantos I Paul Zuidberg I Pei Gui I Philipp Becker I Philip Braselmann I Philip Klasing I Raoul van Herwijnen I Rouja König I Richard Siegers I Richard Ziegler I Robert Bönsch I Rouja König I Rus Carnicero I Ruth Gierhake I Ruth Montejo I Saadet Kahraman I Sabine Piechotta I Sabrina Lupero-Reichert I Sara Hengsbach I Savina Mavrodontidou I Sebastian Dewerenda I Sebastian Fuchs I Sebastian Kimmer I Sebastian Kemper I Sebastian Rübben I Sebastian von Dreusche I Shara Haues I Shidokht Shalapour I Silke Flassnöcker I Simone Heil I Sina Wolpert I Sofia de Mello I Songlin Li I Sonia Goebels I Sonja Gvozdenovic I Sophia Peters I Stefan Dahlmanns I Stefan Haupt I Stephan Hugen I Stephan Paschen I Stefan Peterek I Stefan Weisweiler I Stefanie Driessen I Stephanie Henke I Sung-Jean Park I Susanne Drehsen I Susanne Janssen I Susanne Küppers I Thi Ha Linh Le I Thi My Diem Nguyen I Thomas Behr I Thomas Jansen I Thomas Nachtsheim I Thomas Schmidt I Thorsten Burgmer I Thu Hang Ta I Til Jaeger I Till Oel I Tilmann Sick I Tim Daniel I Tina Schütte I Tobias Bley I Tobias Unterberg I Ulrich Baierlipp I Ursula Vollmert I Vadim Burmann I Vasiliki Failadi I Vivien Bastian I Volker Bähr I Westley Hoffman I Xavier Osorio I Xenia Pohl I Yanlin Ma I Ye Li I Yeliz Uzunemin-Cay I Yihea Ashkar I Yinglin Fan I Yildiz Atilgan I Yilmaz Yilmaz I Yohanna Vogt I Young Kang I Yunke Zheng I Yvonne Mitschke I Zhen Zhang I Zhizhe Zhang

Autoren
Authors

Gastautoren und Gesprächspartner
Guest Authors and Conversation Partners

UTA WINTERHAGER

Nach dem Architekturstudium an der RWTH Aachen sowie Diplom und Master an der Londoner Bartlett School ist Uta Winterhager (*1972) bei der Theorie geblieben. Seither berichtet sie als Rheinlandkorrespondentin mit Schwerpunkt Köln für verschiedene Magazine – in Buchform, im Netz und persönlich vor Ort – über Architektur, Kunst und Städtebauthemen. Überdies erklärt und illustriert sie auch gerne Kugelhäuser, fliegende Städte und DADA für Kinder.

After studying architecture at RWTH Aachen, and attaining both a diploma and a masters at the Bartlett School in London, Uta Winterhager (b. 1972) stuck with theory. She works for various magazines as a Rhineland correspondent with a focus on architecture, art and urban planning in Cologne—in book form, online and personally on site. She also likes to explain and illustrate spherical houses, flying cities and DADA for children.

NILS BALLHAUSEN

Nils Ballhausen (*1969) studierte Architektur an der Universität der Künste Berlin. Von 1998 bis 2015 arbeitete er als Redakteur der Architekturfachzeitschrift *Bauwelt*. Von 2016 bis 2018 forschte er an der TU Dortmund zu den Themen Sakralbau der Gegenwart, Schulbautypologie und Digitale Lehre. Als Architekturpublizist, Moderator und strategischer Berater unterstützt er private wie institutionelle Auftraggeber.

Nils Ballhausen (b. 1969) studied architecture at the Berlin University of the Arts. From 1998 to 2015 he worked as an editor for the architecture magazine *Bauwelt*. From 2016 to 2018, he conducted research at the TU Dortmund about contemporary sacred buildings, school building typologies and digital teaching. He supports private and institutional clients through his work as an architecture journalist, moderator and strategic consultant.

PROF. VOLKWIN MARG

Gründungspartner von gmp Architekten von Gerkan, Marg und Partner, Hamburg

Founding partner of gmp Architects von Gerkan, Marg and Partner, Hamburg

CLAUDIA GOLDENBELD

Sprecherin der Geschäftsführung der Vivawest GmbH und der Vivawest Wohnen GmbH

Spokeswoman for the management of Vivawest GmbH and Vivawest Wohnen GmbH

PROF. DR. JOHANNES BUSMANN

Herausgeber und Chefredakteur der Zeitschrift *polis*

Publisher and editor-in-chief of the magazine *polis*

ANDREAS RÖHRIG

Geschäftsführer moderne stadt, Gesellschaft zur Förderung des Städtebaues und der Gemeindeentwicklung mbH, Köln

Managing director of moderne stadt, Gesellschaft zur Förderung des Städtebaues und der Gemeindeentwicklung mbH, Cologne

ARNE HILBERT

Geschäftsführer Art-Invest Real Estate, Köln

Managing Director Art-Invest Real Estate, Cologne

GERALD BOESE

Vorsitzender der Geschäftsführung der Koelnmesse GmbH

Chief Executive Officer of Koelnmesse GmbH

PROF. DR. MED. JENS SCHOLZ

Vorstandsvorsitzender und Vorstand für Krankenversorgung des UKSH

Chairman of the Board and Executive for Health Care at the UKSH

DR. LUCIO BLANDINI

Vorstand und Partner der Werner Sobek AG, Schwerpunkt „Innovation & Knowledge Management"

Board member and partner of Werner Sobek AG, with a focus on "Innovation & Knowledge Management"

WALTER GRASMUG

Partner bei Chaix & Morel et Associés, Paris, Frankreich

Partner at Chaix & Morel et Associés, Paris, France

Dank
Acknowledgement

Wir schauen mit diesem Buch auf 20 spannende und erfolgreiche Jahre JSWD Architekten zurück und werfen darin auch einen Blick in die Zukunft. Das möchten wir zum Anlass nehmen, allen an der Planung und Durchführung unserer Projekte Beteiligten zu danken.
Zunächst gilt unser Dank unseren Bauherren und Auftraggebern, die uns das Vertrauen geschenkt haben, in ihrem Sinne und nach ihren Bedürfnissen neue Lebens- und Arbeitswelten zu schaffen. Stolz sind wir auf unser leistungsstarkes und zuverlässiges Team, bestehend aus mehr als 150 Mitarbeitern aus 30 Nationen. Jeder Einzelne ist mitverantwortlich für das Gelingen der Bauaufgaben und das Umsetzen unserer Visionen.
Wir danken den beteiligten Fachingenieuren und Architekturbüros, die als Planungspartner in unterschiedlichen Konstellationen zum Erfolg der vielfältigen Verfahren und Bauaufgaben beigetragen haben.
Unsere Entwürfe werden von Visualisierern und Modellbauern, mit denen wir seit vielen Jahren vertrauensvoll zusammenarbeiten, in 3D umgesetzt. Die realisierten Projekte werden von Fotografen, deren Bildsprache wir schätzen, ins rechte Licht gesetzt. Das entstandene Bildmaterial fand ebenfalls Eingang in dieses Buch. Einen großen Dank dafür!
Unser Jubiläumsbuch ist auch das Ergebnis eines intensiven und bereichernden Austausches mit dem Autorenduo Uta Winterhager und Nils Ballhausen. Ihre Idee, die Projekte nicht nur im Sinne eines Werkberichts vorzustellen, sondern in Magazinteilen geschichtlich und projektübergreifend einzuordnen, haben wir gerne aufgegriffen.
Dem Team des JOVIS Verlag in Berlin danken wir für die wiederholt gute Zusammenarbeit! Abschließend danken wir allen, die mit Texten und Interviews zu diesem Buch einen Beitrag geleistet haben. Insbesondere Prof. Volkwin Marg, unserem Lehrer und Mentor, danken wir für sein kollegiales Vorwort!

In this book we look back on 20 exciting and successful years at JSWD Architects and also take a look into the future. We would like to take this opportunity to thank everyone involved in the planning and implementation of our projects.
First of all, we would like to thank our clients, who have given us the confidence to create new living and working environments to meet their needs.
We are proud of our formidable and reliable team, which today is made up of more than 150 employees from 30 nations. Each individual is jointly responsible for the success of the construction tasks and the implementation of our vision.
We would like to thank, too, the specialist engineers and architectural offices who have contributed to the success of the diverse processes and construction tasks as planning partners in various constellations.
Our designs are translated into 3D by visualizers and model builders, with whom we have been working closely for many years. The realized projects are then put in the right light by photographers, whose visual language we appreciate and who have contributed the resulting images to this book. For which, many thanks!
Our anniversary book is also the result of an intensive and enriching exchange with the author duo Uta Winterhager and Nils Ballhausen. We were happy to take up their idea of not only presenting the projects in a report format, but also of contextualizing them historically and across projects in magazine sections.
And, of course, we would like to thank the team from JOVIS Verlag in Berlin for their cooperation once again!
Finally, we would like to thank everyone who has contributed to this book with texts and interviews. In particular, we would like to take the opportunity to thank Prof. Volkwin Marg, our teacher and mentor, for his friendly foreword!

Frederik Jaspert, Konstantin Jaspert, Jürgen Steffens, Olaf Drehsen

Bildnachweis
Picture Credits

ZEICHNUNGEN
DRAWINGS

Alle All: JSWD
Lagepläne Maps: Maßstab Scale 1:5.000;
außer except Koelnmesse: Maßstab 1:10.000
Grundrisse und Schnitte Floorplans and sections: Maßstab Scale 1:200 bzw. or 1:500

FOTOGRAFIEN UND RENDERINGS
PHOTOGRAPHS AND RENDERINGS

Neues Kesselhaus, Gelsenkirchen
19, 21 oben above, 25, 26–27, 30: Christa Lachenmaier
17, 21 unten below, 30 unten below: Michael Wolff
28: Berenika Oblonczyk
29 oben above: Silke Sobotta; 29 unten below: Euroluftbild Hans Blossey
30 oben above: JSWD
31: Stadtarchiv Gelsenkirchen

Haus der Europäischen Geschichte, Brüssel
House of European History, Brussels
35, 36, 40: Christa Lachenmaier
39, 45, 48–51: Christian Fabris
42, 47: Christian Richters
46, 52: Didier Boy de la Tour

Koelnmesse 3.0, Köln Cologne
57, 60–61, 66 (Renderings): JSWD/ Rendertaxi
58, 62, 64 oben above, 67: Koelnmesse
63 oben above: Deutscher Werkbund NW;
63 unten below: hdak
64 unten below: JSWD
65: HOCHTIEF

The Icon Vienna, Wien
70, 76, 78: DERFRITZ
74, 79, 80–81: Rupert Steiner
82, 83: JSWD
84, 85: unbekannt unknown

Neue Mitte Porz, Köln Porz' New Center, Cologne
89–93 (Renderings): JSWD/ Rendertaxi
95–97: moderne stadt

UKSH, Kiel/Lübeck
101–108, 116, 117: Christa Lachenmaier
111–113: Jörg Schwarze
114: Tom Körber
115: F. Schneider

Haus und Platz Building and Square
120, 125 (Renderings): JSWD/ Mohan Karakoc
123, 127 (Modell Model): JSWD/ Leistenschneider
128 (Postkarte Postcard): Verlag Paul Sprenger
129: JSWD
130: unbekannt unknown
131: Jens Willebrand

Ecole Centrale Clausen, Luxemburg Luxembourg
134–145, 149 links oben + unten bottom + top left: Steve Troes
148 links oben top left: Archiduc.lu; 148 links unten bottom left: Firma Rinn
146: sonstige other
148–149: Uta Winterhager

Neuer Kanzlerplatz, Bonn New Chancellor Square, Bonn
153, 154, 157, 165: JSWD
156, 160–161 (Renderings): JSWD/ Bloomimages
162 (Postkarte Postcard): Archiv Archive Uta Winterhager
163: Art-Invest
164 links left: unbekannt unknown; 164 rechts right: Bundesbildstelle

Konversionen Conversions
169 oben above (Modell Model): JSWD/ Leistenschneider
169 unten below, 171 unten below, 173 (Rendering): JSWD/ the third
171 oben above, 172, 175–177, 180–181: Christa Lachenmaier
182, 183, 184 unten below: Jens Willebrand
184 oben above: Rainer Perrey
185 oben above: Felix Krumbholz

Thyssenkrupp Quartier, Essen
Thyssenkrupp Quarter, Essen
189, 203: Thyssenkrupp AG
190–191: Michael Wolff
192, 202 unten rechts bottom right: Thomas Lewandowski
195: Ardex
196: JSWD
197, 200–201, 202 links + mitte + oben left + middle + above: Christian Richters
204–205: JSWD/ Chaix & Morel

Haus und Hof House and Yard
Alle All: Christa Lachenmaier; außer except
216: Archiv Archive Dr. Peter Pies

Bundesumweltministerium BMU, Berlin
222 (Modell Model): JSWD/ BBR/Winfried Mateyka
226–227 (Rendering): JSWD/ Rendetaxi
228, 231 unten: unbekannt unknown
229 links left: Wolkenkratzer; 229 rechts right (Modell Model): JSWD
230 oben above (Modell Model): JSWD
230 unten below: moderne stadt
231 oben above: Christa Lachenmaier
232, 233 (Renderings): JSWD/ Rendertaxi

Ausgewählte Bauten und Projekte 2000–2020
Selected Buildings and Projects 2000–2020
1, 2, 3, 5, 22: Rendertaxi
4: Bloomimages
6, 9, 21, 24, 30, 33, 37, 48: JSWD/ Leistenschneider
7: Loomn
8: Artform
10, 15: Mohan Karakoc
11, 38: JSWD
12: BBR/Winfried Mateyka
13: euroluftbild.de
14: Rupert Steiner
17, 23, 29, 31: Christa Lachenmaier
18: Jens Willebrand
19: Axel Hartmann
20: Christian Fabris
25: Thomas Lewandowski
26, 32: Dirk Matull
27: Steve Troes
28: Thyssenkrupp
34: Raumgleiter/Losinger Marazzi
35, 41, 42, 47: Eddie Young
36: Felix Krumbholz
40: Hervé Abbadie
43: Lukas Roth
44: HOCHTIEF
4: Aymeric Fouquez
46: Daniel Sumesgutner

Gruppenfotos Group Photos
240, 241: Christa Lachenmaier
242–243: JSWD

Die Herausgeber haben sich bemüht, alle Copyright-Vorschriften zu beachten und die Bildnachweise korrekt zu führen. Sollten dennoch Ansprüche bestehen, so wird um Kontaktaufnahme gebeten.

The publishers have endeavored to comply with all copyright regulations and to provide correct photo credits. Should there still be claims, please contact us.

Impressum
Imprint

© 2020 by jovis Verlag GmbH
Das Copyright für die Texte liegt bei den Autoren.
Das Copyright für die Abbildungen liegt bei den Fotografen/Inhabern der Bildrechte.
Texts by kind permission of the authors.
Pictures by kind permission of the photographers/holders of the picture rights.

Alle Rechte vorbehalten.
All rights reserved.

Umschlagmotiv Cover: Skizze sketch Icon Vienna, JSWD

Projektmanagement Project manager: Nina Kathalin Bergeest, jovis
Redaktion Editing: Kim Karen Steffens, JSWD
Plangrafik Graphics: Yeliz Uzunemin-Cay, JSWD
Lektorat Copy editing: Miriam Seifert-Waibel
Übersetzung ins Englische Translation into English: Mary Dellenbaugh-Loss
Gestaltung und Satz Design and typesetting: Susanne Rösler, jovis
Lithografie Lithography: Bild1Druck, Berlin
Gedruckt in der Europäischen Union
Printed in the European Union

Bibliografische Information der Deutschen Nationalbibliothek
Die Deutsche Nationalbibliothek verzeichnet diese Publikation in der Deutschen Nationalbibliografie; detaillierte bibliografische Daten sind im Internet über http://dnb.d-nb.de abrufbar.
Bibliographic information published by the Deutsche Nationalbibliothek
The Deutsche Nationalbibliothek lists this publication in the Deutsche Nationalbibliografie; detailed bibliographic data are available on the Internet at http://dnb.d-nb.de

jovis Verlag GmbH
Kurfürstenstraße 15/16
10785 Berlin

www.jovis.de

jovis-Bücher sind weltweit im ausgewählten Buchhandel erhältlich. Informationen zu unserem internationalen Vertrieb erhalten Sie von Ihrem Buchhändler oder unter www.jovis.de.
jovis books are available worldwide in select bookstores. Please contact your nearest bookseller or visit www.jovis.de for information concerning your local distribution.

ISBN 978-3-86859-477-5